Canada Among Nations

1989
The Challenge of Change

Canada Among Nations

1989
The Challenge of Change

Edited by
MAUREEN APPEL MOLOT
and
FEN OSLER HAMPSON

THE NORMAN PATERSON SCHOOL OF INTERNATIONAL AFFAIRS

CARLETON UNIVERSITY PRESS
Ottawa, Canada
1990

ISBN 0-88629-106-2 paperback
      0-88629-112-7 casebound

Printed and bound in Canada

Carleton Public Policy Series #2
The National Library of Canada has catalogued this publication as follows:

Canada among nations
1984-
Annual.
Each vol. has also a distinctive title.
1984-1988 eds. edited by Brian W. Tomlin and Maureen Appel Molot;
    1989-   edited by Maureen Appel Molot and Fen Osler Hampson.
1984-1988 eds. published by J. Lorimer; 1989-   published by Carleton
    University Press.
Produced by the Norman Paterson School of International Affairs at Carleton
    University.
Includes bibliographical references.
ISSN 0832-0683
    1. Canada—Foreign relations—1945-   —Periodicals. 2. Canada—
Politics and government—1980-1984—Periodicals. 3. Canada—Politics and
government—1984-   —Periodicals. I. Tomlin, Brian W., 1944-
II. Molot, Maureen Appel, 1941- III. Norman Paterson School of International
Affairs.

FC242.C345   _67589_   327.71   C86-31285-2 rev.

Distributed by: Oxford University Press Canada
                70 Wynford Drive
                Don Mills, Ontario
                Canada M3C 1J9
                (416) 441-2941

Cover design: Y Graphic Design

Cover photo: Courtesy of Bill McCarthy, P.M.O.
             Brian Mulroney and Mikhail Gorbachev
             meeting in The Kremlin, Nov. 21, 1989.

Acknowledgement
Carleton University Press gratefully acknowledges the support extended to its
publishing programme by the Canada Council and the Ontario Arts Council.

Table of Contents

List of Tables

Canada Among Nations 1989

List of Contributors

Chris Brown is an assistant professor in the Department of Political Science, Carleton University

Robert E. Clarke is an adjunct research professor in the Department of Sociology and Anthropology, Carleton University

Lenard J. Cohen is an associate professor in the Faculty of Political Science, Simon Fraser University

John M.Curtis is an adjunct professor in The Norman Paterson School of International Affairs, Carleton University

Tim Draimin is director of Development Policy at the Canadian Council for International Cooperation

Lorraine Eden is an associate professor in The Norman Paterson School of International Affairs, Carleton University

Fen Osler Hampson is an associate professor in The Norman Paterson School of International Affairs, Carleton University

Roger Hill is director of research at the Canadian Institute for International Peace and Security

Carl H. McMillan is a professor in the Department of Economics, Carleton University

Dan W. Middlemiss is an associate professor in the Department of Political Science, Dalhousie University

Maureen Appel Molot is a professor in The Norman Paterson School of International Affairs and in the Department of Political Science, Carleton University

Liisa North is an associate professor in the Department of Political Science, York University

Jeremy T. Paltiel is an assistant professor in the Department of Political Science, University of Alberta

Ron Purver is a research associate at the Canadian Institute for International Peace and Security

Tariq Rauf is a senior research associate at the Canadian Centre for Arms Control and Disarmament

Preface

This is the sixth volume on Canada in international affairs produced by The Norman Paterson School of International Affairs at Carleton University. As in the past the book is organized around the most recent calendar year and contains an analysis and assessment of Canadian foreign policies as well as the environment that constrains and shapes them. Our intention is to contribute to the continuing debate about appropriate policy choices for Canada.

The theme of the 1989 edition is "the challenge of change." Contributors examine many of the very significant events of this past year—among them the changes in the Communist world, in the global economy, in Southern Africa and Central America—and the Canadian responses to them. In a rapidly changing global environment selection of the calendar year as an organizing focus for the volume admittedly imposes constraints on authors because the events chronicled, both foreign and domestic, are ongoing. Nonetheless, some structure is required for the undertaking and the calendar year provides an appropriate time frame for analysis. Continuity over time is generated by the series.

Financial support for this volume has been provided by The Norman Paterson School of International Affairs, the Social Sciences and Humanities Research Council of Canada and the Canadian Institute for International Peace and Security. The editors appreciate the willingness of the contributors to participate in an undertaking which itself posed the challenge of coping with the rapidity of change, and the guidance and assistance offered by the faculty and staff of The Norman Paterson School of International Affairs. We are particularly indebted to Brenda Sutherland for her help in producing the manuscript, to Janet Doherty for her patience in organizing the workshop which is an important part of the volume's preparation and to Judith van Walsum for her help in putting the manuscript together. This is the first volume of *Canada Among Nations* to appear under the auspices of Carleton University Press and we are pleased to be part of Carleton's new series on public policy.

Maureen Appel Molot
Fen Osler Hampson
Ottawa, February 1990

1 The Challenge of Change

Maureen Appel Molot and
Fen Osler Hampson

By any measure, the year 1989 was an extraordinary one in international affairs. Changes occurred at a pace in Eastern Europe and in the Soviet Union which caught observers in the West by surprise and fundamentally altered some of the basic premises on which Canadian foreign policy had rested since the end of World War II. The destruction of the Berlin Wall symbolized for many Canadians the changes underway in Eastern Europe, as the communist regimes in Poland, Hungary, East Germany, Czechoslovakia, Bulgaria, and Romania fell under the sway of popular pressures for reform. As the year drew to a close Canadians watched the drama of change unfold in Romania, as that country's leaders were tried and executed. Despite the euphoria generated by the changes in Eastern Europe, the events in Tiananmen Square in June 1989 served as a dramatic reminder of the extreme fragility of the process of change.

These changes in the global environment, and others discussed in this volume, provided real challenges for the Mulroney government during 1989. As critical for Canada as the demise of communism in Eastern Europe were the steady progress in the European Community (EC) toward 1992, the growing economic power of the East Asian political economies and the continuing high debt levels and impoverishment of much of the Third World. All of these changes required policy responses from the Mulroney government, responses which, in the eyes of many observers, were all too slow in coming.

As we enter the next decade there is a need to develop appropriate policies to position Canada for the increasingly competitive international economic environment of the 1990s. Not only must we understand the implications of change in Eastern Europe for the future economic and political shape of Europe as a whole, but we have also to appreciate what they will mean for Canada. In short, the challenges that will continue to face the Mulroney government in the future are formidable. Its capacity to handle these challenges in 1989, and the constraints under which it operated, are the subject of this volume. Among the assessments and conclusions about Canada's international policies and the environment in which they are formulated drawn from calendar 1989 are:

- the Mulroney government was overwhelmed by the pace of change in Eastern Europe and the Soviet Union during 1989 and at year's end was still trying to assimilate the changes and their meaning;
- Prime Minister Mulroney's November 1989 visit to the Soviet Union, the first full-scale trip by a Canadian prime minister in some sixteen years, marked a new stage in the Canadian response to the Gorbachev experiment;
- it is unlikely that we will see any dramatic improvement in Canada's relationship with China in the very near future. Ideology and economics will conspire to limit Canadian enthusiasm for dealings with China;
- in contrast to the earlier détente period when the upswing in relations between Canada and the Soviet Union was clearly following a path set by the government, in recent months the Canadian business community has seized the initiative in responding to the new opportunities created by the opening up of the Soviet economy;
- the rapid change in East-West relations signified by the end of the Cold War has created pressures on governments to seek further reductions in both strategic and conventional armaments, as a means of reducing the defence burden;
- the current negotiations over troop reductions in Europe are not likely to end with the signing of an agreement in 1990, but will continue with the aim of achieving further reductions in force levels by both NATO and the Warsaw Pact;
- during 1989 Canada played an active role in fostering bilateral and multilateral cooperation in several areas of Arctic international relations, and raised relations with its two most important Arctic neighbours, the United States and the Soviet Union, to a new level of friendliness;
- the political and strategic uncertainty that surrounds Canadian defence policy is reflected in the Department of National Defence's long delay in formulating a new statement of priorities and equipment requirements;

- the United States is still the only complete great power, but its ability to lead is severely constrained by market forces, in particular by the U.S. reliance on foreign borrowing and the rise of regional blocs. Market forces are reducing the United States to the status of first among equals, a leader instead of a ruler, while Japan remains the enigmatic power behind the U.S. throne;
- the Conservatives adopted a two-track trade policy, the negotiation of a free trade agreement with the United States and active participation in the largest multinational trade negotiations (the Uruguay Round) ever undertaken;
- Canada's active involvement in international environmental programs in 1989 will soon have to be backed up by action to address urgent environmental problems at home;
- dramatic cuts in the budget of the Canadian International Development Agency suggest clearly that the objectives of austerity and federal deficit reduction come before the maintenance of Canada's commitment to development assistance;
- unable to impose new sanctions on South Africa, the Canadian government found itself subject to a string of embarrassments in 1989 as it struggled to live up to the inflated expectations created by Prime Minister Mulroney's 1985 United Nations speech;
- with Canada's decision to join the Organization of American States (OAS) demands for an independent role in hemispheric affairs will certainly grow, as will the pressures on Ottawa to commit more resources, increase the size of its diplomatic representation, and upgrade the region's profile in the Department of External Affairs and International Trade (DEAIT).

Canada Among Nations 1989

Each of the chapters in **Canada Among Nations 1989** addresses one or more of the challenges that a year of change posed for the Mulroney government as the first full year of that government's second term came to an end. Each chapter either examines the international environment that shapes and constrains foreign policy alternatives, or evaluates specific foreign policy issues and the implications of policy choices. The remainder of this introductory chapter examines the challenges to Canadian foreign policy engendered by the dramatic events of 1989 and suggests that the need to respond to the changes in Europe highlighted the organizational tensions and stresses within the Department of External Affairs and International Trade. It also notes that, change in Europe notwithstanding, Canada's relations with the United States remain paramount, and reviews the bilateral trading relationship during the first year of the free trade agreement (FTA).

The next three chapters focus on changes in the Communist world during 1989. Chapter 2 discusses the dramatic changes in the Soviet Union and Eastern Europe and their implications for Canada. The chapter argues that, although political changes in the Soviet Union have indeed been far-reaching, reforms in the economic sector have been limited with the result that there is widespread public dissatisfaction with deteriorating economic conditions and consumer shortages. Chapter 3 examines political upheaval and repression in China during 1989, suggesting that political and economic change in China were the subject of deep differences among the ruling gerontocracy. From the Canadian perspective, the repression of the democracy movement has diminished interest in Canadian economic linkages with China, particularly on the part of the active Canadian ethnic Chinese community. In chapter 4 attention is focused on Canada's economic ties with the Soviet Union and Eastern Europe. The chapter analyses the evolution of Soviet-Canadian trade during the 1980s, with particular attention to the years after 1985. What is especially noteworthy is the diversification of the economic relationship through successful Canadian bids for capital projects and the establishment of Soviet Union-Canadian joint ventures.

Developments in arms control are the subject of the next two chapters. Chapter 5 examines the process of the Nuclear and Space Arms talks during 1989 and suggests that progress was made on arms reductions and verification during the year. Though commitments to reduce weapon stockpiles have been made on both sides, the reduction of East-West tensions may well lead in the future to more significant reductions in nuclear armaments. In chapter 6 the progress of conventional arms control talks is assessed. There were a number of important proposals during 1989 to reduce troop and weapons levels in Europe; formal agreement on an initial treaty on conventional arms control is expected in 1990.

Chapter 7 discusses the North in Canada's international relations, suggesting that events of relevance to the Arctic occurred in a number of foreign policy areas in 1989: defence, sovereignty, arms control, and environmental relations, to cite but a few. The chapter devotes considerable attention to the series of agreements relating to the Arctic which were signed by Prime Minister Mulroney during his visit to Moscow in November 1989. The difficulties of Canadian defence policy are the subject of chapter 8. In attemping to plan a Canadian defence policy for the next decade Canadian defence planners are caught between the domestic realities of severe fiscal constraint and a rapidly changing global political security environment.

The global political economy is the focus of the next two chapters. Chapter 9 analyses three important ongoing changes in the global economy: the shift to multipolarity among the developed market economies, the growing importance of technology in production, and the increasing globalization of firms and markets. Also discussed in this chapter are three concurrent alterations in the organization of international trade—the multilateral Uruguay Round talks under the auspices of the General Agreement on Tariffs and Trade (GATT), the move toward heightened European economic linkages (1992), and the predeliction of the United States for unilateral responses to import competition. Chapter 10 continues the theme of the global trading system by examining the philosophical and practical similarities and differences between the Canada U.S. free trade agreement and the GATT. Although there were many bilateral differences that the FTA could not overcome the chapter suggests that, in some ways, the agreement may have set the tone for the last year of the Uruguay Round talks. Chapter 11 addresses a variety of environmental concerns, arguing that, although progress is being made slowly on the international level to meet the challenge of environmental degradation, Canada's performance in cleaning up its own environment is rather weak by international standards.

The final three chapters of the book are devoted to the developing world. Chapter 12 examines the challenge the neo-conservative ideology poses for the historically positive Canadian attitude toward development assistance. The chapter argues that reduced development assistance budgets, and the advocacy by the leadership of the Canadian International Development Agency (CIDA) of the structural adjustment philosophy of the International Monetary Fund, may well result in a change in Canadian development assistance, to the detriment of Third World aid recipients. Chapter 13 traces events in Namibia and in South Africa during 1989, highlighting the Namibian transition to independence and the slow dismantling of apartheid in South Africa under F.W. de Klerk. From the Canadian perspective, while the events themselves were positive, Canada found its own credibility in regard to both issues severely tested. In chapter 14 Canada's relations with Central America are analysed and the tensions under which Canadian policy labours are noted. Although Canada joined the Organization of American States in 1989, this move alone will not be sufficient, in the eyes of most Latin American governments, to demonstrate both a Canadian commitment to the region and a Canadian willingness to distinguish its policies from those of the United States.

No attempt has been made in this book to express a common view of Canada in international affairs during 1989. Rather, what unites the volume is the focus of all the authors on events and issues in the world which pose a challenge for Canadian policymakers. No review can possibly touch on all events and localities of significance for Canada. We have selected those regions and issues which force both Canadians and their government to re-examine the premises on which Canadian external relations have rested and to fomulate new responses as we enter the 1990s.

The Challenge of Change

The Mulroney government's ability to successfully implement an ambitious foreign policy agenda during its first term in office was facilitated by relatively favourable global conditions (Tomlin and Molot 1989:19). There were rough spots to be sure, but the larger environment was still characterized by the postwar realities of a bipolar world. By the time the government began the first full year of its second mandate a number of the premises which underlay Canada's long-time external behaviour had become shaky. By the end of 1989 it was abundantly clear that an era of international redefinition had begun. The current and continuing challenge for the Mulroney government would be its ability to adapt to the variety of critical events unfolding in many places around the world. What transpired in 1989 suggests that the government had considerable difficulty formulating policies appropriate to a changing global scene. While planning in times of uncertainty is always stressful, the government did have the advantage of one term of foreign policy experience and a leader with considerable international activity to his credit. Moreover the signs of change in the Soviet Union and the significance of moves in Western Europe toward 1992 were evident well before calendar 1989 began. Why did Canada lag in articulating an appreciation of their relevance?

The Demise of the Cold War

The bipolar perception of the world took a long time to dissipate in Ottawa. That this bipolar perspective appeared in the government's May 1985 Green Paper, *Competitiveness and Security* (Department of External Affairs 1985) was not surprising. Gorbachev's reforms in the Soviet Union had not yet begun, and it was therefore part of the expected, and accepted, discourse that the Soviet Union was targetted as the source of "the most direct threat to Canadian security" (Department of External Affairs 1985: 37). That this same vision of East-West rivalry and the military threat posed by the Soviet Union formed the basis of the 1987 defence White Paper (Department of National Defence 1987) suggested some distance between the perceptions of policymakers in the Department of National Defence (who had their own procurement reasons for employing the language of deterrence) and cabinet about the global security environment on the one hand and the realities of détente and improving superpower relations on the other. Indeed, it took Ottawa rather longer than its allies to recognize the breadth and significance of the changes underway in the Soviet Union.

The reasons for this lag are both personal and institutional. As Lenard Cohen discusses in chapter 2, in the early years of *glasnost* and *perestroika* the prime minister and the government were preoccupied with the negotiation of the free trade agreement. What other time the prime minister had to devote to foreign affairs was consumed by his involvement with the Commonwealth, la francophonie and South Africa. Moreover, by personal philosophy neither the prime minister nor his secretary of state for external affairs was predisposed to look with sympathy upon events in the Soviet Union. Mr. Mulroney was a small "c" conservative in his world view. As for Mr. Clark, though he was on many questions a "red Tory," on issues such as the meaning of change in the Soviet Union his views reflected his Alberta origins and his attentiveness to the attitudes of Canadians of East European origin. In the absence of leadership from Washington on how to respond to Gorbachev's reforms, the government experienced little pressure to re-examine its perspective on the Soviet Union. Reinforcing the political reluctance to alter the traditional Canadian view of East-West relations was the caution advised by senior members of the Department of External Affairs. Headed until close to the end of 1989 by James Taylor, a long-time diplomat with extensive experience in European affairs and with security issues, the Department remained uncertain about the staying power of Gorbachev and his reforms. When finally both political leaders and their departmental advisors decided that "Gorbachev was for real" the new perspective was reflected both in positive statements about the importance of Gorbachev's reforms (Department of External Affairs 1989) and the Prime Minister's November 1989 trip to the Soviet Union.

Once in Moscow the prime minister was enthusiastic about what he boldly proclaimed was a new era in Soviet-Canadian relations. As a number of chapters in this volume discuss, the two countries signed a variety of bilateral agreements. Indicative of the prime minister's perception of the depth of change in the Soviet Union was his suggestion that he would recommend to his G-7 industrial summit partners that the chair of each year's summit brief Mr. Gorbachev on the content of the G-7 discussions (*Financial Post* 1989a). Also significant was the Prime Minister's revelation that he had advised the Soviet Union to seek observer status at talks held under the General Agreement on Tariffs and Trade (*Globe and Mail* 1989a).

If Ottawa experienced difficulties in adjusting to what in retrospect was the relatively slow pace of change in the Soviet Union, the rapid, domino-like fall of communist regimes in Eastern Europe left officials and politicians alike struggling to keep up. To its credit the government acted quickly in pledging a substantial aid package for Poland and Hungary to promote industrial restructuring. Among the measures are food assistance for Poland, an economic development fund to support free-market reforms in Poland and Hungary, and a projected export credit insurance facility for Poland (*Financial Times* 1989). Canada has agreed to forgive Poland's interest payments on its $2.5 billion debt until mid-1991 (an amount of some $500 million). Furthermore, Canada has sought a position as a founding shareholder in the proposed European Bank for Reconstruction and Development being promoted by the European Community (*Financial Times* 1990). On the disarmament side Canada supported the Open Skies proposal of the superpowers, promoted it amongst its North Atlantic Treaty Organization (NATO) partners, and organized the first conference on the subject in Ottawa.[1]

The ongoing changes in the Soviet Union and Eastern Europe pose a number of challenges for Canadian policy. The situation in both locales is likely to be unstable for some time, as the populations come to grips with new political opportunities and serious national economic weaknesses. Although the situation at the year end justified optimism, the outcome is by no means guaranteed. Within this context of uncertainty decisions have to be made about Canadian military spending and priorities, the future of Canada's military presence in Europe (see chapter 8), the nature and role of NATO, and additional assistance to strengthen the desperately weak economies of Eastern Europe. In the current environment of fiscal restraint in Canada, financial assistance to Eastern Europe has a potential impact on the monies available to assist Canada's traditional aid recipients in the Third World. To facilitate the fashioning of new policies toward the Soviet Union and Eastern Europe the government has ordered a foreign policy review which it expects to receive in the early part of 1990.

The Challenge of Economic Change

If changes in Eastern Europe posed for Canada the challenge of adjusting to the end of the cold war division of Europe, events in Western Europe were engendering a different, if not more significant, provocation. Here the challenge is not the demise of linkages but rather their growth—the intensification of economic ties among the twelve members of the European Community as they adopt policies that will move them toward a single European market,[2] a market which may well be more restrictive of foreign trade than it is at present (Dobell 1989: 24). Though Canadian trade with Western Europe remains a small and declining percent of overall Canadian trade—some 7.4 percent in 1987—what is at stake for Canada in the growing integration of Europe is the continued, if not increased, access of Canadian firms to this lucrative market. With mergers and takeovers, joint ventures and partnerships, Europe is quickly emerging as one of Ohmae's powerful "triads" (Ohmae 1985) in which investment is replacing trade as a means of economic activity. Although a number of Canadian firms have invested in Europe to secure a future position for themselves within this enlarged market, overall interest in the EC on the part of Canadian business is limited.[3] Whether or not a new "Fortress Europe" emerges (*Financial Post* 1989b) what is important is the changing character of the global economy and its implications for the future of Canadian trade. The Canadian government has stated that its "action plan for 1992" is the continued use of the GATT as a framework for Canadian-EC trade relations (*Financial Post* 1989c). It is this continuing expectation that trade will remain the preferred mode of international economic activity, and that this trade will be carried on in accord with the multilateral philosophy of the GATT, that raises questions about the appropriateness of Canadian international economic policy.

The global economy is changing in ways that pose serious challenges with respect to trade policy and competitiveness for a small open economy such as that of Canada. This country has, in recent years, pursued a two-track trade policy (support for GATT and for bilateral free trade) as chapter 10 suggests. Whatever the outcome of the Uruguay Round of GATT talks Canada needs to re-examine this two track policy in light of a rapidly evolving international trading system in which the norms of the GATT will continue to be threatened by the increasing resort to both reciprocity and unilateralism on the part of many countries, most notably the United States (Ostry 1990). Given the pace of economic growth among the Pacific Rim countries and the fact that Canada's trade with Pacific countries is now greater than that with Europe how Canada will structure its economic relationships with that part of the world will be of enormous importance (Dobell 1989: 24). Also of significance is the question of competitiveness, the ability of Canadian firms to survive at home and abroad in an increasingly competitive global environment. Despite much discussion about "competitiveness" dating back to the Conservatives' foreign policy green paper (Department of External Affairs 1985), the government has not developed a strategy on the subject. Here the Tories face a dilemma that derives from the tension between their political philosophy—that of a preference for market forces—and the reality of neo-mercantilism under which governments in most of the developed market economies have adopted policies to promote the competitiveness of their domestic industry.

Canada-U.S. Economic Relations during 1989

Free trade with the United States was seen by the government as one way to secure market access and enhance Canadian competitiveness. From the perspective of many industries, the first full year of the FTA was a success, so much so that there was an agreement to accelerate tariff reductions on a number of products (*Financial Post* 1989d). Labour, on the other hand was very much less enthusiastic, pointing to the loss, according to its estimates, of some 70,000 jobs as plants closed and production was shifted to U.S. locations (*Globe and Mail* 1990).

On closer examination, the lessons of the first year of the FTA may be that the negotiation of the agreement was but the first of many bilateral economic challenges with which the government must deal. Though many of the plant closures have little to do with the free trade agreement and were the result of previously planned corporate reorganizations, there will be considerable restructuring under free trade, a fact which the government has not yet faced directly. The public, if not the government, expected that U.S. harassment of Canadian exports would decline with the implementation of the agreement. This has not occurred: in fact, a variety of Canadian products, ranging from agricultural exports (pork in particular) to processed foods to manufactured goods, have encountered difficulty in entering the United States as a result of U.S. protectionist measures. Moreover, as discussed in chapter 9, the potential for continued harrassment of Canadian exports exists under section 301 of the 1988 Omnibus Trade and Competitiveness Act. Even if injury to U.S. producers is not proven, section 301 permits petitions by American firms that force Canadian companies to incur legal costs and the uncertainties of subsequent market access.

The lobster dispute that erupted at the end of 1989 typifies the current realities of bilateral trade. A rider attached to a piece of U.S. legislation prohibits the importation into the United States of what are defined as undersized Canadian lobsters. What is at issue is the method of lobster fishing and the difference in conservation regimes between the two countries. Canada argues that lobsters caught legally by Canadian fishers should not be kept out of U.S. markets, while the United States maintains that the smaller sized Canadian lobsters pose a threat to the Maine-based industry (*Financial Post* 1989e). Whatever the outcome of the case (it was referred for resolution to a binational panel under chapter 18 of the FTA), to Canadian officials the issue appeared to be an instance of U.S. bullying. The case was eminently manageable; instead, however, from the Canadian vantage point it was seen as reflecting the consistent responsiveness of Congress to constituency pressures for industry protection and the readiness of the administration to condone the resort to unilateral trade action.

The decision of the first dispute settlement panel under the FTA (on West Coast Canadian salmon and herring) also generated some disquiet in Canada.[4] Although the Canadian ambassador to Washington noted that "dispute settlement panels are better than retaliation" (*Financial Post* 1989e), the panel ruling, which was not binding, found against Canadian landing requirements for fish prior to export, and demonstrated that the dispute settlement mechanism cannot substitute for the political resolution of differences, at least not yet. Canadian reaction to the outcome—which presumably would have been different had the ruling been in Canada's favour—suggests that for both sides there is a learning experience ahead that is part of any trade agreement. But in an environment of protectionism the decision to accept or reject rulings that in effect reduce a government's ability to protect its domestic interests constitutes a significant challenge.

Little progress was made during 1989 on the definition of subsidy codes under the FTA. Both sides recognize that subsidy codes are under discussion at the Uruguay Round (which will conclude by the end of 1990) and that the outcome of these negotiations will have to be factored into the bilateral dialogue. Given the five-to-seven year time frame permitted under the FTA for the subsidy negotiations neither government feels any urgent need to push the discussions ahead. When the talks do begin, Canada will have considerable difficulty in persuading the United States that both governments engage in subsidizing practices, since Washington's traditional position is that it does not subsidize its industries.[5] For its part, the Canadian government will be under domestic pressure to protect regional development programs.

Institutions under Challenge

The rapidly changing international environment of the last few years and the increasingly complex foreign policy agenda have placed the foreign policy decision-making mechanisms in Ottawa under considerable stress. Although it is tempting to blame the problem on personalities, many of the current difficulties in the management of Canadian foreign policy have institutional and bureaucratic origins. The overwhelming number of issues, combined with divided bureaucratic responsbility and the concentration of ultimate decision-making authority in the Prime Minister's Office (PMO), are the source of much of the tension. The Department of External Affairs and International Trade in Canada is not alone in facing this challenge; foreign policy bureaucracies in many countries have found their traditional preeminence in foreign affairs diminished by the foreign policy agenda, which now includes such diverse issues as fisheries, the environment, energy, trade, aid, and culture. For DEAIT the pressures under which the department is functioning emanate from (i) the heterogeneous foreign policy agenda, (ii) the continuing interest and activity of the prime minister in foreign policy, (iii) the isolation of the department from the rest of the Ottawa bureaucracy and its exclusion from some of the major foreign policy initiatives of the 1980s, and (iv) budget cuts imposed on the department.[6]

Because so many dossiers are now shared between departments and agencies, the ability of DEAIT to have an impact on specific outcomes is limited. The need to be familiar with a wide range of international problems and thus to maintain relations with a number of relevant line departments, as well as the requirement for sensitivity to the domestic political ramifications of a mulitple agenda, has strained the department's resources. Although the departmental reorganization in the early 1980s to include trade and aid (as well as immigration) was a recognition of the new complexities of foreign policy, the addition of ministers (and deputy ministers) with responsiblities for these portfolios has produced a top-heavy department in which the room for manoeuvre by the secretary of state for external affairs is constrained.[7]

Though he came to office with very limited familiarity with foreign policy issues (Kirton 1985), Prime Minister Mulroney has demonstrated both a continuing interest in foreign policy and a growing adeptness at it. Regular summit meetings of the G-7, the Commonwealth and la francophonie, as well as institutionalized discussions with the U.S. president provided the prime minister with the opportunity first to master a myriad of issues important to Canada and then to be more assertive with regard to them. With a domestic agenda fraught with problems it is hardly surprising that the prime minister found the international arena enticing and potentially useful for domestic political purposes. Given the prime minister's high profile with respect to the most significant foreign policy questions for Canada in recent years— relations with the United States, summit diplomacy, South Africa, and, most recently, ties with the Soviet Union and the decision to join the OAS—and the difference in perspective of a PMO attentive to the potential domestic political capital of foreign policy and that of a Department of External Affairs focused on the routine analysis of information and policy evaluation, tension between the two organizations has been endemic almost from the outset of the Conservatives' tenure in 1984.

DEAIT has not, in recent years, been a regular player in the Ottawa bureaucracy. Because of their corporate culture or their personalities, recent undersecretaries of state have not been comfortable with the networking game so important among senior bureaucrats and this contributed to the department's marginalization wthin Ottawa. The new Undersecretary of State, deMontigny Marchand, comes to the position with a greater appreciation of the bureaucratic environment and therefore may be able to reconnect the department in Ottawa. What has been perhaps the most telling evidence of DEAIT's status within the Ottawa bureauracy is the periperhal role the department played in some of the more controversial foreign policy initiatives of the decade. When Prime Minister Trudeau undertook his peace initiative in 1984 it was organized by an interdepartmental task force of mid-career level officials, with only limited input from the senior ranks of DEAIT (von Riekhoff and Sigler 1985: 57-58). The free trade negotiations were conducted by the Trade Negotiations Office, a structure which pulled officials from a number of departments and which was headed by a former public servant (Simon Reisman) with no connection to DEAIT. In the eyes of some of the participants this special office was of critical importance for the pursuit of Canada's interests. In both these cases the initiatives were driven by prime ministers, who created the arrangements they saw as necessary to execute the policies.

Finally, DEAIT is facing the challenge of fiscal restraint. The department had $70 million spread over the next four years cut from its budget in December 1989 and will have to decide how that loss will be accommodated. On the one hand government priorities have targetted the opening of four new posts in Asia as part of the Going Global strategy, the prime minister announced the establishment of a consulate in Kiev (*Globe and Mail* 1989b), and there is the question of implementation of renewed interest in Latin America. On the other hand, foreign posts are expensive to maintain and the decision to close missions may redound negatively on relationships with governments in whose countries Canadian representation has been reduced. A departmental review, underway at the end of 1989, is addressing ways of absorbing the budget reductions and changes in structure which will enhance organizational capacity to respond to the diversity of current demands.

Conclusion

Changes in the environment of Canadian foreign policy during 1989 generated a range of policy and institutional challenges for the Mulroney government. As this chapter suggests the government did not meet many of those challenges with ease. Most will continue into 1990.

In the political security arena the government faces the need for accommodation to an undivided Europe and the possibility of one Germany, with the consequent requirements for new definitions of security. Developments in the international security system have clear ramifications for the global economy, insofar as NATO members will have to respond to requests for economic assistance from Eastern European states concerned with economic restructuring. With respect to the global economy the challenge is that of continuing adjustment to growing globalization in the context of uncertain economic prospects, at least in North America. At the end of 1989 observers were predicting an economic slowdown in 1990 and 1991 with the attendant stresses that this will impose on Canada. High interest rates in Canada intended to restrain inflation, were dampening corporate investment, and the high dollar has made Canadian goods less attractive to foreign purchasers. Given Canada's export dependence on the United States (some 75 percent of total Canadian exports go to the U.S.) any economic downturn in that country has the potential for negative consequences for Canadian exports, and carries with it the possibility of increased resort by American producers to contingency protection. In terms of the Third World, the challenge for Canada is to bear its share of the responsibilities for ameliorating the economic situation of most of the South. Here concern for improvement in the conditions in the less developed countries clashes with the realities of domestic budgetary constraints and the need to protect Canadian industries against import competition. Finance Minister Wilson reduced the aid budget in his April 1989 budget and there are fears that 1990 will see a further slide downward in the monies Canada spends on official development assistance; moreover, Canada continues to impose restrictions on imports from a number of Third World countries (North-South Institute 1990:1). As the government seeks to shape Canada's foreign policy for the 1990s, it will have to develop a clearer set of priorities than it has done so far in order to cope with the major challenges created by the extraordinary changes in East-West relations, the fast-moving global economy, and recent developments in North-South relations. If 1989 was a year marked by the challenge of change the 1990s surely represent a decade of new directions for Canada and Canadians.

Notes

[1] The Open Skies conference was held in Ottawa in February 1990.

[2] In March 1985 the European Council agreed that the Community should constitute a single market by 1992. In June 1985 the European Commission published a White Paper detailing the actions necessary to implement this pledge. Though the 1992 goal will not be met in all areas—and the concern to support East European economic restructuring might direct attention away from 1992 in the immediate future—the process is nonetheless well underway. For details see Hoffman 1989, Kelly *et al.* 1988 and *Economist* 1989.

[3] Interestingly Quebec firms have shown a greater appreciation of the opportunities the new Europe offers than firms based in other provinces.

[4] This panel, also established under the provisions of Chapter 18 of the Agreement, reported in mid-October 1989. As a result of the decision all salmon and herring caught off the west coast of Canada no longer have to be landed in Canada prior to export.

[5] Government subsidy policies are different in the two countries. Canadian subsidies tend to be "transparent"—program grants or other assistance to industry—whereas subsidization in the U.S. is more ad hoc, designed to help a particular company and typically hidden in tax measures (*Financial Post* 1990).

[6] Some of the material in the next few paragraphs was obtained from interviews.

[7] Although trade promotion and negotiations now lie within the mandate of DEAIT, the Department of Finance retains some trade policy responsibilities.

References

Canada. 1985. Department of External Affairs. *Competitiveness and Security: Directions for Canada's International Relations.* Ottawa: Supply and Services Canada.

_____. 1987. Department of National Defence. *Challenge and Commitment: A Defence Policy for Canada.* Ottawa: Supply and Services Canada.

_____. 1989. Department of External Affairs. Statement by the Right Honourable Joe Clark. "What's at stake for us in today's Russian Revolution?" Canadian Speeches 3, no. 4, June-July: 23-28.

Dobell, Rod. 1989. "The Global Bargain." *Policy Options* December: 19-28.

Economist. 1989. "A Survey of Europe's Internal Market." July 8.

Financial Post. 1989a. "Gorbachev urges faster change." November 23: 3.

_____. 1989b. "Fortress Europe will pose new problems for Canadian exporters." (Gordon Pitts) December 25: 5.

_____. 1989c. "Ottawa unveils policy for 1992." (Victor Fung) April 11: 3.

_____. 1989d. "Canada, U.S. to cut tariffs affecting $6 billion in trade." (Alan Toulin) December 1: 3.

_____. 1989e. "Canada-U.S. fish disputes boiling over." (Rod McQueen) December 18: 4.

Financial Times (Toronto) 1990. "A peace dividend is likely to be omitted in the new budget." (Giles Gherson) January 15: 7.

Globe and Mail. 1989a. "Soviet tour a new start in relations, PM says." (Craig McInnes) November 28: A3.

_____. 1989b. "Millions from External Affairs." (Jeffrey Simpson) December 19: A6.

_____. 1990. "The economic costs outweigh the benefits." (Tony Clarke) January 2: A7.

Hoffman, Stanley. 1989. "The European Community and 1992." *Foreign Affairs* 68, no. 4. Fall 1989: 27-47.

Kelly, Margaret et al. 1988. *Issues and Developments in International Trade Policy.* Washington: The International Monetary Fund.

Kirton, John. 1985. "Managing Canadian Foreign Policy" in *Canada Among Nations 1984: A Time of Transition*, edited by Brian W. Tomlin and Maureen Appel Molot. Toronto: James Lorimer & Co: 14-28.

North-South Institute. 1990. *Review '89/Outlook '90.* Ottawa.

Ohmae, Kenichi. 1985. *Triad Power: The Coming Shape of Global Competition.* New York: Free Press.

Tomlin, Brian W. and Maureen Appel Molot. 1989. "The Tory Record: Looking Back, Looking Ahead." In *Canada Among Nations 1988: The Tory Record*, edited by Brian W. Tomlin and Maureen Appel Molot. Toronto: James Lorimer & Co: 3-20.

Von Riekhoff, Harald and John Sigler. 1985. "The Trudeau Peace Initiative: The Politics of Reversing the Arms Race." in *Canada Among Nations 1984: A Time Of Transition*, edited by Brian Tomlin and Maureen Appel Molot. Toronto: James Lorimer & Co: 50-69.

2 The Soviet Union and Eastern Europe in Transition: Trends and Implications for Canada

Lenard J. Cohen

> Tensions are at their peak ... the problem is that the old is dead and the new is still being born.
> Mikhail Gorbachev (November 1989)

At the end of the 1980s the Soviet Union and the East European states underwent dramatic socio-political and economic changes which profoundly altered their organizational and ideological make-up. In this chapter the following questions will be addressed: what are the major dimensions of the renewal and transformation occurring in the U.S.S.R. and in the neighbouring states which formerly constituted the "Soviet orbit" or "East Bloc?" How successful has the Soviet regime been in carrying out its proposed reforms, and what obstacles have impeded the implementation of the new policies? What is the general pattern of political evolution in the diverse East Central European and Southeastern European regions? How have the changes in Soviet policy affected Moscow's relationship to the East European regimes, as well as its attitudes to developed capitalist countries such as Canada? Finally, how has Canada responded to recent developments in the Soviet Union and Eastern Europe?

Reorienting the Soviet System: Major Dimensions and Problems

The advent of the Gorbachev regime in March 1985 marked the start of an ambitious experiment in transforming the Soviet system. That experiment is grounded on three closely related facets of reform: 1) *economic rejuvenation*, which calls for major changes in the Soviet Union's industrial and business sectors, organization of agricultural production, and foreign trade practices; 2) *political liberalization*, consisting of measures to create electoral and legislative systems with a more participatory character, changes in the role of the Communist Party, a more candid and pluralistic media sector, and legal reforms to enhance the rights of citizens; and 3) *a reform of Soviet foreign policy*, both in terms of the doctrinal principles which guide Moscow's external relations, and the actual behaviour of the U.S.S.R. in world affairs. The now relatively well-known concepts of *perestroika, glasnost*, and "new political thinking" in international relations provide the broad theoretical underpinnings for Gorbachev's comprehensive effort to reorient the U.S.S.R.

Domestic Reforms: Trends and Prospects

The Gorbachev experiment constitutes a peaceful revolution which is designed to rid the U.S.S.R. of the totalitarian practices inherited from the Stalin era, and also of the neo-Stalinist glosses elaborated during the anti-reformist Brezhnev period. Recognizing that his country was beset by serious economic deterioration and a "pre-crisis" situation during the first part of the 1980s, and faced with an atmosphere of tension and distrust in East-West relations, Gorbachev endeavoured to change course and ensure the future development of the U.S.S.R. as a modern, respected, and constructive member of the international community.

By the end of 1989 Gorbachev and his *perestroika* elite had achieved a very promising—albeit still only partial—record of success in transforming the U.S.S.R. The economic sphere has been the most disappointing area of reform. Although the government produced a blueprint for radical economic recovery, efforts to provide Soviet citizens with a higher standard of living, and in particular to make more consumer goods and foodstuffs available, fell short of regime promises and rising expectations. After an initial period, which witnessed the proliferation of efficient and productive enterprises in the non-state directed cooperative sector, such businesses were stifled by restrictive and anti-reformist legislation. Agriculture remained the Achilles' heel of the Soviet economic system. Despite ambitious plans to establish new incentives and methods of production in the agrarian sector, the U.S.S.R. continued to allocate a large portion of its foreign currency earnings for the importation of grain, thereby depleting the funds available for the purchase of badly needed technology and industrial products.

The Soviet population's seemingly infinite patience in enduring economic privation continued in 1989 and early 1990, but there were also signs of widespread dissatisfaction with Gorbachev's economic program. For example, in a fall 1989 poll of Soviet citizens, commissioned by one of Gorbachev's major economic advisors, 52 percent of the respondents claimed that the economic situation in the U.S.S.R. had grown significantly worse in the last two or three years, and another 23 percent said the situation was only "slightly worse." Eighty-six percent of the respondents claimed that the supply of food and other consumer goods had deteriorated. While public understanding of the need for radical economic reforms had apparently grown, the poll also revealed considerable fear regarding the consequences of major change, such as a growth in social differentiation, unemployment and inflation. The majority of those surveyed felt that the best way to bring about improvements in the economy was for the leadership to bring "firm order to the country," and a large majority of respondents opposed the termination of state-controlled prices, i.e., the centrepiece of any genuine reform of the old Stalinist-type command economy. Moreover, an overwhelming majority of Soviet citizens do not foresee any substantial improvement in their standard of living for at least ten years, if ever (*New York Times* 1989: 1, 13). Near the end of 1989, Soviet policymakers and economists discussed plans to breathe new life into Gorbachev's stalled market-oriented reforms, setting 1991-1995 as the target period for implementation.[1] Gorbachev's program of political reform proved more successful than his efforts to restructure the Soviet economy. By revamping the electoral and legislative systems, and reducing the scope of the system of censorship and press control, he significantly broadened opportunities for the expression of different political ideas and interests in the U.S.S.R. The plethora of individual and group opinions articulated in the electoral campaigns of 1989, in the new Congress of People's Deputies and Supreme Soviet, and through the media, completely transformed the nature and influence of political participation in the Soviet Union. Up to the first part of 1990 Gorbachev's new brand of "socialist pluralism" was still confined within a single-party framework, but the party apparatus had become only one player—albeit still a formidable player—in an increasingly multi-sided political game.

While Gorbachev's reform initiatives pluralized Soviet political life in an unprecedented manner, they also triggered developments jeopardizing the political liberalization of the U.S.S.R.. The most dangerous by-product of Soviet reform in this regard has been the mounting pattern of conflict between various Soviet nationalities, and also between regionally based nationality groups and the central political authorities. After decades of political centralization, assimilatory Russification, and the maintenance of a largely spurious federal system, the explosion of ethnic and regional protests was not surprising. Unfortunately, inter-ethnic conflicts and demands for the rapid devolution of power to the republics, as well as more extreme demands for independence in the Baltic region and the Caucasus, placed an enormous strain on Gorbachev's plans for a unified and incremental approach to Soviet reform. Violent inter-ethnic conflicts, nationalist and separatist protest demonstrations, strikes, and even the blockade of entire regions (e.g. the predominantly Armenian Nagorno-Karabakh area in Azerbaijan), not only required the use of scarce resources for security management and disrupted economic production schedules, but also created an impression that Gorbachev's program is fundamentally destabilizing and potentially threatening to the very territorial cohesion of the country (Lapidus 1989).[2]

The explosion of ethnic unrest, together with the multiplicity of freely expressed opinions, which has been encouraged by the policy of *glasnost* in the Soviet media and has included the denunciation or re-evaluation of almost all facets of Soviet ideology and history, provided ammunition for Gorbachev's conservative opponents who urged that restructuring should be kept within strictly defined limits. A major Soviet reform strategist persuasively argued in 1989 that the most powerful resistance to comprehensive reform in the U.S.S.R. does not derive from the dwindling reactionary or neo-Stalinist forces, but rather from the "liberal-conservative" elements of the *perestroika* elite who seek to limit the pace and scope of change (Zaslavskaia 1989).

Gorbachev's poor record of economic achievement, and also the feeling in some quarters that political developments in 1989 had acquired a quasi-anarchical character, even led some reform-oriented members of the Soviet intelligentsia to suggest that the transition from totalitarianism to democracy must be engineered by means of a strong leader, empowered to use authoritarian methods if necessary. According to such views, the resistance to market-oriented economic reforms is so strong it is necessary to install a "democratic dictatorship" to restructure the economy (Klyamkin and Migranyan 1989). Up to early 1990 Gorbachev rejected such formulations and remained committed to a more benign *perestroika* vision. He has also, however, pointedly discouraged the idea of evolution towards a multi-party system in the U.S.S.R., and warned separatist-oriented radical forces in the Baltic area and elsewhere against attempting the fragmentation of the Communist Party, or the established federal state.[3]

In less than five years, Gorbachev had made enormous strides in transforming the U.S.S.R., but the innovative and pluralistic features of his fledgling liberal communist regime were still only weakly institutionalized and remained under attack by conservative opponents. By 1990 considerable *liberalization* had taken place, but only tentative steps were made towards the genuine redistribution of power entailed in fundamental regime *democratization*. As the Soviet playwright A. Gel'man observed: "Liberalization is an unclenched fist, but the hand is the same, and can be clenched into a fist at any moment. Liberalization resembles democratization only outwardly, but in fact it is a fundamental and inadmissible substitution" (Gel'man 1989). While Gorbachev persistently reiterates his commitment to democratization his prudent habit of steering between the extremes—reactionary conservatives and radical reformers (the *ultra-perestroishchiki*)—gave his political initiatives a distinctly "liberal-conservative" hue. "The situation is complicated and unpredictable," claimed the editor of a pro-reform weekly newspaper, who refused to resign despite being attacked by Gorbachev for publishing a poll from which it appeared that the Soviet president was not among the ten most popular legislators.

> The [party] apparat is not going to give up without a fight, although I do not share the view that catastrophe or civil war is inevitable.... Mr. Gorbachev understands all of this and is therefore pursuing a middle course ...You ask where we are going? We will live and see (Starkov 1989: A15).

The International Dimension of Soviet Reform

Gorbachev's reform program has achieved its most positive results in the area of foreign policy. Recognizing that the Soviet Union's impressive gains in military power and global offensive capability under Brezhnev had been paralleled by a serious deterioration in the domestic economy, Gorbachev and his new team of foreign policy specialists committed themselves to establishing a new relationship between domestic and external policies. The economic slump or "pre-crisis" situation of the early 1980's could not be attributed solely to heavy defence expenditures, but Soviet economic recovery was now seen to require a much greater concentration of investment funds in non-military sectors (Kaufman 1989). Indeed, Gorbachev's entire program of eliminating Soviet inferiority in terms of economic and technological achievement is linked to the respite and savings he hopes to obtain from improved East-West relations and arms control. As a major "new thinker" in the Soviet academic community put it: "In pursuing our foreign political aims for many long years, we lost sight of the real opportunities for fulfilling them. Yet our possibilities proved very modest compared with those of the forces opposing us, with the result that we undermined our economy and confrontation with the West almost bled us white" (Dashichev 1989: 125).

A good deal of Soviet "new thinking" on international relations is designed to serve the urgent demands of economic modernization. According to the revised view of domestic priorities, the allocation of funds to economic "restructuring" requires a substantial reduction in the costly arms race with the Western alliance, as well as decreased Soviet economic and military outlays to economically depressed countries in the Third World. Moscow's aggressive pursuit of military parity with the United States during the second half of the 1970s and early 1980s is now viewed by Soviet specialists as unrealistic, because it ignored the different economic potential of the two superpowers. High defence expenditures and "showy international activities" are alleged to be factors contributing to the stagnation of the Soviet economy (Izyumov and Kortunov 1988). As one Soviet observer remarked: "Putting the blame, out of habit, for all world evils on the U.S. military-industrial complex, the bureaucrats who were ready to place departmental interests above those of society not only followed, but also brought grist to the mill of the arms race...which, in the final analysis, damaged our own interests" (Kozyrev 1988: 7).

The notion that economic security rather than sheer military growth must become the central factor in overall security policy led to the reorientation of Soviet military doctrine around the new concept of "reasonable sufficiency" (*razumnaya dostatochnost*). Briefly, the concept of reasonable sufficiency posits that political factors such as negotiations and diplomacy, rather than the maintenance of military parity with the West, have become the prime components of Soviet security. Arms can therefore be reduced to levels sufficient to cope with the tasks of defence, that is, levels far below those currently maintained by the two major alliances. As articulated by Soviet civilian specialists and leading members of the military, reasonable sufficiency suggests the mutual reduction of armaments to the point where neither the Warsaw Pact nor NATO would possess the capability of conducting offensive operations or surprise attacks against the other. As the Deputy Chief of the Soviet General Staff observed: "Now military doctrine concentrates on the prevention of war ... the new political mentality and existing realities in the field of defence means that all arms of the services in the Soviet Union are now oriented only to the retaliation against political aggression" (Gareyev 1988: 30, 31). Previous Soviet concentration on primarily offensive military operations is now attributed by scholars in the U.S.S.R. to an "absolutizing of the experience of the Great Patriotic War (for all of its unquestionable value)," while pre-World War II writers who showed an appreciation for the political and economic aspects of military strategy and particularly the problems of strategic defence are now being rehabilitated (Kokoshin 1988).

During the second half of the 1980s Gorbachev's new thinking in foreign policy provided the basis for major improvements in superpower relations and East-West arms control, as well as the Soviet Union's constructive participation in international organizations such as the United Nations and the World Court. The Soviet leader's bold proposals for unilateral reduction in the U.S.S.R.'s military strength, put forward at the United Nations in December 1988, were a direct outgrowth of the "new thinking" about military strength and national security. As the Soviet leader put it: "no country can achieve omnipotence, however much it builds upon its military might. More than that, emphasis on that might alone will in the final analysis undermine national security in other aspects" (Gorbachev 1988). Gorbachev's decision included a reduction of Soviet troop strength by 500,000 over two years, and involved the withdrawal of six tank divisions and other offensively configured military units from the GDR, Czechoslovakia, and Hungary. The plans provided that Soviet forces stationed in those countries would be reduced by 50,000 men and 5,000 tanks, while remaining military units would be restructured in "a strictly defensive" manner.

The East European Revolution of 1989

> Every East European country is now a social laboratory.... Our chief principle is non-interference. This does not mean we are indifferent. But we do not want to repeat past mistakes.
>
> Nikolai Shislin (CPSU, Central Committee Aide
> for East European Countries, September 22, 1989)

During 1989, Gorbachev's re-orientation of Soviet domestic and foreign policy became dramatically linked to developments in Eastern Europe. Early on in his reform program Gorbachev hoped that by reducing Soviet military and economic commitments in Central Europe and also encouraging his Warsaw Treaty Organization allies to jettison politically unpopular and economically inefficient of their regimes, the Kremlin would be able to reap savings for the U.S.S.R.'s domestic modernization without sacrificing the ability to guide the overall pattern of East European development. Particularly at the outset of his rule, Gorbachev feared that any loosening of Soviet control in Eastern Europe might unleash the kind of "anti-socialist" political turbulence which proved so costly to his reformist predecessor, Khrushchev, during the mid-1950s. At the same time, however, the economic burden of controlling Eastern Europe was recognized by the Soviet elite even before Gorbachev assumed power. Thus, Moscow was especially sensitive to economic losses incurred as a result of Soviet subsidies to its European allies (related primarily to the under-pricing of Soviet energy exports to the region prior to 1986), the sub-standard quality of East European machinery and other exports to the U.S.S.R., and East Europe's marginal contribution to the costs of the Warsaw Pact.

Faced with uneven and cautious enthusiasm for *perestroika* on the part of Eastern Europe's communist elites—Hungary and Poland were the most accepting, the GDR and Romania the most hostile, with the Bulgarian and Czechoslovak regimes somewhere in between—Gorbachev initially tried to engender a climate of incremental change and a looser model of Soviet-led coordination. As Gorbachev told a mid-November 1988 meeting of cultural and scientific personnel in Poland: "The notion that there are not diverse ways to build a new society has been relegated to the archives once and for all. We realize full well that it is the ability to draw useful lessons from diversity, rather than unification and general levelling, that make up the most reliable basis for unity" (Gorbachev 1988). Moscow also made an effort to abandon its "big brother" mentality by crediting East European and other socialist states for many of the reforms incorporated into the Soviet *perestroika* program. In many respects, the Soviet leadership had no choice but to adopt a more relaxed and detached approach to Eastern Europe. The economically strongest and most politically assertive regimes, such as East Germany and Hungary, already had an established record of successfully obstructing Soviet efforts to dictate policy specifics; while for the U.S.S.R. to have assumed a deeper and more active involvement in the affairs of the economically most depressed communist regimes, such as Poland and Romania, would have involved an intolerable drain on the Soviet exchequer. Gorbachev was faced with a situation in which he had few carrots to offer his allies, and the use of the stick to influence their internal affairs would completely destroy his regional and international credibility as a supporter of "socialist pluralism."

In the fall of 1989, with a suddeness that surprised both participants and observers, the momentum of political change in Eastern Europe went far beyond the limits of the reforms sought by Mr. Gorbachev within a Soviet-inspired communist framework. The Kremlin's decision in August to permit the installation of a Solidarity-led coalition government in Poland, following the massive defeat of communist candidates in that country's June election, was an important signal to both communists and non-communists in Eastern Europe that prior Soviet restraints on change in the region were no longer operative. The Hungarian regime's demolition of its barbed-wire border barriers with Austria, its promises to hold free elections in 1990, and its relabelling of the 1956 anti-communist uprising as a popular rebellion, and not a counter-revolution, also helped to generate rising political expectations throughout Eastern Europe. Encouraged by Polish and Hungarian developments in the first half of 1989, and Gorbachev's visible distaste for unreformed communist leaders, the citizens and reform elite factions took advantage of the situation. After years of "asymmetrical verification" (Kapuscinski 1985: 216) in which the communist elites had evaded accountability for their actions, but had prodded their subjects to demonstrate loyalty, it was now the rulers who were being forced to answer to the ruled. In East Germany and Czechoslovakia popular demonstrations expressing pent-up frustration and resentment toppled entrenched conservative communist elites in just a few weeks. In October 1989, only ten days after hosting Mr. Gorbachev's visit to the GDR, East German communist leader Erich Honecker was forced to step down from his post, expelled from the ruling party, and, together with several of his colleagues, placed under house arrest.[4] Honecker's departure was preceded and followed by a mass exodus of East German citizens to the West via Hungary, and also mass street demonstrations, throughout the GDR, in opposition to the regime. As the already tenuous legitimacy of the communist state evaporated, Honecker's former lieutenant and successor, Egon Krenz, was forced to open the Berlin Wall and promise free elections. Despite Krenz's instant conversion to *perestroika* he was forced to resign within less than two months (and shortly thereafter expelled from the party), as control passed to a new team of communist reformers who promised to consult with the newly legitimized and increasingly assertive non-communist political forces.

In mid-November the anti-reform Czechoslovak communist leadership that had been installed in 1986 by Soviet-led invasion forces resigned after only one week of demonstrations. This event was quickly followed by further mass protests which catapulted the leaders of the non-communist opposition into the most influential posts in the political system. The departure of the Czech neo-Stalinists followed closely upon warnings from Moscow that delay in initiating reforms would create the scenario that had occurred in East Germany only weeks before. By the beginning of December the severely weakened Czechoslovak communist party disavowed the 1968 invasion of their country ordered by Brezhnev, a move quickly duplicated by Mikhail Gorbachev and the Warsaw Treaty Organization. The "Brezhnev Doctrine" justifying earlier Soviet military interference in Eastern Europe had been dead in spirit for some time, but the formal disavowal of such practices legitimated and stimulated the ongoing process of regime transformation at the end of 1989.[5]

Events in Southeastern Europe were equally dramatic, but the region's limited experience with non-violent and democratic political change seriously complicated the process of regime transformation. In Bulgaria, the longest surviving East European communist leader, Todor Zhivkov, was removed from power in mid-November by a younger elite faction who committed themselves to free multi-party elections and by non-communist participation in the government. The non-communist counter-elite, however, was much weaker and more disorganized than in Central Europe, and the outbreak in January 1990 of mass protest against the regime's decision to rescind repressive policies towards the country's Turkish minority indicated that the creation of a liberal political order might not be easy. In Romania the toppling of the Ceaucescu dictatorship departed radically from the uniform pattern of bloodless regime change elsewhere in Eastern Europe: it was preceded by a massacre of dissenters, ordered by the regime and a violent conflict between the army and the security forces in which thousands of citizens were killed, and concluded with the star-chamber execution of the former leader and his wife. The new Romanian government consisted initially of an uncomfortable coalition of former communists, communist reformers, and non-communists, functioning in an atmosphere of distrust and demands for revenge against associates of the previous regime.

The prospects for peaceful and democratic change were also uncertain in the two communist states in the region which were outside the Warsaw Pact: former reform front runner Yugoslavia, and staunch anti-reformist Albania. In the Yugoslav case, the linkage between continuing economic deterioration and serious inter-ethnic conflicts, stimulated by elite-led nationalism and the mobilization of mass protests in Serbia, seriously threatens the future cohesion of the country and the survival of the communist regime. Competitive elections in 1990 may lead to the advent of non-communist regional governments in Slovenia and Croatia, and the development of secessionist pressures in the two republics. In isolated and xenophobic Albania, the conservative communist regime seemed to relish its position as the last bastion of neo-Stalinism, although even in this repressive regime in a remote corner of Eastern Europe pressure for reform and transformation seemed to be bubbling to the surface.

While the festival of democratic change and aspiration seemed to draw the Cold War to a conclusion in the very same region in which it had begun four decades earlier, enormous problems and outstanding issues still confronted Eastern Europe at the onset of the 1990's. The prospect of German reunification generated considerable anxiety and controversy in both Western and Eastern Europe, especially since the possibility of revived German political and economic strength in Central Europe had arisen so suddenly. Another troubling issue was the extent of the East Europeans' ablility to successfully institutionalize the emergent democratic forces and establish viable economic structures; failure to accomplish this task might lead to the alternating political turbulence and authoritarian solutions which had characterized so much of the region's pre-World War II history. Moscow was particularly concerned that Germany's development and that of the rest of Eastern Europe would proceed in a manner consistent with Soviet security interests. Thus, while the Kremlin's recently revised security perspectives no longer emphasized the direct military control of East European real estate, the Soviet Union was hardly indifferent to the region's political development or to its relationship with the U.S.S.R.

The relatively peaceful course of East European political transformation, at least in Central Europe, and the fact that initially all of the newly established regimes—even those led or dominated by non-communists—maintained their nominal membership in the Warsaw

Treaty Organization, were certainly reassuring to the leaders of the U.S.S.R.[6] Indeed, the Soviet Union indicated that the Warsaw Pact was now a political, rather than a military or political alliance, and opened negotiations with Czechoslovakia regarding the withdrawal of Soviet troops from that country (Hungary and Poland have made similar requests on the same subject). The possibility of a precipitate surge towards German unity, or of the ascendancy of radically "anti-socialist" East European elites that might seek to accelerate the political, military and economic decoupling of their country's links with the Soviet Union, nevertheless remained very much on the minds of Mr. Gorbachev and his colleagues. In a speech to the European Parliament on December 19, 1989, Soviet Foreign Minister Shevardnadze expressed the Kremlin's desire for caution with respect to the future balance of power in Eastern Europe:

> East Germany is our strategic ally and a member of the Warsaw Pact. It is necessary to proceed on the basis of post-war realities, namely, the existence of two sovereign German states. . . . A retreat from that is fraught with destabilization in Europe. . . . Surely the peoples of the Soviet Union are entitled to know what any changes in Central Europe would mean to their future and their security. We paid the price of 20 million lives for the existing European stability (Shevardnadze 1989b: A10).

Whether the fluid developments in Eastern Europe would continue to satisfy Moscow's liberalized security expectations, especially in the case of East Germany, and how the "virus of pluralism" sweeping the region would impact on the U.S.S.R.'s increasingly volatile internal political dynamics, were very open questions at the onset of the 1990's. It was Mikhail Gorbachev's "new political thinking" which had set the stage for the 1989 East European revolution, but as that region entered its post-communist phase its own future, and Mr. Gorbachev's personal political fate, remained closely linked and uncertain. For the moment one thing was clear, as was aptly observed by a leading Soviet analyst: "It is in the cards that the East European countries will veer appreciably towards the West" (Bogomolov 1990: 12-13).

Capitalism and Canada in the Soviet Elite Mindset

> . . . we were willing to deceive ourselves with regard to capitalism. But it disclosed a potential that was still far from exhausted, and it proved capable of looking at itself self-critically and restructuring a great deal in the organization of societal life.
>
> Aleksandr Yakovlev (July 1989)

The Soviet Reconceptualization of Capitalism

The reorientation of Soviet views concerning international affairs has had a major impact on Moscow's perception of capitalist states and of Canada in particular. In a groundbreaking speech to the Social Sciences Section of the Presidium of the U.S.S.R. Academy of Sciences in mid-1987, Aleksandr Yakovlev, now a key Gorbachev adviser, remarked that at the onset of the 1980s the "theoretical consciousness" of the Soviet elite was in many ways "still at the level of the 1930s." "Forecasts," Yakovlev added, "regarding the development of the capitalist system, the limits of its viability, and its capacity for survival turned out to be greatly oversimplified. All this has to be discarded, which is not so easy to do" (Yakovlev 1987: 8, 10). Yakovlev's encouragement of "new thinking" about capitalism was similar to views advanced by other leading reconceptualizers in Gorbachev's circle of experts, a group whose innovative perspectives and research had failed to receive top level sponsorship or official recognition during the Brezhnev period.

The recent reconceptualization of capitalism by Soviet specialists includes the notion that, although militarism has been connected with the evolution of capitalist societies, the degree of militarization differs significantly from one capitalist country to another. As foreign policy specialist Yevgenii Primakov has argued, in some capitalist countries, especially smaller ones, the "militaristic component" of the economy is very inconsequential while in others, such as Japan, "militarism is not necessarily a fellow traveller" of economic growth. Moreover, even in highly militarized capitalist countries such as the United States, Primakov suggests, it might be possible to reverse the militarization of the economy through the conversion of military to civilian output. The opportunities for reversing the military features of capitalist societies, and appealing to the more "sober-minded" elements within the elites and general publics of capitalist states, broaden the overall prospects for peaceful East-West cooperation and by implication permit the reduction of Soviet defence expenditures. According to Primakov, the present "correlation of forces" in the world reveals a "certain balance" between the capitalist and socialist systems. Thus earlier Soviet prognoses of the "general crisis" and imminent demise of capitalism reflect "simplistic theoretical approaches" stemming from "the underestimation and occasional total neglect of development potentialities of capitalist production relations" (Primakov 1987: 105, 106, 109).

Vadim Medvedev, a member of the Politburo and chairman since September 1988 of the Central Committee's ideological commission, has also emphasized that capitalist countries have undergone important positive changes, including the ability to reduce their internal class antagonisms, employ elements of planning in economic development, and coordinate the overall activities of the capitalist world. Capitalism, according to Medvedev, has managed to "make up the losses" resulting from the creation of the "world socialist system." It survived the collapse of the colonial system, "using neo-colonial dependence and drawing the majority of newly independent countries into its economic system" (Medvedev 1988: 9-10). Medvedev's last observation reaffirms a viewpoint frequently advanced in recent Soviet commentaries on the Third World, namely, that the majority of developing nations are not only "leaning on the Western model of development," but are also "suffering not so much from capitalism, as from its shortage" (Kozyrev 1988: 6).

Canada and the "Yakovlev Line": Origins Of "New Thinking"

There is some basis for arguing that the Kremlin's new attitudes toward capitalism were in part shaped by changing Soviet perceptions of Canada. The key link in such speculation is undoubtedly Aleksandr Yakovlev, who served as Soviet Ambassador to Canada from 1973 to 1983 (Cohen 1989). Shortly after Gorbachev's visit to Canada in May 1983, Yakovlev was brought back to Moscow to take an active part in the Soviet re-evaluation of international affairs. There is some evidence, for example, that, along with his experience in the United States, Yakovlev's long and high-level associations in Canada helped to shape his ideas about the capitalist world—its defects, vitality and foreign rivalries. Because Yakovlev is the number two foreign policy-maker in the U.S.S.R., such influence and images acquire added significance. In many respects the historian and diplomat, Yakovlev, is the U.S.S.R.'s major Canadianist, and Gorbachev his most prominent pupil. Indeed, a large measure of recent Soviet rethinking about Western capitalism, and especially the importance attached to exploitation, by the Soviet Union, of "inter-capitalist contradictions" to adoption of a less American-centred approach in international affairs, has been aptly described as the "Yakovlev line" (Gellman 1986).

The exploitation of inter-capitalist rivalries is, of course, an old Leninist precept (Lynch 1987), but it is Yakovlev who has spurred the conceptual modernization of that notion. Important aspects of the Yakovlev approach to world affairs include the need for Soviet policy makers to treat particular states which comprise the "world capitalist economy" in a more differentiated manner, and also the notion that the economic and political power of the world has become more fragmented and multipolar. It is difficult to determine to what degree Yakovlev's special sensitivity to Canadian-American disagreements may be responsible for his portrayal of Western capitalism, but the influence of such factors certainly warrants consideration. Long before he arrived in Canada Yakovlev was far from enamoured with the United States and American hegemony, but his experience in Ottawa, including private lunches with Pierre Trudeau,[7] undoubtedly heightened his awareness of the utility of driving wedges between the United States and its allies.

The Gorbachev leadership's enhanced awareness of diversity and conflict in the capitalist world does not, of course, necessarily translate into greater Soviet attention to Canadian affairs, or even a more favourable image of Canada. Moscow is clearly more sensitive to Canadian distinctiveness than it was in earlier periods. When Yakovlev talks about a multipolar world, he is referring primarily to major constellations of capitalist polycentrism, namely, Japan, Western Europe, and the United States, and not the two poles of the Ottawa-Washington axis. While Canada and the United States are now seen by Soviet specialists as two quite separate capitalist countries with many conflicting interests, the two states are also frequently described as part of a single "North American centre of imperialist rivalry" with other regional capitalist combinations such as the European Economic Community (EEC). Moreover, although Yakovlev has grave reservations about American capitalism he in no way sees Canadian capitalism or democracy as a model for his own country. Commenting recently on the value of Western-style democracy, Yakovlev derisively remarked that he found parliamentary activities in Canada to be a "disgusting spectacle" in which "you see a member hammering away at a minister of a ruling party" (*Globe and Mail* 1989a: A5).

While the Soviet elite has reservations about the transferability of Canadian institutions to the U.S.S.R., its image of Canada has been quite favourable since March 1985. Despite some bumpy episodes related to Soviet intelligence gathering in Canada, relations improved noticeably in the second half of the 1980s. The Soviet media consistently rebuked Canada for "back door" cooperation in the United States "star wars" program (the Strategic Defence Initiative), and also for helping to test cruise missiles, but Canadians have also been complimented for trying to "win as much 'freedom to manoeuvre'" as possible within the framework of the military-political alliance with the United States (*Izvestiya* 1986: 5). The trend towards improved relations was illustrated by the reinstatement of the Canadian-U.S.S.R. academic exchange, non-military cooperation in the Arctic, the extension of sport exchange agreements, a growing number of joint business ventures, and preparations for Prime Minister Mulroney's November 1989 visit to the Soviet Union (see Chapter 7).

Meanwhile, Soviet scholarly and policy-oriented commentaries on Canada have continued to manifest the improved scope and analytical quality first observed in the decade after 1974. Book-length Soviet studies have recently been completed on the Canadian state and the economy, Canadian federalism, Canada's role in World War II, the relationship between Canadian and American economic cycles, the strategy of the New Democratic Party, Canadian internal politics, Canadian foreign trade, and Canadian-American relations. Articles in the Soviet professional periodical literature have included topics as diverse as the Canadian cinema, Catholicism in Canada's political life, Canadian-Chinese relations, and the political activities of the Canadian women's movement (Cohen 1989: 45). Dogmatic capitalist-bashing and amateurish Ottawology are still not totally absent from Soviet media reports but a more sophisticated and subtle approach to Canadian affairs has become the norm in Soviet commentary and scholarship.[8]

Canadian Perspectives on Perestroika

> The Soviet Union before Mr. Gorbachev was an entirely different place than the Soviet Union today.
>
> Brian Mulroney (November 25, 1989)

Gorbachev's audacious attempt to transform Soviet domestic and external relations has both fascinated and perplexed Western observers. Like most citizens of Western countries, Canadians have generally been very optimistic and enthusiastic about the *perestroika* program. Public opinion polls in Canada indicate that Mr. Gorbachev's foreign policy initiatives have contributed to a striking decline in the number of Canadians who feel that the Soviet Union is trying to increase its area of influence in the world. For example, although 87 percent of the Canadians surveyed in 1980 (shortly after the Brezhnev-ordered invasion of Afghanistan) viewed the Soviet Union as an expansionist power, only 49 percent of those polled in 1989 felt the same way (Bozinoff and MacIntosh 1989). Canadian support for defence spending also declined significantly during the second half of the 1980s (see Table 1).

Table 2.1*
Public Views of Current Levels of Defence Spending in Canada

% Response

	Dec. 1983	March 1986	Sept. 1987	Dec. 1989
Too Much	17	18	25	34
Right Amount	35	38	37	35
Too Little	47	44	37	29
No Opinion	1	0	1	2

* Generally speaking would you say that Canada spends too much, about the right amount or too little on the military and defence? (Decima 1989: 30).

In contrast to the striking shift in public opinion during the past decade official Canadian reaction to reform in the U.S.S.R. has exhibited considerable caution. At a point when Soviet foreign policy pronouncements and actions were beginning to undergo major alteration in mid-1987, the government's 1987 White Paper on defence characterized the Soviet Union as an essentially expansionist power which still represented the "principal direct threat" to Canadian security (see Chapter 8). "Soviet strategic planners," the authors of the White Paper informed Canadians, "must regard Canada and the United States as a single set of military targets no matter what political posture we might assume" (Department of National Defence 1987: 5, 10). As Mr. Gorbachev's personal popularity soared in the West following the major arms control breakthroughs and summit meetings of 1988, and as the thrust of Soviet internal reform accelerated noticeably, Canadian foreign policymakers continued to express serious reservations about the potential success of reform in the U.S.S.R. In a January 1989 speech, for example, External Affairs Minister Joe Clark stressed that, despite many encouraging signs of change in the U.S.S.R. "in the direction of a more free and open system," Canadians "have to look at all the faces of the Soviet Union." Mr. Clark drew special attention to the considerable impediments which Russian history and Soviet political culture create for the democratic evolution of the U.S.S.R. Cautioning against euphoria in evaluating Soviet intentions, Clark called for the solidarity of the Western alliance in negotiations with the U.S.S.R., and for continued Canadian commitment to the defence of the West (Clark 1989a).

Canada's very reserved and cautious official response to changes in the U.S.S.R. during the second half of the 1980's was partially the result of the divergent perceptions and rivalries exhibited by different segments of Ottawa's foreign policy-making establishment.[9] Some senior officials in the Department of External Affairs suggested that Prime Minister Mulroney's preoccupation with negotiations for the U.S.-Canada free trade agreement during 1987-1988 made him reluctant to take any initiatives toward the Soviet Union which might have ruffled feathers in Washington. Officials in the Prime Minister's Office, however, were more likely to blame the Minister of External Affairs, Mr. Clark, for excessive caution with respect to *perestroika*, and for having allowed Canada to become "marginalized" in the accelerating East-West dialogue. The latter view was also expressed by some members of the Department of External Affairs, who felt that Mr. Clark's Western Canadian orientation, and his close association with conservative Canadians of East European origin, clouded his recognition of changes occurring in the Soviet Union. One thing that officials in both the Prime Minister's Office and the Department of External Affairs usually did agree upon was that the major obstacles to the improvement of Canadian-Soviet relations could be found in the upper reaches of the Department of National Defence. Justifiably or not, the top echelons of the military bureaucracy were frequently accused of having an occupational devotion to the maintenance of East-West tension, and of not being able to adjust to a "world without an enemy." Such critics admitted, nevertheless, that the rather "hawkish" 1987 White Paper on defence matters could not have been issued without the approval of both the Prime Minister's Office and Mr. Clark. In the final analysis, the responsibility for any Canadian "marginalization" with regard to Gorbachev and the U.S.S.R. up to mid-1989 appears to be shared by a cross-section of the cautious Tory government team, whose initial priorities did not include the active pursuit of closer cooperation with the Soviet Union.

In any case, by May 1989 Canadian official policy seemed to be catching up with domestic public opinion and foreign perceptions of the U.S.S.R. Conceding that Mr. Gorbachev was not just "tinkering" but had "undertaken to remake Soviet society," Mr. Clark now emphasized that it is in Canada's interest to see Gorbachev succeed. "Canada and the West have a big stake in Mr. Gorbachev's success," Clark remarked, adding that Canadians must be "alert" to the "real change occuring in the Soviet Union" and also "conscious of the probability" that we may be part of a "genuine watershed in modern history." Laying the groundwork for Mulroney's November 1989 visit to the Soviet Union, Mr. Clark also stressed Canada's eagerness to expand commercial ties with the U.S.S.R. (Clark 1989b).[10]

While Ottawa's recognition of *perestroika's* potential evolved rather more slowly than views in other Western capitals, Canadian government policy did exhibit constancy with regard to three crucial assumptions. First, that the cohesion of the Western alliance has been a major factor—although not the only factor—responsible for the radical changes in the Soviet Union's perceptions regarding domestic and foreign affairs. Secondly, that at a time of delicate transition in the history of a long-entrenched authoritarian system such as the U.S.S.R., Western policymakers are wise to negotiate a middle course between excessive enthusiasm and debilitating over-cautiousness. And thirdly, that although the U.S.S.R. is in the throes of fundamental reform, Mr. Gorbachev's long-term "success cannot be taken for granted." Legitimate differences exist about whether Canadian policy was sufficiently "accommodationist," or even sufficiently coherent with respect to the initial phase of the Gorbachev experiment, but in view of the complexity and questionable sustainability of the changes occurring in the Soviet Union, Ottawa's very "prudent" policy from 1987 to 1989 may not have been entirely unjustified.[11]

Prime Minister's Mulroney's November 1989 visit to the Soviet Union marked a new stage in the Canadian response to the Gorbachev experiment. Describing Mr. Gorbachev as "one of the genuine reformers of modern history," the Prime Minister praised the major changes that were emerging in Soviet domestic and foreign policy, and stressed that Canada "would like to invest in this process" (*Canadian Press Newstex* 1989b and 1989d). Canadian-Soviet commercial ties were significantly strengthened in Moscow as the 240 business people who accompanied the Prime Minister on his trip took part in launching the Canada-U.S.S.R. Business Council, and proceeded to sign a number of important investment projects with their Soviet hosts. Several intergovernmental agreements between Ottawa and Moscow were also signed during the visit, the most important being a Political Declaration which called for joint Soviet and Canadian efforts in a number of important areas including environmental policy, the Arctic, anti-terrorism policy, the campaign against illegal drug trafficking, and the debt problems of developing countries. The Soviet Union and Canada also agreed to "strengthen their cooperation in the fields of trade, economy, science, technology, agriculture, fisheries, and civil aviation."

Soviet Foreign Minister Shevardnadze observed that, as a result of Prime Minister Mulroney's visit, more agreements had been signed between Canada and the U.S.S.R. than in the previous twenty years, and that "unlike their counterparts in other Western countries Canadian businessmen feel [there is] strong backing on the part of the government." Shevardnadze also emphasized that "the concept of new political thinking, advanced by the Soviet Union, and the Canadian concept of constructive internationalism are consonant philosophically and in other regards" (Shevardnadze 1989a: 2,4,5-6). According to the Prime Minister's Office, the Political Declaration represents an agreement "formalizing a joint vision of the world as an interdependent community of nations" (*Globe and Mail* 1989b: D6). Departing from the conventional view of the Soviet Union as Canada's "principal" adversary, the tone and content of the new Declaration provide a strong basis for the extension of Canadian-Soviet cooperation on serious global issues, and for a significant expansion of bilateral ties.[12] At the onset of the 1990's, Canadian-Soviet relations had certainly taken a major step forward. It nevertheless remained to be seen whether the promise and potential of the understandings reached during the Prime Minister's visit to the U.S.S.R. would be fulfilled and lead to tangible long-term benefits for Canada.[13]

Notes

[1] Economic reform in the U.S.S.R. took a major *de jure* step forward in February and March, 1990 when the Soviet central legislature adopted new laws permitting the farming population to lease land, and also giving private citizens the right to own small-scale factories and other businesses.

[2] In mid-March 1990, following their massive electoral victory, Lithuanian nationalists prepared to initiate the secession of their republic from the U.S.S.R. Although Gorbachev warned that the Kremlin would present the republic with a massive financial bill—21 billion rubles—if Lithuania proceeded to declare independence, the Soviet leader seemed unlikely to use force in order to prevent such a move.

[3] At a dramatic Central Committee plenum held in early February 1990, Gorbachev abandoned his earlier public condemnation of multi-party politics, and obtained support for ending the Communist Party's constitutional monopoly of power. Although Gorbachev's advisors warned that "extremist" and "anti-socialist" forces would not be permitted to exploit the new pluralist framework, the long-standing hegemony of the Communist Party apparatus appeared to be waning. The plenum also endorsed a proposal to create a popularly-elected and strengthened state presidency, a post custom-made to provide Gorbachev with an independent power base outside of the Communist Party. It remained unclear whether Gorbachev's triumph at the plenum and enhanced prerogatives would offset the potential chaos of expanded pluralism under the very difficult socio-economic circumstances in the country.

[4] Gorbachev is reported to have advised Honecker that Soviet troops would not be used to repress internal dissent (Ash 1989: 14).

[5] Gorbachev had, prior to the popular revolt against East European anti-reformist elites, carefully refrained from any formal repudiation of the Brezhnev doctrine.

[6] Non-communist East European leaders are very conscious of Soviet sensitivities on this question. Commenting on plans for a trip to the United States, Vaclav Havel, the new President of Czechoslovakia, said he had to try to develop American "understanding for some peculiarities of Czechoslovak foreign policy" (*New York Times* 1990: A6).

[7] In interviews with Bill Keller, Trudeau's foreign policy advisor, Ivan Head, related how he would arrange lunches with Yakovlev at which the prime minister would sometimes drop around, and that the two men hit it off well: "I think Trudeau saw in Yakovlev the best of what the Soviet Union had to offer." According to Keller, these private lunches "drove some bureaucrats in the Canadian External Affairs Department wild with curiosity" (Keller 1989: 31, 42).

[8] As Soviet Canadianists prepared for Mr. Mulroney's November 1989 visit, their enthusiasm and professional stake in better U.S.S.R.-Canadian relations was highly visible. For example, Dr. Bagramov, the head of the Canadian Department of the U.S. and Canada Institute has suggested that Moscow had "invited Mulroney because he's the head of—and I emphasize this—an independent and highly developed state that plays an important role in world politics ... In many respects, Canada is more important to us than the United States" (*Canadian Press Newstex* 1989b).

[9] The views in this section are based on discussions with Ottawa-based Canadian government officials and foreign policy specialists in November 1989.

[10] In a mid-October 1989 speech in Los Angeles, Mr. Mulroney praised Gorbachev's reform program and stressed that Canada wanted to encourage "the revolution sweeping Eastern Europe." He added that "the pace of change in [Eastern Europe] is both breath-taking and astounding ... but its outcome, particularly in Poland, remains in doubt..." (*Canadian Press Newstex* 1989a).

[11] On the difficulties faced by Western policy-makers in assessing and influencing Soviet policy changes see Snyder 1989.

[12] A forthcoming foreign policy review announced by the government in 1990 will undoubtedly present Ottawa's official post-Cold War evaluation of the Soviet Union and Eastern Europe.

[13] In early December 1989, at a meeting of NATO leaders, Mulroney stressed the enormous economic difficulties facing Gorbachev: "His economy is in such god-awful shape it would take the treasuries of everyone around the table to fix it—and then some" (*Globe and Mail* 1989c). While Canadians generally welcomed the 1989 democratic revolutions in Eastern Europe, polls indicated that two out of three citizens were opposed to Canada immediately providing foreign aid to the new governments in the Warsaw Pact countries (Decima 1989: 29-30). Some Canadian bankers also expressed a reluctance to finance projects in Eastern Europe without "firm" official guarantees from Ottawa (Cox 1990: 17).

References

Ash, Timothy Garton. 1989. "The German Revolution." *New York Review of Books* 36, no. 20 (December 21): 14.

Bogomolov, Oleg. 1990. "East Europe: A Painful Step Forward." *Moscow News* no. 1: 12-13.

Bozinoff, Lorne and Peter MacIntosh. 1989. "Soviet Union Viewed as Less Expansionist Than in the Past." Gallup Canada Inc. March 16.

Canadian Press Newstex. 1989a. October 13.

———. 1989b. November 15.

———. 1989c. November 19.

———. 1989d. November 20.

Clark, Joe. 1989a. "Why we can't be sure of Soviet peace and freedom." *Canadian Speeches* 2, no. 10 (February): 35-39.

———. 1989b. "What's at stake for us in today's Russian revolution?" *Canadian Speeches* 3, no. 4 (June-July): 23-28.

Cohen, Lenard J. 1989. *Canada and the Soviet Elite Mindset: A Case Study of "New Political Thinking."* Toronto: Centre for Russian and East European Studies, University of Toronto, Working Paper no. 3.

Cox, Kevin. 1990. "Scotia Bank Wary of Aiding Eastern Europe." *Globe and Mail*, January 17: B9.

Dashichev, Vyacheslav. 1989. "Openness in Politics." *International Affairs* no. 8: 125.

Decima Research and Public Affairs International. 1989. *Decima Quarterly Report*: 29-30.

Department of National Defence. 1987. *Challenge and Commitment: A Defence Policy for Canada*. Ottawa: Canadian Government Publication Centre.

Gareyev, Makhmut. 1988. "The Revised Military Doctrine." *Bulletin of the Atomic Scientists* 44, no. 10 (December): 30-31.

Gel'man, A. 1989. Quoted in T. Zaslavskaia, "On the Strategy of Social Management." *Soviet Sociology* 28, no. 4 (July-August): 21-22.

Gellman, Harry. 1986. "Gorbachev's Dilemmas and His Conflicting Foreign Policy Goals." *Orbis* 30, no. 2. (Summer): 231-248.

Globe and Mail. 1989a. August 26: A5.

⸻. 1989b. November 25: D6.

⸻. 1989c. December 6: A4.

Gorbachev, Mikhail. 1988. "Speech by Mikhail Gorbachev at the UN General Assembly." *Moscow News* no. 51 (3351), Supplement (December 18): 2.

Izyumov, Alexei and Andrei Kortunov. 1988. "The U.S.S.R. in the Changing World." *International Affairs* no. 8 (August): 46-56.

Izvestiya. April 29, 1986: 5.

Kapuscinski, Ryszard. 1985. "A Warsaw Diary." *Granta* 15: 214-223.

Kaufman, Richard F. 1988. "Economic Trends and Defence Burdens in the United States and the Soviet Union." In *Macroeconomic Management and the Enterprise in East and West*, edited by Christopher T. Saunders. London: Macmillan: 357-361.

Keller, Bill. 1989. "Moscow's Other Master Mind." *New York Times Magazine*, February 19: 31, 42.

Klyamkin, Igor and Andranik Migranyan. 1989. Quoted in Elizabeth Teague, "Does the Soviet Union Need 'An Iron Hand'." *Report on the U.S.S.R.* 1, no. 41 (October 13): 7-8.

Kokoshin, Andrei. 1988a. "Alexander Svechin: On War and Politics." *International Affairs* no. 11 (November): 118-126.

Kozyrev, Andrei. 1988b. "Confidence and the Balance of Interests." *International Affairs* no. 11 (November): 6-7.

Lapidus, Gail. 1989. "Gorbachev's Nationalities Problem." *Foreign Affairs* 68, no. 4 (Fall): 92-109.

Lynch, Allen. 1987. *The Soviet Study of International Relations.* Cambridge: Cambridge University Press: 108-116.

Medvedev, V. 1988. "K poznaniyu sotsializma." *Kommunist* no. 17 (November): 9-10.

New York Times. 1989. November 5: A1, 3.

———. 1990. January 12: A6.

Primakov, Yevgenii. 1987. "Kapitalizm vo vzaimosvyazannom mire." *Kommunist* no. 13 (September): 105-106, 109.

Shevardnadze, Eduard. 1989a. "Common Concerns—Close Partnership." *News Release, Press Office of the U.S.S.R. Embassy in Canada* no. 90, November 30.

Shevardnadze, Eduard. 1989b. *New York Times.* December 20: A10.

Starkov, Vladislav. 1989. *New York Times.* November 11: A15.

Snyder, Jack. 1989. "International Leverage on Soviet Domestic Change." *World Politics* 62, no. 1 (October): 1-30.

Yakovlev, Aleksandr. 1987. "Dostizheniye kachestvenno novogo sostoyaniya sovetskogo obshchestva i obshchestvennyye nauki." *Kommunist* no. 8 (May): 8, 10.

Zaslavskaia, T. 1989. "On the Strategy of Social Management." *Soviet Sociology* 28, no. 4 (July-August): 16-24.

3 Rude Awakening: Canada and China Following Tiananmen

J.T. Paltiel

On June 3, 1989, tanks rolled into Tiananmen square at the centre of Beijing, putting an end to six weeks of defiant demonstrations against communist policies and the Chinese government. With that brutal repression of democratic opposition the Chinese government drew a jagged line across its reform policies of the past decade. The roots of the contestation and the repression lie in the inability of China's communist régime to adapt to the processes which it had itself set in motion. The process of reform had been applauded and supported by all Western nations, and by none of them more enthusiastically than Canada, which was particularly active in supporting China's entry into the community of nations and the international market.

Canada's Relations With China

Canada had cultivated what it declared to be a "special relationship" with China from the time when, at the end of the cultural revolution, Prime Minister Trudeau established diplomatic relations with the People's Republic. Both Liberal and Conservative governments fostered friendly relations with China—the former originally viewing this policy as a showpiece of independent Canadian diplomacy, and the latter seeing it as part of an aggressive attempt to pursue economic opportunities as part of the coming "Pacific Century." Both these policies were supported by a substantial domestic consensus.

The Trudeau initiative came in the wake of changing Canadian immigration policies which led to a rising wave of immigration from the ethnic Chinese communities of East Asia, particularly from Hong Kong at the end of the 1960s. Canada's recognition of China lent dignity to Canada's ethnic Chinese community, which subsequently became very active in cultural exchange initiatives, provincial and municipal twinning projects and various business ventures of varying scale. Despite some initial friction within the Chinese community between supporters of the People's Republic of China (PRC) and older groups with lingering loyalties to the Kuomintang régime on Taiwan, Trudeau's policy was very easily integrated with the new policy of multiculturalism. One highly visible symbol of the new approach was an agreement on the reunification of families concluded during the very first prime ministerial visit to China in 1973. Under this policy some 40,000 Chinese have immigrated to Canada over the past decade and a half.

The Trudeau policy was also welcomed by business interests eager to exploit the potential "China market." Trade relations with the People's Republic of China predated the establishment of diplomatic relations by a decade, for the Diefenbaker government had initiated wheat sales to China in 1960. Thus both major political parties can lay claim to pioneering this special relationship.

Trade relations continued to be dominated by wheat well into the 1980s, and for this reason Canada has always enjoyed a healthy trade surplus with China. However, Canadian exports to China have become much more diversified in recent years. A Canada-China Trade Council has been in existence since June 1978, actively pursuing diversified trade. Exports of finished products finally overtook those of primary products in the mid-1980s. Among the high technology items in Canada's trade balance are Canadair Challenger aircraft, digital switches for telecommunications and oilfield equipment.

Canada's surpluses in trade have been offset to some extent by Canada's willingness to provide development assistance to China. Bilateral government-to-government aid has averaged about $30 million in recent years; if aid given through various multilateral organizations is included it totalled some $100 million in 1988. When Prime Minister Mulroney paid his official visit to China in May 1986 he announced a doubling of the Canadian International Development Agency's (CIDA) bilateral aid program to $200 million for the 1987-92 period (Department of External Affairs 1988: 45).[1] Canada has laid particular stress on education, a number of programs being aimed at human resource development, among them a management training school staffed by Canadians in the Chinese city of Chengdu. One controversial Canadian aid project has been the feasibility study on the construction of a giant hydroelectric project in the picturesque Three

Gorges area of the Yangtse River, a proposal attacked by environmentalists both inside China and abroad, but one on which CIDA spent $13 million in the hope of gaining significant Canadian engineering participation should the project ever go forward (*Globe and Mail* 1988a). Thousands of Chinese students have studied in Canada in recent years and several thousand are still involved in various programs with or without government support.

One particular feature of Canada's relations with China has been the active participation of several provincial governments. Alberta and the Chinese province of Heilongjiang have enjoyed a twinning relationship since 1983; Ontario has an extensive relationship with the Chinese coastal province of Jiangsu and Saskatchewan with Jilin, while other Canadian provinces have sent trade delegations to China.

Canada is not one of the more important investors in China, although there are a number of well-known joint ventures involving some of Canada's best-known firms. Northern Telecom has a joint venture for producing digital switches in the Special Economic Zone of Shekou, Alberta's Nova Corporation has a number of energy and petrochemical ventures in China, and there are joint venture hotels as well. One peculiar feature of the Canadian business relationship with China is the presence of significant Chinese investment on Canadian soil. The most important example is the Celgar pulp mill in Castlegar B.C., in which the China International Trade and Investment Co. is a significant investor (*Globe and Mail* 1989a).

Canada's relationship with China became a key point in our network of relations with Asia. In 1988 China became the fourth largest market for Canadian goods, with exports reaching $2.6 billion and Canadian imports from China slightly less than $1 billion (Department of External Affairs 1989).

The tragedy in Beijing has ramifications extending beyond Chinese politics. By putting the pace and extent of reform in China in question, the crackdown in Beijing impacts on the stability of the entire East Asian region, and in particular on that of the dynamic colony of Hong Kong, which reverts to Chinese sovereignty in 1997.

Background to the Crackdown

The trouble in China did not come about overnight, nor were the student demonstrations and the support they received just a matter of abstract demands for freedom. For months prior to the outbreak of demonstrations the Chinese political and economic systems were under severe strain. The Chinese reforms reached an important crossroad just at a time when the succession to Deng Xiaoping was pending. Although he held only the titular position of Chairman of the Party's Military Affairs Commission he was really China's commander-in-chief and supreme political arbiter. At this critical juncture controlling the succession really meant controlling the direction of reform. While the power struggle inside the Forbidden City appeared to the casual observer to be incidental to the demonstrations, the latter were in fact the culmination of political deadlock at the centre.

The Chinese political system had grown increasingly unstable since the student demonstrations of 1986 which led to the removal of the then Party General Secretary Hu Yaobang. Hu had already been found unacceptable as Deng's successor by senior members of the Military Affairs Commission. The struggle over "political reform" was merely the pretext to eliminate him as a candidate. Zhao Ziyang, who moved from the post of Premier to succeed Hu as General Secretary, never really wished to relinquish control over economic reform which had been his main responsibility as Premier. Yet, as General Secretary, he lacked a strong power base inside the Party apparatus. He too wished to move forward on political and economic reforms. Specifically, he wanted to decrease the role of the Communist Party in the economy and in administration generally, to strengthen the legal position of the state and state institutions and to expand the role of the market by moving towards wide-ranging price reforms while severely limiting the scope of planning. The net effect of all these changes would have been to reduce the role of the state in the economy and of the Party in running the state. These reforms, Zhao felt, would incidentally also ease China's entry into such international organizations as the General Agreement on Tariffs and Trade (GATT) (*Globe and Mail*, 1988b;1988c).

This course generated powerful misgivings among veteran conservative interests who were able to check Zhao's plans by having a conservative protegé, Li Peng, named to the post of Premier. Li, an adopted son of the late Premier Zhou Enlai, maintained close personal connections with veterans in the Party and government. In addition, his background as a Soviet-trained power engineer led him to favour traditional planning over the market economy.

Zhao's plan to accelerate price reform occurred at a time when the economy, stimulated by a vast consumer boom and rising incomes, was overheating dangerously. When the intention to pursue radical price reform was announced in late July 1988, panic buying erupted throughout China. Shoppers scrambled to buy up all available goods before feared price rises.

This panic accelerated inflation still further. Fearing a Polish-style outbreak, the leadership decided to back Li against Zhao, to back off political and economic reforms and to institute a traditional "re-adjustment," characterized by centralization of investment decisions and tighter control over resource allocation, beginning in September 1988. Zhao's reforms were left on the drawing board as Li attempted to reassert central control over an economy which had been undergoing growing decentralization for years.

The example of Poland also caused a retreat from promised political reforms. The Party anticipated civil unrest long before the student demonstrations. Inflation was already eating into real income, especially for employees of public institutions, including universities. Just when the retreat from reform became evident, real grievances of the urban population, especially the intellectuals, were building up dangerously. This powder keg was all the more explosive because the clumsy mix of administrative planning and markets offered numerous opportunities for official corruption. Low-priced centrally allocated materials were turned over at inflated market prices. Government appeals to control inflation by public frugality were being openly flouted by profiteering officials. At the same time, an impatient populace was told the time was not ripe to introduce democratic reforms which might allow public scrutiny to unearth and deter official corruption.

Encouraged by the changes in the Soviet Union certain public figures, notably the dissident scientist Fang Lizhi, felt the time had come to mount a public offensive for democracy. In the six months following the announcement of an austerity program in September hardly a dent was made in inflation. April marked the tenth anniversary of the closing down of "Democracy Wall"[2] while May would mark the seventieth anniversary of the May Fourth Movement, the first mass movement for democracy in Chinese history.[3] Fang Lizhi began a petition campaign to release political prisoners. In February 1989, this petition garnered signatures from leading writers, journalists, and social as well as natural scientists. By March the movement had gained adherents among activist students on the campus of Beijing University. In the meantime, conservative members of the régime were reported to be plotting the ouster of Zhao Ziyang (*Cheng Ming* 1989).

On April 15, 1989 former Party General Secretary Hu Yaobang died suddenly. Rumour spread that he had had a heart attack in the middle of a Politburo meeting, following an attack by Li Peng. Taking a cue from the 1976 Tiananmen protests which criticized the Gang of Four by focusing on their attacks on Premier Zhou Enlai, students mounted a memorial to Hu as a means of protesting against the current regime and the slow pace of political reform. The government, which had anticipated anomic violence and food riots, was not prepared for principled opposition in this form. It could hardly ban memorial services for a senior Party official. Moreover, Tiananmen was loaded with symbolism for the reform-minded regime of Deng Xiaoping, which had risen to power by linking Deng to the martyrdom of the protesters of 1976. More and more students joined the movement, calling for an official explanation of Hu's death. In the wake of the demonstrations, independent student unions were set up on the main campuses of the universities in the capital (the leading campuses being Beijing University and Beijing Normal University). Very quickly the movement spread throughout the country. Demonstrators called for wide-ranging democratic reforms, including revision of the constitution to remove the infamous references to the "four basic principles" enjoining the Chinese to uphold socialism, Marxism-Leninism, the dictatorship of the proletariat, and the leadership of the Communist Party.

The student calls for democracy and human rights were rebuffed in an April 26 editorial in the People's Daily, the main Party newspaper, entitled "With Clear Banners We Must Oppose the Disturbance." The editorial charged that the student movement was manipulated by a small number of persons conspiring to create a counter-revolutionary disturbance with the aim of overthrowing the leadership of the Communist Party and socialism. This editorial was written under the express orders of Premier Li Peng at a time when the Party general Secretary Zhao Ziyang was out of the country in North Korea (*Renmin Ribao* 1989a).

Notwithstanding the strong threats implied in this editorial, the movement exploded in subsequent days, as students demanded a retraction of the statements implying that their demands were not patriotic. Other sectors of society joined in supporting the students, who now went on strike. The anniversary of the May Fourth movement was an opportunity to mobilize large masses of people behind calls for democracy. On this important anniversary Zhao Ziyang made a public statement appearing to uphold the legitimate aims of the student movement, contradicting the April 26 editorial and splitting the Communist Party. Subsequent moves by Deng Xiaoping and the "hard liners" were aimed as much at Zhao and his supporters inside the Party as at the students outside in the square.

The demonstrations took on the appearance of a people's power movement confronting an apparently impotent government. As the students targeted Premier Li Peng for criticism in addition to the gerontocracy headed by Deng Xiaoping, Li and the conservative veterans were pushed together into an alliance, while Zhao was isolated. Ultimately, Zhao let the initiative slip into the hands of hard-line conservatives struggling, they felt, for the integrity of the régime as well as their own power.

China's gerontocracy suffered deep humiliation when the historic summit with Gorbachev was overshadowed by the demonstrators who skillfully capitalized on the attention of the world media. Zhao, in his public talks with Gorbachev, pointed out the extra-constitutional position of Deng Xiaoping. This admission, intended as a subtle call for Deng's retirement, egged the students on. By the time Zhao Ziyang appeared at the square in the early hours of Friday May 19, a decision in principle to declare martial law had already been taken by the Politburo.

The declaration of martial law at noon on May 20 was followed by a "phoney war" in which ordinary townspeople seem to have foiled attempts to overawe them. No one outside China knows for certain how the consensus was forged which resulted in a decision to use a massive degree of violence against the protesters. Zhao Ziyang was not seen in public after May 19, and his efforts to have the declaration of martial law nullified by the National People's Congress (China's parliament) failed.

The Chairman of the National People's Congress, Wan Li, was on an official visit to the United States and Canada when martial law was declared. While in Canada he is reported to have supported the aims of the students. He cut short his visit to the United States, rushing back to China on May 25, but was held in Shanghai "for reasons of health" (*Renmin Ribao* 1989b). A confident Li Peng then showed determination to put an end to the disturbances.

Troops entered Tiananmen square in the early hours of June 4. While there is no way of accurately gauging the numbers killed or injured, they are certainly very high. Many of the dead were killed by random shooting into side streets. The leadership's initial fears of civil strife breaking out between rival factions of the military did not materialize. The massive presence of foreign media gathered in China during the weeks of upheaval in anticipation of the Gorbachev summit ensured that pictures and sounds of the bloody repression would be broadcast throughout the world. China's international reputation was not en-hanced by troops firing into diplomatic compounds and on buildings housing foreign businesses along Beijing's main thoroughfare, Changan Avenue.

Canadian and Western Reactions

Canada's official reaction came swiftly on the floor of the House of Commons on June 5, 1989. All parties joined the Prime Minister in condemning the Chinese government's action. The Secretary of State for External Affairs, Joe Clark, announced an immediate series of steps, among them the recall of Canada's ambassador to China (*Globe and Mail* 1989b). After consultation with interested citizens and academics Mr. Clark elaborated Canada's official reaction to the massacre on June 30, 1989. Having already condemned Chinese action in the House of Commons on June 5, he developed a policy line which distinguished between relations with the Chinese government on the one hand, and "people to people" relations on the other. He expressed concern that China not be isolated and pledged to work together with other countries to maximize the effect of the sanctions on China.

Specific measures taken by the Canadian government included cancellation of agreements to provide help for a television transmission facility, the co-production agreement between the CBC and Radio Beijing, and a program to train Chinese civil servants. In contrast to these government sanctions was the special treatment Mr. Clark accorded the hundreds of Chinese students in Canada, many of whom had participated in pro-democracy rallies and demonstrations. The government announced a relaxation of visa requirements and promised to renew the visas of students already in Canada (Department of External Affairs 1989). American sanctions were somewhat less extensive than those of Canada. The United States immediately suspended arms sales to China and urged postponement of new loans by multilateral agencies such as the World Bank, in which the U.S. has strong influence. Like Canada, the United States suspended high level contacts with the Chinese government (*Washington Post* 1989). The Japanese government, China's largest aid donor and trade partner, suspended all bilateral aid, but did not follow the U.S. in discontinuing all high level contacts (*Financial Times* 1989a).

The Madrid summit of the European Community (EC) took place shortly after the massacre and issued a strongly worded condemnation of the massacre (*Financial Times* 1989b). Member nations of the EC including France, Italy and West Germany issued their own sanctions as did the U.S. The Paris summit of the group of Seven in July further strengthened this condemnation (*Globe and Mail* 1989c).

The strong reaction of the West had little effect on the Chinese government. As the official government spokesman put it just a few days after the massacre:

> ... It must be said that with regard to this counter-revolutionary violence and the struggle to end this violence, at present international opinion is not quite the same. Already there are people openly accusing us, saying we will not be given this and we will restrict that ... and institute so-called sanctions against us. As far as that is concerned, I have been authorized by the State Council leaders to explain two things before international opinion. First, we are not afraid. No matter whatever means, whatever accusations and whatever sanctions are levelled against us the Chinese government will never agree to any and people will never agree to any interference in our internal affairs. We are not soft spined. Even if this causes us some temporary difficulties, we will get by.... Second, we hope that international opinion and foreign governments will take a long term view... If they take a long term view they will see that it is not enough reason to take extreme measures to excite the feelings of the Chinese government and people (*Renmin Ribao* 1989c).

Despite this defiant attitude, Chinese officials continued to insist that the open door was still open and that foreign business should continue to invest in China (*Renmin Ribao* 1989d). The most dramatic effect of the crackdown on the Chinese economy has been on tourism, a major source of foreign exchange in recent years. As a result of revulsion and fear, tourism to China has all but collapsed (*Globe and Mail* 1989d).

The bloody crackdown has had far-reaching implications for China's domestic policy and for its international relationships. There is no doubt that the entire episode of upheaval and repression has grievously undermined the legitimacy of the regime. This is confirmed by the continuation of martial law months after the initial action. Even more important, it has all but precluded a smooth succession to Deng Xiaoping, whose death is likely to occur soon. It is clear that the repression was largely supported and encouraged by the octogenarian generation of veteran revolutionaries (Bixu 1989: 20-22).

In removing Zhao Ziyang, Deng had now removed both of his designated successors Hu Yaobang and Zhao. Ironically, Deng now attempted to retain some of the faith of his associates in his tattered version of reform by elevating Jiang Zemin (instead of Li Peng) to the position of general secretary of the Party. Jiang, Party Secretary in Shanghai, was expected to display continued commitment to the policies of the open door and economic reform. However, the elevation of someone whose base within the Party was even weaker than that of Zhao simply demonstrated the weakness of Party institutions and opened up a new power struggle. In any impending succession Li would be left as the potential scapegoat, an outcome he was determined to avoid by concentrating as much power as he could in his own hands.

The policies of economic reform were scaled back as part of Li's austerity program. While the reforms already promulgated were not repudiated, the vilification of Zhao signalled a return to traditional planning, a policy with which Li and Vice-Premier Yao Yilin were much more in sympathy. They were aided by the repressive ideological atmosphere, in which militant adherence to the principles of socialism was demanded from all levels and which was therefore highly inimical to market experimentation. In successive months, as the foreign investment and tourism dropped off, the central government concentrated resources in its own hands. This in turn further discouraged foreign investment.

Effects on Hong Kong

Outside the territory of the People's Republic of China the crackdown seems to have had its greatest impact in Hong Kong. The declaration of martial law in China set off the largest demonstrations in Hong Kong's history. Up to a million residents are said to have marched on May 21, 1989. On June 4, the day of the crackdown several hundred thousand demonstrated in Hong Kong, and there was near panic about Hong Kong's future. Voices were raised inside and outside the colony about the Sino-British agreement to return the colony to Chinese sovereignty in 1997. Hong Kong residents were not reassured when, in the wake of events in China, several Hong Kong journalists were detained, in addition to well-known political activists from Hong Kong. Calls for revision of the treaty were not heeded by the British government. Moreover, attempts by Britain to extract from China a promise not to station troops in Hong Kong after 1997, and efforts to institute democratic elections before that year, have been greeted with vituperative condemnation by the Chinese authorities. These responses caused jitters throughout the already nervous colony. Denied any reassurance about their own future, and having no confidence in the willingness of the Chinese government to guarantee basic human rights, Hong Kong residents are besieging foreign consulates in the hope of emigrating. This has a direct impact on Canada, as it is the country of choice for Hong Kong emigrants.

Prior to the Tiananmen crackdown, all signs had pointed to an increasing spirit of co-operation in the region. Not only had the historic summit between Deng Xiaoping and Soviet President Gorbachev sealed the end of a quarter-century of bitter enmity between the two great communist powers, but also cautious steps had been taken to reduce tensions and foster economic ties elsewhere in the region. Both China and the Soviet Union had participated in the Seoul Olympics in September 1988, and both were building trade relations with South Korea. Trade relations between the People's Republic and South Korea had begun to reach significant figures, and in recent months there had also been indications of interest in substantial investment in China on the part of South Korean businesses in search of secure supplies of raw materials and lower labour costs (*Globe and Mail* 1988d). On the southern border Vietnam, with which China had fought a brief but bloody border war in 1979, was pulling its troops out of Cambodia after ten years of occupation. India, another country with which China had clashed, had improved relations to the point that its Prime Minister, Rajiv Gandhi, was able to pay a visit to China in December 1988 (*Economist* 1988).

Even the long-drawn-out civil war across the Taiwan Strait had shown significant signs of détente prior to June 1989. The Kuomintang government on Taiwan had relaxed its policy of no contacts with the mainland to such an extent that in two years, from June 1987 to June 1989, there were almost half a million visitors from the island to relatives in the People's Republic. In May the Taiwan government allowed a high-level official delegation to attend the Asian Development Bank meetings in Beijing. Formerly illegal trade relations were being formalized, with cross-strait trade expanding rapidly and significant investment flows beginning. Trade for 1989 was slated to rise by over US$1 billion. Taiwan manufacturers were being lured to China to locate low-skill labour-intensive activities which were no longer profitable because of Taiwan's appreciating currency and rising wages (*Economist* 1989).

The crackdown has dashed hopes that China would constitute a dynamic and powerful link in a chain of booming East Asian economies along the Pacific littoral. Its growing market and increasingly trade-related economy could have inherited the low-technology end of the manufacturing processes in these export-driven and rapidly maturing East Asian economies. The political and economic fallout from the repression has certainly soured the investment climate. While China has proclaimed loudly that "not one" business has pulled out (which sounds suspiciously like the phrase "not one student killed at Tiananmen" so vociferously repeated after the massacre), there have been numerous reports of prospective investments which have been abandoned (*Globe and Mail* 1989e).

Ever since the normalization of relations in 1970 Canada has made China an important focus of its trade relations with East Asia. Canada was for a long time extremely cautious in its dealings with Taiwan and has attempted to increase manufactured exports to the People's Republic of China. Indeed, it could be argued that China is the only important market for Canadian manufactured goods in the region. Canadian multicultural ethnic organizations have been strongly encouraged to take the lead in forging business and trade links with their countries of origin, and nowhere has this been more strongly evident than in the case of China. Federal trade strategy has also linked up with provincial and municipal twinning projects, all of which have been strongly supported by members of the Chinese Canadian community.

The repression of China's democracy movement has led these organizations to turn strongly against the Chinese government. Far from encouraging trade with China, they have—the Chinese Canadian National Committee[4] among them—been urging the Canadian government to impose severe sanctions on China, and they were incensed when the federal cabinet decided to go ahead with a $130 million loan for telecommunications equipment to China in July (*Toronto Star* 1989). By alienating the Chinese Canadian community the Chinese government altered the political basis of Sino-Canadian relations. This generally hostile stand toward the Chinese government has been evident throughout Canadian society, as evidenced by the critical domestic reaction to loans for telecommunications and hydroelectric equipment.[5]

The Canadian government justified the loans on the grounds that they were approved in principle before the June crackdown. With regard to the telecommunications loan specifically, the government argued that the free exchange of information should be fostered and not hindered (*Globe and Mail* 1989f). External Affairs Secretary Joe Clark argued eloquently against isolating China, and reminded Canadians that the worst periods of communist repression in China were precisely those when China had been most isolated from the international community (*Edmonton Journal* 1989b).

Canada is not alone in allowing some departure from its stated sanctions policies. In mid-December 1989 it was revealed that U.S. National Security Advisor Brent Scowcroft had travelled secretly to Beijing in July (*New York Times* 1989a). Soon afterwards the United States announced a slight relaxation of its sanctions policies (*New York Times* 1989b). As early as September, a high-level Japanese delegation had journeyed to China to discuss both trade and investment. Japan was clearly determined to keep close relations with its neighbour regardless of that country's internal policies (*Globe and Mail* 1989g). Under these circumstances Canada could not afford to isolate itself and allow economic advantages to accrue to its competitors.

Conclusion

It is difficult to see the climate significantly improving unless there are dramatic and substantial moves by the Chinese government to engage its own people in a democratic dialogue. The changes in Eastern Europe merely spotlighted Chinese policy as a brutal exception and place the government in the company of the minority of crude and violent political systems, alongside the defunct Ceaucescu regime in Romania. It is unlikely that we shall see a dramatic improvement in Canada's relationship with China in the near future. While the feelings of revulsion are shared by Canadians generally, it is important to note that the organized ethnic associations constitute a permanent interest group seeking to influence Canadian policy towards China. While the interest of other Canadians in the issue may wane, it will probably continue to attract the attention of ethnic activists. Canada's "special relationship" with China is over, as two Canadian academics declared on the fortieth anniversary of the People's Republic (*Globe and Mail* 1989h). At the same time, Canada has not been singled out by the Chinese authorities for a special place as villain (*Globe and Mail* 1989f).

It is now conceivable that Canada's relations with Taiwan will be significantly upgraded so that advantage may be taken of the island state's huge foreign exchange reserves. Such action would, moreover, be a way of recognizing the significant improvement in Taiwan's human rights situation, to which recent events across the Strait of Taiwan offer a sad contrast. Ideology and economics will conspire to limit Canadian enthusiasm for China for a significant time to come.

Notes

[1] This figure was in any case not reached, due to the severe cutbacks to Canada's aid program in April 1989.

[2] Democracy Wall was the name given to a strip of wall near a major bus terminal in Beijing, where in late 1978 and early 1979 young intellectual activists posted up their proposals for accelerated democratic reform in China. The leaders of this movement were arrested and jailed in March and April 1979.

[3] On May 4, 1919, word came back to China that the Chinese delegation to the Versailles Peace Conference had signed the treaty which ceded to Japan former German possessions in China, despite the hopes of the Chinese that their own sovereignty would be restored as a result of their entry into World War I on the allied side. Protests against this perceived act of betrayal by the Chinese government grew into a nationwide movement in favour of democracy and against the traditional Chinese culture.

[4] This is the national umbrella group for all Chinese ethnic organizations in Canada.

[5] For comments on the policy of loans to China see the *Edmonton Journal* (1989a) and the *Hamilton Spectator*, (1989). For Joe Clark's reply, see, the *Edmonton Journal* (1989b).

References

Bixu Qizhi Xianmingde Fandui Dongluan. 1989. Beijing: Renmin Chubanshe: 20-22.

Canada. 1988. Department of External Affairs. *Annual Report 1987/88*. Ottawa: Supply and Services Canada.

_____. 1989. Department of External Affairs. "China and Canada: The Months Ahead." Statement by the Right Honourable Joe Clark. Canadian Foreign Policy Series no. 18. June 30.

Cheng Ming. 1989. "Notes on a Northern Journey." (Luo Bing) 138: pp. 8-11.

Economist. 1988. "Warily Towards Their Himalyan Pass." December 24.

_____. 1989. "Taiwan: Curiously Ungloating." July 1.

Edmonton Journal. 1989a. "A Hypocritical Return to Business." August 8.

_____. 1989b. "China Policy Intact—Clark." August 21.

Financial Times (London). 1989a. "Japan Caught Between Awe and Contempt for China." June 22.

_____. 1989b. "Chinese Repression Condemned." July 15.

Globe and Mail. 1988a. "Canadians May Have Inside Track if Hydro Project Succeeds." April 27.

_____. 1988b. "China Plans Case for GATT." April 28.

_____. 1988c. "China Eager to Join Feuding GATT Gang." December 14.

_____. 1988d. "China Quickly Firming S. Korea Ties." August 4.

_____. 1989a. "Chinese Canadians Mourn and Plan Protests." June 6.

_____. 1989b. "Ottawa Recalls Envoy Home." June 13.

_____. 1989c. "China Accuses G-7 of Gross Interference." July 8.

_____. 1989d. "Xian Hoteliers Ask Government to Save Them from Themselves." October 24.

_____. 1989e. "GM and Fuji Scrap Joint Ventures with Chinese." October 24.

_____. 1989f. "Even Remembrance of Bethune Affected by Chill in Chinese Canadian Relations." October 7.

_____. 1989g. "Business Delegation from Japan Visits China." November 13.

_____. 1989h. "End of a Special Relationship." (B. Michael Frolic and Paul Evans) September 30.

Hamilton Spectator. 1989. "A Disgraceful Deal: Don't Lend to Them." August 5.

New York Times. 1989a. "Two U.S. Aides Visited Beijing in Month After Killing." December 19.

_____. 1989b. "Bush Lifts Some Sanctions." December 20.

Renmin Ribao. 1989a. "The True Picture of the Counter-revolutionary Violence." (Chen Xitong) July 7.

_____. 1989b. May 26.

_____. 1989c. "State Council Spokesperson Yuan Mu's Press Conference." June 8.

Toronto Star. 1989. "Groups Urge Trade Sanctions on China." June 22.

Washington Post. 1989. "Bush Bars High-level Contacts with Beijing." June 21.

4 Canada's Response to the "New Détente" in East-West Economic Relations

Carl H. McMillan

A s the 1980s drew to a close, the drama of change in the eastern half of Europe captured the world's attention and imagination. By the end of the decade new, reformist regimes had come to power in all of the European member-states of the Council for Mutual Economic Assistance (Comecon).[1] Although the pace of change was more rapid everywhere in the political than in the economic sphere, a new basis for the reform of traditional economic structures had been established.

The transformation in the East was also creating conditions for a new relationship with the West. The West viewed the changes in the domestic and foreign policies of the Comecon countries with mounting enthusiasm, and sought ways of responding which would reinforce the process. The new governments in the East gave high priority not only to the expansion of trade with the capitalist countries, but also to the creation of new investment links with them. The result was the emergence of a new détente at the end of the decade, a much improved political climate for the further development of relations in the 1990s.

This chapter examines Canada's role in the rapid revival of East-West economic relations in the second half of the 1980s. It will concentrate on relations with the Soviet Union, because the new Soviet course has served as a catalyst for change in Eastern Europe, and because relations with the Soviet Union continue to dominate Canada's political and economic relations with the area as a whole. I shall argue that while recent developments have radically altered the premises on which Canada's previous policies were based, the Canadian government has been slow to respond to the new situation.

Canada's Traditional Policy and Its Abandonment in the Early 1980s

As a relatively small, trade-dependent economy, Canada has for the most part adopted commercial objectives in its bilateral relations with the Comecon countries. These objectives have necessarily been pursued in the context of efforts to coordinate Western policies towards the East. Within the Western alliance, Canada has often perceived its interests to lie somewhere between those of Europe on the one hand and the United States on the other. Canada's close political relationship with the United States and the considerable integration of the two economies have, however, created certain constraints on the independent pursuit of economic relations with "the other superpower" and its allies.[2]

The expansion of East-West economic relations in the early 1970s, fostered by a "détente" between the two superpowers, found the Liberal government in Ottawa, under the leadership of Pierre Elliott Trudeau, anxious to develop new directions in foreign policy. The Eastern drive to import Western equipment and technology, financed in substantial part by Western credits, coincided with the Trudeau government's goal of restructuring Canadian foreign trade to reduce dependence on the U.S. economy (the "Third Option"), and to diversify the structure of exports by raising the share of manufactures. By the end of the decade, however, Trudeau's détente policies had begun to lose momentum; the Soviet Union was slipping increasingly into the policy stagnation of the end of the Brezhnev era, tensions were reemerging in U.S.-U.S.S.R. relations and domestic, constitutional questions were preoccupying the government in Ottawa to an increasing extent.

In developing economic relations with the East in the 1960s and 1970s Canada was guided by certain basic policy considerations. A brief review of what may be regarded as the "principles" applied over the postwar period under governments in Ottawa which were mostly Liberal will provide the context for the discussion that follows.

First, since the 1955 visit to Moscow of Lester B. Pearson, at that time Secretary of State for External Affairs, an event that launched the process, the federal government has led the way in the development of relations. Official visits, government-sponsored trade missions, trade and economic cooperation agreements, mixed commissions and working groups—these all reflected the impetus that official policy, over a long period, gave to the expansion of such ties. In view of the centralized nature of the systems on the Eastern side, the Canadian approach meant that bilateral relations have in the majority of cases, taken the form of transactions between states. In the important sphere of the grain trade, for example, negotiations have been conducted by state trading monopolies on both sides.

Secondly, Canada has long sought to "normalize" economic relations with the Comecon countries, by subjecting them to the same regulations as those which it applies to its other trading partners. The few exceptions prove this rule. Given Canada's strategic commitments within the Western alliance, exports to the U.S.S.R., Eastern Europe and other "communist countries" have been subject to stricter provisions, under the Export and Import Permits Act, than have exports generally.[3] Moreover, because the non-market nature of prices in the Comecon countries makes it difficult to determine when dumping has occurred, Revenue Canada resorts to special investigation procedures to ascertain whether imports from those countries have arrived in violation of the anti-dumping regulations.[4] Otherwise, Canada's trade and financial relations with the Eastern countries have been free from the myriad of restrictions and regulations that the U.S. government, to take an example, has imposed on its economic relations with them.

This difference in policy approach has derived, in turn, from differing perceptions of national interest in trade with the East. For reasons already cited, Canada has viewed its principal interests as commercial in nature, and it has sought to promote trade with the East through a "business for business' sake" approach. For the United States, all dealings with countries belonging to the "bloc" headed by its rival superpower are inescapably political, and U.S. policy on economic relations with the East has for the most part consciously incorporated political considerations.

Finally, a certain ambivalence has long existed in Canada's export promotion policies towards the East. This ambivalence has hinged on the continued importance of the grain trade to Canadian agriculture; with 75 percent of its grain production destined for export, the agricultural sector is highly dependent on foreign trade. In the 1980s the U.S.S.R. alone purchased over one-fourth of Canada's grain exports. Grain has been the dominant element in trade not only with the U.S.S.R., but with Eastern Europe as well, and has tended to generate large trade surpluses, especially with the former. At the same time, the government has wished to diversify the composition of exports through a variety of official programs, including export credit support, to promote the export of manufactures, especially machinery and equipment. The areas of greatest success in this regard have been equipment and technology for the energy sector—oil, gas, nuclear power—and for forestry activities. Sensitive to the problem of expanding exports of manufactures, while maintaining grain exports, in view of the large trade surpluses that have resulted, the government has sought to treat grain as separate from other areas in state-to-state negotiations.

These long established policy principles underwent significant erosion in the 1980s. Conservative governments in Ottawa, sharing many of the philosophical premises underlying U.S. policy, were less interested than their predecessors in maintaining a differentiated Canadian stance. As a result, the principle of insulating economic relations from politics was quickly abandoned. In response to the Soviet invasion of Afghanistan, and in consort with Washington, the Canadian government applied a wide-ranging set of sanctions against the U.S.S.R. The measures, announced by Prime Minister Joe Clark in January 1980, included a partial grain embargo, tighter export controls, suspension of all official visits and programs and the decision not to renew the official line of credit to the U.S.S.R.[5] The sanctions were slowly removed and official relations gradually restored after the death of Soviet leader Leonid Brezhnev in November 1982, but Ottawa showed little interest in returning to the pro-active East-West trade policies of the 1970s except with regard to the grain trade.[6] Its interest in trade policy was focused elsewhere, on the application of sanctions to South Africa and on the development of new economic relationships—especially with the United States, but also with the dynamic Pacific Rim area and with the rapidly expanding European Common Market.

The Situation at Mid-Decade

By the end of 1984, relations between Canada and the Soviet Union had considerably recovered from the three-year hiatus in official intercourse that had followed the 1980 sanctions (McMillan 1989). Fortuitously, the frequent state funerals of aged Soviet leaders played a role in the restoration of official relations, bringing the Canadian prime minister to Moscow on each occasion and providing recurrent opportunities for at least brief contact between the two governments at the highest level. In March 1985, a new Canadian prime minister, Brian Mulroney, was to make his first official visit to the U.S.S.R. and to meet the new Soviet leader, Mikhail Gorbachev, on the occasion of the funeral of Konstantin Chernenko. Some vestiges of the economic sanctions remained in effect, notably the absence of an official line of credit to the Soviet Union and the continued suspension of scientific and technical exchanges between the two countries.

The recovery of relations was largely formal, with a marked absence of new policy initiatives.[7] The Canada-U.S.S.R. Mixed Economic Commission had resumed its annual meetings in 1983. Negotiations begun in the early 1970s, and subsequently interrupted, had finally come to fruition with the conclusion of a bilateral fisheries agreement and a protocol on Arctic cooperation in 1984. Only in the sphere of the grain trade was there a new, long-term agreement, concluded in 1981, which was, ironically enough, the result of the Western grain embargo and of consequent Soviet determination to secure a diversified source of future supply. The agreement guaranteed Canada minimum sales of 25 million metric tons of grain over a five-year period and established a mixed agricultural commission which met for the first time in 1982. While this was new "machinery," there was little new in the way of substance.

The slow restoration of the official framework and the absence of new policy initiatives can hardly be called surprising if we recall the circumstances in which relations were being re-established. The succession to Brezhnev had created a leadership vacuum in Moscow; in the twilight of the Trudeau era Ottawa was caught up in its own succession preoccupations, and Washington had meanwhile embarked on its new Cold War under Ronald Reagan. Nor did Eastern Europe offer much scope for initiative. This was a period of crisis and martial law in Poland, bankrupt political leadership elsewhere and deep economic difficulties throughout the region, characterized, in relations with the West, by balance of payments crises and even, in some cases, the forced rescheduling of external debt (Joint Economic Committee 1985; Hardt and McMillan 1988).

Paradoxically, as Table 4.1 illustrates, Canadian-Soviet trade reached an historic high in 1984 at $2.15 billion. The paradox is easily explained by the strong Soviet demand for imported grain, stimulated by continuing domestic production shortfalls. The value of Canadian grain exports to the U.S.S.R. alone exceeded two billion dollars in 1984, generating a record trade surplus and an export-import ratio of nearly 75 to 1. Wheat continued to account for the overwhelming bulk (94 percent) of Soviet purchases of Canadian grains. Meanwhile imports from, and non-grain exports to, the U.S.S.R. suffered, falling well below their averages for the preceding ten years.

Table 4.1
Canada's Trade with the U.S.S.R.
(Values in millions of current $ Can.)

Year	Exports	Imports	Trade surplus	Trade with U.S.S.R. as % total trade	Non-grain exports	Growth in non-grain exports (1979=100)
1969-73*	162.7	14.5	148.2	0.48	12.5	4
1974-78*	381.7	40.0	341.7	0.54	87.9	25
1979	773.5	64.1	709.4	0.66	346.0	100
1980	1,534.9	59.3	1,475.6	1.11	247.1	71
1981	1,865.6	77.7	1,787.9	1.22	138.2	10
1982	2,068.7	41.9	2,026.8	1.41	159.4	46
1983	1,760.8	33.3	1,727.5	1.09	135.6	39
1984	2,119.0	28.7	2,090.3	1.05	79.9	23
1985	1,607.9	27.7	1,580.2	0.74	114.7	33
1986	1,215.6	25.5	1,190.1	0.54	277.0	80
1987	800.6	35.6	765.0	0.35	105.1	30
1988	1,141.9	156.2	985.7	0.49	161.1	47

* Figures in these rows are annual averages for the periods given.
Source: Statistics Canada, *Exports and Imports by Country*, various years.

Total Canadian trade with the six East European Comecon countries stood at $520.2 million in 1984. Here again, grain accounted for an important share, especially in trade with East Germany and Poland (Canada's principal trading partners among the six). Trade with Eastern Europe was more balanced than with the Soviet Union, and in some cases trade balances were in the Eastern favour.

Although, as the result of grain exports (sold for cash, not on credit), Canada enjoyed cumulative surpluses amounting to $9.1 billion in the first half of the 1980s, both sides recognized that these surpluses constituted a major structural weakness in bilateral trade. Excessive reliance on grain exports produces not only a short-term instability in trade, but also a long-term vulnerability to trends in Soviet demand, given Canadian supply and competitive conditions on the international grain market.

The New Climate of East-West Relations

Meanwhile, political events in the East increasingly demanded Ottawa's attention. Under dynamic new leadership, the Soviet Union emerged dramatically from its long period of policy stagnation. The initiatives launched by Gorbachev after his election as Soviet Communist Party leader were intended to address the serious domestic, political, economic and social problems that his predecessors—in part because of age and ill health—had allowed to accumulate. Gorbachev's initiatives quickly spilled over into external relations, and also served as a catalyst for change in Eastern Europe.

These developments have radically altered the climate for East-West economic relations. Gorbachev's efforts to settle differences and to establish a basis for cooperation rather than confrontation initially encountered a cautious reception in the West, but scepticism has increasingly given way to enthusiasm. The "end of the Cold War" has been the story of the decade for the world press, and is discussed by Lenard Cohen in Chapter 2. The present chapter will focus more closely on the policy measures that have been adopted, on both sides, to facilitate commercial and financial relations between East and West.

The East has taken important steps to dismantle its traditional system of "state trading." This process began in the more trade-dependent East European economies in the 1970s, but the addition of the huge Soviet economy to the reformist ranks gave the process renewed momentum in the late 1980s. The highlights of these changes in the institutions through which the Comecon countries conduct their external economic relations, both with each other and with the rest of the world, are:[8]

1) *Reorganization.* The government ministries of foreign trade, for long almost solely responsible for both trade negotiations and operations, have been transformed into policymaking and supervisory agencies. State banks for foreign trade have been placed on a more commercial basis.

2) *Decentralization.* The authority and responsibility for conducting foreign trade has been shifted to the domestic enterprises (state, cooperative and private) that are the producers and end-users of traded goods and services. Under the radical reforms, foreign trade rights have been granted automatically to all enterprises, thus allowing practically unrestricted competition among them on foreign markets.

3) *Ownership.* All of the Comecon countries, with the exception of East Germany, which has indicated its intention to follow suit in 1990, have opened their economies to foreign direct investment.[9] Investment by private capitalist firms has been particularly sought. The regulations have been liberalized to allow majority—and even wholly foreign-owned companies to be established.

4) *Convertibility.* The dismantling has also extended to exchange controls that have in the past severely limited the convertibility of Comecon currencies. None of the countries is in a position economically to eliminate controls quickly, and their ability to do so depends to a significant extent on the success of domestic economic reforms. Nevertheless, the goal of convertibility has been officially espoused, and initial steps toward it have been taken, including the establishment of more meaningful rates of exchange for long overvalued currencies.

Reforms of this nature, adopted by the Comecon countries in varying degrees and at a varying pace, are designed to complement the domestic reform process by exposing hitherto sheltered domestic state enterprises to the forces of foreign competition. They are also intended to improve lagging export performance and to attract foreign capital and technology in support of domestic modernization goals.

Meanwhile, the West (with Europe strongly in the lead) has become increasingly persuaded of the genuineness of the Eastern reforms. The sweeping changes in Eastern Europe in the fall of 1989 were no doubt the decisive factor in shaping this new attitude. The concrete response in the economic sphere has taken varied forms, but has on the whole been cautious about linking assistance to the progress of reform. The response has not been limited to the allocation of additional credits to ease the balance of payments problems of heavily indebted Eastern economies. Special investment funds of a longer-term nature have been established; quantitative restrictions on imports from the East have been relaxed; tariff preferences have been granted; and, in some cases, controls on technology exports have been liberalized. Schemes to provide economic advice and business training have also been launched.

The improving climate of East-West relations is also reflected in other developments. The Soviet Union's 1986 request for observer status at the Uruguay Round of the General Agreement on Tariffs and Trade (GATT) negotiations was rejected, but by the end of 1989 the U.S.S.R. had established diplomatic relations with the European Community (EC), under a new EC-Comecon accord, and had signed a long-term trade and cooperation agreement with Brussels. Although no formal Soviet demarche had been made to the International Monetary Fund (IMF) and the World Bank, a member of the board of the Soviet State Bank attended the annual meeting of the Fund and the Bank in Washington in September 1989 (*New York Times* 1989). After the Malta Summit, the granting of most favored nation (MFN) tariff treatment to Soviet products entering the U.S. market seemed increasingly likely. This concession, which would remove a long-standing irritant in Soviet-American relations, would be an important symbol of the new policy climate.

Policy Evolution in the Second Half of the 1980s

With the sanctions imposed in 1980 a Tory government had set the tone for Canada's East-West trade policy in the first half of the decade. The return of the Progressive Conservative party to power in Ottawa, in the fall of 1984, was followed six months later by the accession of Gorbachev to the party leadership in Moscow. It thus fell on a Conservative government to set Canadian policy in response to the growing "revolution" in the East that followed. The government of Brian Mulroney showed itself reluctant to accept that challenge.

The new government continued the process of slowly putting back together the pieces of the policy that had been shattered in 1980. It was Joe Clark, the author of the sanctions policy, who now presided over this process as Secretary of State for External Affairs in the Mulroney cabinet. The Moscow meeting of the Mixed Economic Commission in June 1985 provided the occasion for the new Canadian

Minister for International Trade to visit the Soviet Union.[10] The Commission met again in 1986, in Ottawa, and renewed the ten-year agreement on economic, scientific and technical cooperation, first signed in 1976. Other high-level contacts were made, including reciprocal visits by the Soviet and Canadian foreign ministers. A further major step in the restoration process was the signing in late 1986 of the General Exchanges Agreement, the predecessor of which, dating from 1971, had fallen victim to the 1980 sanctions.[11]

In certain areas the restoration of relations was particularly slow. The official line of credit to the U.S.S.R., which had lapsed at the end of 1979, was not re-established until late 1988, although credit had been extended by the Export Development Corporation (EDC) to all of the Soviet Union's East European allies. The line was reinstituted by cabinet decision, at the request of EDC, in the original (1975) amount of $500 million (in the form of medium- and long-term credit to Soviet purchasers of Canadian goods and services, for the most part capital goods and technology).

The long-term cooperation agreement had also not been fully reactivated, and most of the sectoral working groups set up by the Mixed Economic Commission remained dormant. Canadian officials were reluctant to restore these mechanisms, which, in their view, had not proved very effective in the 1970s. The opening up of direct enterprise-level contacts as a result of *perestroika* had meanwhile removed the rationale for such channels. At the seventh session of the Commission in September 1988 both sides agreed not to reactivate the dormant groups.

The 1980 sanctions laid the groundwork for a tightening of Canada's system of strategic export controls for which Washington was continually pressing. The list of embargoed items was revised in conformity with the new COCOM doctrine of "higher walls around smaller areas". At the same time, the administration of the control system was expanded and strengthened, providing for tighter enforcement at the border and more active prosecution of offenders.[12]

Although the process of restoring relations was virtually complete by the end of 1988, no new policy initiatives in relations with the Soviet Union and Eastern Europe had been undertaken. The few statements on developments in the Eastern countries that emerged from Ottawa were of a cautious nature, advocating a wait-and-see posture and emphasizing the need for a concerted NATO policy position (Cohen 1989). Moreover, the government's White Paper on National Defence, and its expulsion with considerable public fanfare of Soviet embassy officials in 1988, showed that Cold War proclivities were still strong in official Ottawa.[13] As the Eastern reforms gathered momentum, however, the Mulroney government was under mounting public pressure to take more positive action. The growing contrast between the government's do-nothing stance and the activism of the Canadian business community (see below) was particularly embarrassing for political leaders who looked to business as a major source of political support.

The rapid course of political events in Poland and Hungary finally provoked action from the Canadian side. In October 1989, the Prime Minister announced a $42 million aid package for Poland, combining food aid with a fund to support development of the private sector in the two countries and a projected export credit insurance facility within EDC to facilitate the purchase by Poland of urgently needed imports.[14] The announcement came at a time when the European Community and the United States were announcing their own aid packages.

It was, however, the Prime Minister's scheduled visit to the Soviet Union in November that was perceived in Ottawa as the ideal opportunity to eliminate the growing gap between the government's position and the perceptions of the Gorbachev reforms that were current in Canada and elsewhere. It was to be the first full-scale visit of a Canadian Prime Minister to the Soviet Union since the Trudeau visit in 1971.

During the visit, Mulroney went out of his way to demonstrate support for the reform process under way in the Soviet Union and Eastern Europe. A statement on "Canada in the East-West Context," issued by the Prime Minister's Office in connection with the visit, asserted that "it is clear that the revolutionary changes championed by President Gorbachev offer the best chance for East-West relations in the postwar era." The Prime Minister echoed this sentiment in his address at a Kremlin state dinner on the first day of his visit, affirming his "deep conviction that it is very clearly in everyone's best interest that your reforms succeed." He added that Canada "welcomed the greater integration of the U.S.S.R. into the world economy" and would "support progressive Soviet participation in the international trade and payments system as the reforms of Perestroika create the conditions for success." He specifically mentioned, in this regard, close cooperation between the U.S.S.R. and the Organization for Economic Cooperation and Development (OECD), as well as Soviet observer status and eventual membership in GATT (Office of the Prime Minister 1989a). In a Moscow speech two days later the Prime Minister summed it up as follows: "East-West relations are at their most promising point since the war. And Canada-Soviet relations are poised to make a new beginning" (Office of the Prime Minister 1989b). It can be seen that the official rhetoric of the Mulroney visit clearly abandoned the equivocal tone of the government's previous statements.

The Canadian government was obviously anxious to create the public impression that new substance as well as new rhetoric had emerged from this visit. It arranged for the Prime Minister to sign, while in Moscow, no less than ten bilateral agreements for cooperation in a variety of areas, ranging from peaceful uses of nuclear energy to combatting narcotic drug abuse. While all of these agreements had an economic dimension, two are of particular significance for future commercial intercourse. A full-scale agreement for reciprocal investment protection is clearly designed to encourage Canadian firms to invest in the Soviet economy. This agreement is the first of its kind for Canada, and provides official guarantees not hitherto available to Canadian investors abroad.[15] An umbrella accord authorizes individual Canadian provinces and Soviet republics to establish direct cooperation in economic, scientific, technical and cultural areas. The announcement during the visit of the intended opening of a Canadian Consulate in Kiev took on special economic significance in light of this agreement.

The government's actions in Moscow supported initiatives already undertaken at the provincial and business levels. The agreement on provincial-republican relations formally sanctioned contacts that had already been initiated, notably between the Province of Alberta and the Russian and Ukrainian republics. The positive tone of the Mulroney visit provided justification for sentiment already widely held within the Canadian business community. The business community had clearly demonstrated both its conviction that the Soviet reforms should be taken seriously and its interest in actively exploiting the opportunities they opened up; in 1988 it took the initiative in forming a Canada-U.S.S.R. Business Council. The Prime Minister was accordingly joined, during his visit to Moscow, by a 240-strong Canadian business delegation and, together with the Soviet Prime Minister, he opened the inaugural meeting of the new council. Let us turn, then, to developments at the business level that had occurred in the second half of the 1980s and view them against the mid-decade background of policy stagnation and consequent reinforcement of the traditional structure of grain-dominated trade.

The Course of Economic Relations, 1985-89

Canada's trade with the East declined after 1984. Trade turnover with the six East European Comecon countries stood at $544.3 million in 1988, a fall in real terms. The downward trend in trade with the U.S.S.R. can be seen from by the data in Table 4.1.

The data reveal the powerful effect of grain exports on bilateral trade flows. The decline in grain exports to the U.S.S.R. after their 1984 peak (in value) was due both to demand and to supply factors. Soviet grain output rose above the level of 200 million metric tons (mmt) in the 1985-86 crop year for the first time since 1978 and remained above it in the subsequent two years. In 1988-89, when Soviet grain output fell somewhat, severe drought in the Canadian West pushed grain exports to the U.S.S.R. to their lowest level (2.7 mmt) in ten years.

Trade is not the whole story, however. A number of innovative developments have enhanced the quality of relations and will increasingly make themselves felt quantitatively in flows of goods, services and capital.

After years of unsuccessful Canadian bids for capital projects in the Soviet Union, a breakthrough occurred in 1985. Lavalin Inc., the Quebec-based multinational engineering firm, was successful in winning the first of a series of contracts for the construction of sour-gas gathering systems and processing plants in newly developed gas fields near the Caspian Sea. Meanwhile, a number of Canadian firms in the oil and gas industries won Soviet orders for equipment and technology. Most of these firms were located in the West where, because of the recession in the domestic energy sector, the Alberta government was especially active in assisting efforts to explore foreign markets.

It is such firms that have also taken the lead in opening permanent offices in Moscow, demonstrating their commitment to pursuing business opportunities in the U.S.S.R. on a longer-term basis. Permanent representation in Moscow was an area in which Canadian firms had lagged behind their West European and American competitors. Half a dozen Canadian firms now have representative offices in the U.S.S.R.

Possibilities for maintaining a direct presence in the Soviet Union have greatly expanded since the introduction, in January 1987, of legislation establishing the conditions for foreign equity participation in joint enterprises on Soviet territory. Canadian firms were uncharacteristically swift and enterprising in responding to the new opportunities which the Soviet legislation afforded within a context background of broader reform measures. By October 1, 1989, twenty-three Canadian-Soviet joint ventures had been officially registered, and at least as many more were under discussion. While the registered ventures only constituted 3.1 percent of the 748 joint enterprises between Soviet and OECD partners which were in the official records as of October 1, 1989, this proportion was still considerably greater than the Canadian share (0.27 percent) of the West's non-grain trade with the U.S.S.R.[16] The grain trade, being dominated on both sides by state trading agencies, provides little scope for such ventures; but taken as a whole agribusiness is a promising area of cooperation, and one Canadian-Soviet joint enterprise in animal husbandry has been established.

The Canadian-Soviet joint ventures established as of the end of 1989 tended to be concentrated in the service sector, mostly in hotel and restaurant services. In terms of capital investment, they reflected the small scale of Western investments in joint ventures generally (on average under two million U.S. dollars, according to Soviet official statistics). Only a few investments were in manufacturing: all-terrain tracked vehicles, automotive parts, communications equipment.

It was the momentum generated by the Canadian business response to the Soviet economy's new receptiveness to foreign equity investment that led to the formation of the Canada-U.S.S.R. Business Council. Canadian companies involved in joint enterprises in the U.S.S.R. were among the founding members of the Council (Canadian Foremost, Canadian Fracmaster, McDonald's, Magna International). A major role in its formation, however, was played by Albert Reichman of Olympia & York Developments Inc., whose personal interest served as an important catalyst. As Canadian co-chairman, Reichman presided with his Soviet counterpart (the Chairman of the Soviet Chamber of Commerce and Industry) over the inaugural meeting of the Council which Prime Minister Mulroney attended in Moscow on November 22, 1989. Olympia & York has announced plans for a large office complex in Moscow, covered by one of the commercial protocols signed in connection with the Mulroney visit. The total value represented by these protocols exceeds $1 billion. Although not all of the deals making up this total are firm, and some may never be realized, there is little doubt of the intensity of interest that has developed in the Canadian business community.

The Challenge of a New Relationship

This paper has traced the rise of a new relationship following Canada's first abortive effort to establish detente with the East. The eighties have differed from the preceding decade in that government policy has lagged behind, instead of leading in the development of new ties. Whereas the first detente was imposed from above by the Trudeau government, the second has sprung up from below. It is the Canadian business community, especially certain of its members in Toronto and Calgary aided by a few aggressive law firms, that has taken the initiative away from the federal government. Some provincial and territorial governments, notably in Edmonton and Yellowknife, have also been more active than Ottawa in initiating policies and programs.

The result is a new relationship that is far less dominated by state-to-state agreements and official contacts. This is surely a healthy development. It means that relations are being rid of their bureaucratic character, not only the Eastern side, where decentralizing reforms are taking effect, but on the Canadian side as well. The major exception is the grain trade, which continues to be conducted at the state-to-state level.

The future, however, is rather uncertain. Grain exports to the U.S.S.R. have had their heyday (Hay and Davies 1984; Frank 1988) and had already fallen off in the late 1980s. New Soviet policies are intended to reduce imports further. Self-sufficiency in grains has been a long-standing, though elusive, goal of Soviet policy. It may not be easily attainable, but it is being approached with new vigour and imagination.[17] Even at present output levels, if the Soviet Union could eradicate the excessive losses in harvesting, transport and storage that consume an estimated 20-30 percent of the crop, it would virtually eliminate the need for grain imports. The Canada-U.S.S.R. grain agreement guarantees a minimum of sales until 1991, but the circumstances described support that its renegotiation will be difficult.[18] At the very least, the U.S.S.R. can be expected to demand greater flexibility in any future purchase commitments.

The traditional relationship faces other challenges. Because of *glasnost*, the mega-projects characteristic of past Soviet economic development are coming under mounting criticism in the U.S.S.R. on technical, social, environmental and financial grounds. The last may alone be decisive; the U.S.S.R. simply cannot afford any more massive development schemes. While not spelling the end of capital projects in the Soviet Union, this situation does mean that Canadian firms, especially those in the oil and gas equipment industry, and Canadian governments too, will have to adjust their export development targets.

Canada must be prepared to lose some of its accustomed competitive advantages because of the new Soviet priorities. The areas of greatest promise are consumer goods and services and electronics. Now at the top of import priorities are equipment, technology and know-how, the latter for the expansion and modernization of the long neglected light industries and the distribution of their products to the Eastern populations. In this market Canadian firms will have stiff competition from their counterparts in the United States, Europe and Japan. In the agricultural sector, the downstream areas of agribusiness are those that currently have the greatest export potential.

Financing must necessarily be an important component of the new relationship, given the severe balance of payments difficulties faced by all the Eastern countries. New government credits have been announced, but Canadian commercial banks have not yet emerged from the isolationism into which they withdrew during the financial crisis of the early 1980s.

The traditional imbalance in trade (especially with the Soviet Union) takes on greater significance in the new circumstances. The problem is to reduce it without drastically curtailing the volume of trade. If less use is to be made of credits—and neither side wants to see them playing the dominant role in future trade expansion that they did in the 1970s—this means that Canada will have to buy more from its Eastern trading partners.

Foreign investments are a key feature of the new Eastern development strategies, which emphasize export-led growth. Canadian participation in export-oriented joint enterprises in the Soviet and Eastern European economies can therefore help to create a more balanced and stable long-term commercial relationship. So can Eastern investments in marketing structures in Canada. In 1988-89, for example, the Soviet Union established one new marketing company in Canada, purchased the outstanding equity in two others and used its equity in a fourth to finance a new marketing company in the United States.

Increased flows of investment capital can, however, have only limited effect on trade balances so long as traditional economic systems continue to stifle the competitiveness of Eastern exports in Canadian and other Western markets. In the end, only significant progress in the reform of these systems during the new decade can eliminate the chronic imbalances in East-West trade.

Notes

[1] The Council is an international economic organization with the objective of promoting "socialist economic integration" among its members. The European members are Bulgaria, Czechoslovakia, East Germany, Hungary, Poland, Romania and the Soviet Union. Relations with the non-European members (Cuba, Mongolia and Vietnam) will not be covered in this paper.

[2] The problems of reconciling the sometimes divergent pressures originating in the bilateral (Canada-U.S.S.R.), multilateral (NATO alliance) and trilateral (U.S.-U.S.S.R.-Canada) contexts are treated at greater length in McMillan (1989), especially pages 4-16.

[3] Canada's policies with regard to strategic exports are coordinated with other major industrial exporting nations through the consultative procedures of a special Coordinating Committee (COCOM) established under the aegis of the North Atlantic Treaty Organization (NATO). All NATO countries except Iceland are members of COCOM; two non-NATO countries, Japan and Australia, are also members.

[4] Use of market-economy prices as indicators of the Eastern cost of production often works to the disadvantage of Eastern exports, making them appear to be dumped even when this is in fact not the case.

[5] The sanctions are reviewed and assessed in Nossal (forthcoming).

[6] The partial grain embargo was lifted in November 1980; grain exports boomed, and in 1981 a new long-term grain agreement was signed.

[7] An exception was the founding in 1984, with federal government support, of the Canadian-East European Trade Council, within the framework of the international division of the Canadian Chamber of Commerce. As of May 1989, the Council was made up of 67 Canadian member-firms.

[8] For more detail, see Hough (1988) and Jacobsen (1989).

[9] The new East German government of Prime Minister Hans Modrow has announced that it will present detailed proposals for a joint venture law in 1990 (*Financial Post*, 1990: 9).

[10] Under the aegis of the 1976 Long Term Agreement between Canada and U.S.S.R. on Economic, Industrial, Scientific and Technical Cooperation, the Mixed Economic Commission normally meets annually, alternating between the two capital cities.

[11] This umbrella agreement governs the various academic, scientific and cultural exchanges between the two countries.

[12] Approval of applications for export licenses is administered by the Export Controls Division of the federal Department of External Affairs.

[13] The Soviet retaliation to the expulsions weakened the staff of the Canadian embassy in Moscow at an untimely moment.

[14] The haste with which this announcement was made revealed its minimal advance preparation and lack of detail.

[15] They have, however, been able to look to EDC's Foreign Investment Insurance Program for coverage against exceptional (political) risks.

[16] The trade data are for 1987, the latest available.

[17] Although collective and state farms have been retained as the principal forms of agricultural organization, the measures adopted at the March 1989 Plenum of the Soviet Communist Party introduce some significant innovations, especially the concept of long-term leasing of land to farmers. See Giroux (1989) and Van Atta (1989).

[18] In the first three years, the U.S.S.R. purchased 15 of the 25 mmt to which it is committed over the full five-year term of the agreement.

References

Canada. 1989a. Office of the Prime Minister. Address by the Right Honourable Brian Mulroney, Prime Minister of Canada, November 20, 1989, Moscow, Press Release, Ottawa.

———. 1989b. Office of the Prime Minister. Address by the Right Honourable Brian Mulroney, Prime Minister of Canada, Inaugural Meeting of the Canada-U.S.S.R. Business Council, November 22, 1989. Moscow, Press Release, Ottawa.

Cohen, Andrew. 1989. "Canada's Foreign Policy: The Outlook for the Second Mulroney Mandate." *Behind the Headlines.* Canadian Institute of International Affairs, June.

Financial Post. 1990. "East Germany to seek foreign ventures." January 12.

Frank, James C. 1988. "Who Will Buy Our Wheat? The Next Agricultural Crisis." *Canadian Business Review,* Summer 1988: 16-19.

Giroux, Alain. 1989. "Le Plenum de mars 1989 sur l'agriculture soviétique: un compromis". *Le Courrier des Pays de l'Est,* no. 338, March: 65-9.

Hardt, J.P. and McMillan, C.H., eds. 1988. *Planned Economies: Confronting the Challenges of the 1980s.* Cambridge: Cambridge University Press.

Hay, Keith A.J. and Davies, Robert J. 1984. "Declining Resources, Declining Markets." *International Perspectives,* March-April: 13-18.

Hough, Jerry F. 1988. *The Opening Up of the Soviet Economy.* Washington, D.C.: Brookings.

Jacobsen, Carl, ed. 1989. *Soviet Foreign Policy, New Dynamics, New Themes.* London: The Macmillan Press.

Joint Economic Committee, U.S. Congress, 1985. *East European Economies: Slow Growth in the 1980s.* Washington, D.C.: U.S. Government Printing Office, three volumes.

McMillan, Carl H. 1989. "After Detente: Canada's Economic Relations with the U.S.S.R. in the 1980s." Working Paper no. 4, Centre for Russian and East European Studies, October.

New York Times. 1989. "International bankers told of Soviet reforms." September 29.

Nossal, Kim Richard, (forthcoming). *Canada, Sanctions, and the Soviet Union: The Lessons from Experience.* Kingston: McGill-Queen's University Press.

Van Atta, D. 1989. "Theorists of Agrarian *Perestroika.*" *Soviet Economy*, January-March: 70-99.

5   Strategic Arms Control

Tariq Rauf[1]

Strategic offensive arms control between the United States and the Soviet Union is now in the fourth of the series of phases that began twenty years ago. The four phases are: Strategic Arms Limitation Talks (SALT) I, 1969-1972; SALT II, 1972-1979; Strategic Arms Reduction Talks (START), 1982-1983; and the subsequent Nuclear and Space Arms Talks (NST) since March 1985 (Barton 1976: 172-227; *Arms Control Reporter* 1985: 611.A.1-8). These negotiations have sought to control the size of the two superpowers' intercontinental-range nuclear weapons, comprising land-based ballistic missiles (ICBMs), sea-launched ballistic missiles (SLBMs), and long-range or strategic nuclear-armed bombers. Strategic systems are defined as having ranges in excess of 5,500 kilometres and are capable of hitting the territory of the other superpower.

Background

In mid-June 1989, after a seven-month hiatus, the NST in Geneva were resumed under a new U.S. administration headed by President George Bush. The United States and the Soviet Union had completed ten negotiating rounds by late 1988, and had drawn up the basic framework of a strategic arms reduction agreement consisting of a 360-page Joint Draft Text with associated protocols; the document contained, however, over 1,200 items enclosed in square brackets, being points that required resolution. The two sides started the eleventh round on June 19 with continuing differences over crucial issues in the Strategic Arms Reduction Talks (START), and the Defence and Space Talks (DST), that together make up the Nuclear and Space Talks (Arms Control Association 1989: 63).

The 1985, 1986, and 1987 Reagan-Gorbachev summits had resulted in agreement in principle that each side should reduce its strategic nuclear forces to a maximum of 6,000 accountable nuclear warheads on 1,600 deployed launchers—i.e. a mix of intercontinental ballistic missiles and long-range bombers—and that this reduction should be phased in over seven years. Warheads on ballistic missiles would be limited to 4,900 while nuclear-armed, long-range, air-launched cruise missiles (ALCMs) would not exceed 1,100, and each heavy bomber equipped only for nuclear-armed gravity bombs and short-range attack missiles (SRAMS) would be counted as one warhead. As well, the Soviets would cut by half their force of 308 SS-18 "heavy'" missiles each carrying 10 nuclear warheads, and reduce their aggregate throw weight (the weight that is placed on a trajectory toward the target by the central boost phase of the missile) by fifty percent. The two sides had agreed to deal with the thorny issue of limits on nuclear-armed sea-launched cruise missiles (SLCMs) in a separate agreement.

Major areas of disagreement included: the method for counting nuclear weapons carried aboard strategic bombers, as well as the definition of ALCMs and mobile land-based missiles, verification provisions, the meaning and the future of the 1972 Anti-Ballistic Missile (ABM) Treaty,[2] and the link, if any, between strategic force reductions and the future deployment of strategic defences envisaged in connection with the U.S. Strategic Defence Initiative (SDI).

Bush Administration Policy

The seven-month delay between the tenth and the eleventh NST negotiating rounds was largely the result of president-elect George Bush's announcement, in mid-December 1988, that the resumption of NST tentatively scheduled for mid-February 1990 would be postponed indefinitely pending a review of arms control and security policy.

The much vaunted review was not completed until the summer. In the event, it turned out to be a disappointment because it was not effected within an overall framework for the future of East-West relations. In effect, the new administration decided to respond to events in preference to undertaking any new initiatives regarding strategic arms control. President Bush's foreign policy review turned out to be a series of four major speeches that were marked by their dullness. In his May 12 speech, however, Bush resurrected President Dwight Eisenhower's July 1955 "Open Skies" plan, calling for unhindered aerial surveillance and monitoring of military activities on the territories of the superpowers and other parties to such an agreement (*Barometer* 1989: 5-6). Open Skies is perceived by arms control experts as possibly contributing to the verification of a START agreement. Canada was instrumental in persuading Bush to propose the Open Skies plan (Department of External Affairs and International Trade 1989a: 13).

On resuming NST in mid-June, U.S. administration officials were careful to point out that the negotiations for an accord to reduce conventional forces in Europe (CFE) were now their main priority (*Arms Control Reporter* 1989: 611.B.553). This essentially meant that for the first time since the superpowers began discussions over two decades ago on the limitation of strategic nuclear weapons reductions, such armaments were no longer Washington's main arms control priority, even though the Bush administration had inherited an almost complete framework for 50 percent cuts.

The administration, in another departure from previous U.S. policy, sought to negotiate and implement verification and stability measures prior to a START treaty. These measures would include advance notification of exercises involving strategic missiles and bombers, a ban on low-flying or "depressed trajectory" missiles, and an experimental verification of the number of warheads on ballistic missiles (*Arms Control Reporter* 1989: 611.B.554).

Some Limited Progress

The long overdue first meeting between U.S. Secretary of State James Baker and Soviet Foreign Minister Eduard Shevardnadze took place in late September at Jackson Hole, Wyoming, and, because of Soviet pressure, it resulted in START being accorded the same high priority in Washington as a CFE agreement.

In a surprise move the Soviets dropped their linkage between completing and implementing a START agreement and achieving a DST accord. At Wyoming, Shevardnadze stated that the Soviets were willing to base the START simply on the assumption that the Antiballistic Missile (ABM) Treaty would continue in the form in which it was signed and would have unlimited duration. This clearly was one of the most important Soviet concessions to date. The Soviets also proposed that a violation of, or a withdrawal from, the ABM Treaty would provide a basis for withholding compliance with and implementation of a START treaty on grounds of supreme national interest (*Arms Control Today* 1989: 9).

While the Bush administration did not reject this approach, it continued to declare its support of both the SDI program and the previous administration's unilateral (and controversial) "broad" or permissive interpretation of the ABM Treaty, which allowed for mobile and space-based strategic defences. SDI, however, has been steadily losing support in Congress, and in May even the Joint Chiefs of Staff urged that the United States give up its insistence on the right to deploy extensive strategic defences. As well, Congress has been paring down the SDI budget every year while the projected deployment date of any limited system keeps getting pushed further into the future (*Bulletin of the Atomic Scientists* 1989: 5).

In order to secure a better position from which to insist on a strict interpretation of the ABM Treaty, the Soviets during the Wyoming ministerial meeting, announced their decision to dismantle unconditionally, and completely, the large-phased array radar station at Abalakovo, near Krasnoyarsk in south-central Siberia. The United States had long charged that this installation violated the ABM Treaty because of its inland location (USIS 1989a: 41).

The two sides also reached agreement on a verification and stability package. These two concepts, however, have very different meanings for the United States and the Soviet Union depending on the meaning given to the term associated with them, i.e., predictability. For the United States, predictability means an information exchange on military activities, and reciprocal visits to facilities working on strategic defences as they would be defined under the broad interpretation of the ABM Treaty. (Baker's invitation to the Soviets to visit two SDI facilities was not taken up.)

The Soviets, on the other hand, understand predictability to mean the establishment of numerical limits on research and development of SDI technologies, particularly space-based systems, within the traditional or "narrow" interpretation of the ABM Treaty.

In the Soviet view, strategic stability would be enhanced by reductions beyond those agreed under START and by reinforcing the ABM Treaty with additional limits or measures. The United States, in contrast, considers discussions on strategic stability as enabling it to move along a clearly defined path toward future deployment of strategic defences.

At the Wyoming meeting, the U.S. administration agreed to reverse its longstanding opposition to mobile ICBMs, subject to Congress providing funding for such weapon systems. Under one plan, the United States would have 500 warheads on 50 MX missiles, and another 500 on single-warhead small intercontinental ballistic missiles (SICBMs), for a total of 1,000 warheads on 550 missiles (*New York Times* 1989a; *Toronto Star* 1989b). The Soviets already have deployed some 50 SS-24, and 144 SS-25 mobile missiles (CCACD 1989a).

Other significant developments resulting from the meeting included an agreement on the advance notification of major strategic exercises, and another on defining ballistic missiles in terms of deployed missiles and their associated launchers—thus resolving a major issue of disagreement.

Regarding SLCMs, the Soviets proposed that limits must be agreed upon simultaneously with the signature of START, but that such an agreement need not be an integral part of the START treaty. The precise Soviet position on SLCMs remained unclear, since it varied from a complete ban to a combined limit of 400 nuclear- and 600 conventionally-armed missiles to agreed limits on nuclear SLCMs only. The United States meanwhile continued to maintain its opposition to SLCM limits, citing as reasons its doubts about the possibility of verification and its refusal to accept naval arms control.

It is interesting to note in this regard that in July 1989 physicists from both countries boarded the Soviet guided-missile cruiser *Slava*, at the port of Yalta on the Black Sea, to carry out experiments aimed at determining the ease of detection of the presence of a nuclear warhead the Soviets had hidden in one of the 16 SLCMs on board the warship. Using relatively simple equipment, the scientists easily detected the nuclear warhead. However, it was also evident that such equipment could not easily detect all types of nuclear charges placed in less accessible locations or used at a distance from the vessel (Union of Concerned Scientists 1989: 2; USIS 1989b: 15).

At the close of the twelfth round of NST negotiations in early December, following the Malta summit between Bush and Gorbachev, agreements were reached on two joint verification exercises to begin in advance of a START treaty. These included an agreement to conduct trial inspections of strategic bombers for the purpose of testing each side's ability to distinguish ALCM-carrying bombers from other bombers, and to conduct trial inspections of ballistic missile warheads as one means of verifying compliance with the limit of 4,900 ballistic missile warheads (*New York Times* 1989b; *Ottawa Citizen* 1989).

Informed analysts, in late December 1989, believed that a START treaty would not be ready until late 1990.

Canada's Position

While Canada is not a party to the START and DST negotiations, its pressing concerns in the areas of arms control and defence give it a clear and immediate interest in the outcome of the Nuclear and Space Talks. Over the past few years, mainly because of the insistence of the non-governmental arms control community, Canada has supported, the following positions: limits on ALCMs and SLCMs adherence to a "strict" or "narrow"; interpretation of the ABM Treaty (which prohibits both mobile and space-based SDI anti-missile systems); a negotiated, stable transition to ballistic missile defences; and stabilization of armaments at lower levels (Department of External Affairs 1988a: 62; Office of the Secretary of State for External Affairs 1988b: 7; Roche 1988: 2; Talbott 1988: 62; Office of the Prime Minister 1987; 1989b: 5, and 1989c: 4).

Although these positions are sensible and desirable they do not go far enough to protect Canadian security interests. While Ottawa is actively involved in multilateral security matters, such as conventional force reductions in Europe (see chapter 6 by Roger Hill) and negotiations for a chemical weapons ban at the Conference on Disarmament in Geneva, it is clearly reluctant to emphasize the Canadian view of bilateral relations with the United States which affect security matters. This attitude differs markedly from that of the European allies, who have strongly represented their interests in Washington, as can be seen from the negotiations on the Intermediate-range Nuclear Forces (INF) Treaty in 1987, and the discussions which took place earlier this year on future of U.S. short-range nuclear weapons in Europe.

The belief seems prevalent in Ottawa that, because Canada is not a party to the NST, it is not in a strong position to make suggestions to Washington, or to raise concerns over such issues as U.S. strategic modernization or force structure. It would also appear that the Mulroney government is sensitive, and perhaps even timid, when it comes to discussing strategic arms issues with the U.S. administration. Canadian officials apparently believe that raising Washington's ire on strategic arms control issues may provoke retaliation in other important areas, such as bilateral trade relations and the environment.

The Emerging START Treaty

The present framework of a START treaty raises a number of significant questions for Canadian (and also international) security and arms control interests.

Quantitative Constraints

While both the United States and the Soviet Union say that a START treaty would reduce strategic offensive weapons by 50 percent, generous counting rules for gravity (or air-dropped) nuclear bombs, short-range nuclear-armed attack missiles (SRAMs), and ALCMs mean that the actual reduction in deployed warhead numbers would be about 15 percent rather than 50 percent as claimed. In fact, even after implementing START-mandated reductions, both superpowers will have deployed more strategic warheads than they had at the outset of the negotiations.

The explanation is as follows: the bomber counting rule, as agreed between the two sides, would count each modern strategic bomber carrying up to 24 nuclear-armed gravity bombs or SRAMs as only *one* warhead under the 6,000 warhead ceiling, and not as 24. Thus the United States could deploy some 3,500 SRAMs or gravity bombs that would escape START limits, while the Soviet Union could add some 2,300 such non-accountable nuclear weapons.

If the United States has its way in attributing to bombers with ALCM capability a notional count of only 10 missiles under the 6,000 warhead ceiling, rather than the actual number carried (which could be as high as 16 to 20), both sides would be free to deploy even more non-accountable weapons.

Further, the United States has, at the present time, deployed 1,899 launchers or SNDVs (strategic nuclear delivery vehicles), while the Soviet Union has 2,488. Reductions to a common ceiling of 1,600 deployed launchers each would imply only an 18.6 percent actual cut by the United States as compared to a 36.9 percent reduction by the Soviet Union. A 6,000 accountable warhead ceiling on each side, given the bomber-carried weapon counting rule, would involve a cut of nearly 14 percent in the case of the United States (down to 10,579 from the present 12,570) and a cut of nearly 10 percent in the case of the Soviet Union (down to 8,996 from the current 10,988). In aggregate terms the combined U.S.-U.S.S.R. strategic nuclear warhead arsenal would be reduced from 23,558 to 19,757—that is to say, by only about 16 percent, if non-accountable weapons are included and nuclear-armed SLCMs are not (SIPRI 1988: 302-304; U.S. Congress 1988: 21-23; NRDC 1987: 12-14).

In fairness, however, the START sub-limit of 4,900 warheads on ballistic missiles (within the 6,000 overall ceiling) would mandate cuts of nearly 40 percent for the United States and 50 percent for the Soviet Union (SIPRI 1988: 302). Also, the Soviets have agreed to cut by half their present force of 308 SS-18 ("heavy") ICBMs, with 10 warheads apiece, to 154 launchers with a total of 1,054 warheads. However, the United States' advantage over the Soviet Union in the numbers of deployed warheads and bombers will continue even after a START treaty is implemented, if both accountable and non-accountable warheads and bombers are taken into consideration; this is the effect of the counting rule referred to above.

It follows that Canadians, and others, should not be misled by the myth that a START treaty will bring about an actual 50 percent reduction in the superpowers nuclear arsenals. Although limited reductions would represent a significant step forward, the absence, in the current START documents, of comprehensive qualitative restrictions on strategic arms modernization may simply result in the arms race being channeled along new technological routes which will lead to an even more unstable situation and will be even less manageable by arms control procedures.

Qualitative Restrictions

A START treaty, unlike SALT II, will not ban strategic modernization except in the case of heavy missiles. Neither side will have to give up any of its current nuclear modernization programs. In the case of the United States these include the SRAM II, the low-observable (or "stealth") technology strategic bomber (B-2), the *Trident* II (D-5) SLBM, the *Ohio*-class SLBM carrying submarine (SSBN), the advanced ALCM (AGM-129A and its successor), and the 10-warhead MX ICBM; and in the case of the Soviet Union, the 10-warhead rail-mobile/fixed-silo deployed SS-24 ICBM, the single-warhead road-mobile SS-25 ICBM, the SS-N-20 and SS-N-23 SLBMs, the *Typhoon*- and *Delta* IV-class SSBNs, and the TU-160 (*Blackjack*) strategic bomber. Both sides are also developing long-range nuclear SLCMs.

Some Canadian non-governmental arms control analysts have voiced concerns that a START treaty would enable both sides to carry out open-ended nuclear modernization programs. In the absence of true 50 percent reductions, both sides having the freedom to develop, test and deploy new generations of advanced and more capable weapons, will tend to retire older systems under START, thus assembling in relatively smaller but more capable strategic offensive forces. Post-START forces will therefore be "leaner but meaner."

Canadian (and international) security could be enhanced if a better defined ban on the modernization of START-permitted systems were to be instituted in a START agreement. It is still not too late to demand that the modernization of ICBMs, SLBMs and strategic bombers be limited to only one new type each, with firm restrictions on flight-testing at designated ranges, unencrypted transmission of both ballistic and cruise missile telemetry, and on-site inspections to facilitate verification.

Canada is a "front line" state where strategic arms are concerned since the flight paths of long-range nuclear systems are over the North Pole and Canadian territory. Thus Canada has both the right and every reason to stress the requirement for negotiated, verifiable and radical reductions in strategic offensive arms (CCACD 1987).

Cruise Missiles

Both superpowers are currently developing advanced, long-range, nuclear- and conventionally-armed cruise missiles in both the air- and the sea-launched variants. The introduction of radar-evading "stealth" technology together with light-weight, fuel-efficient, jet engines capable of sustaining supersonic flight, and terrain contour mapping (TERCOM) technologies to guide the missiles to their targets, will produce a significant reduction in attack warning times. These technological developments will further blur the distinction between stabilizing retaliatory weapons and destabilizing first-strike (or surprise attack) weapons. The prospect of the Soviets developing and deploying such systems is particularly daunting to Canadian and North American Aerospace Defence (NORAD) planners.

Projected Soviet deployments of ALCMs and SLCMs capable of hitting targets in North America have already stimulated increasing interest in a buildup of advanced air defences to counter this "air-breathing" threat. Future air defence technologies are currently being explored by the United States, with some Canadian participation, within the framework of the Air Defence Initiative (ADI).

A significant increase in the cost of "thickened" continental air defences would have serious implications for Canadian defence planning and budgeting (CCACD 1989a). It is, therefore, clearly in Canada's interest to encourage both superpowers to negotiate a ban or at least strict limits on the modernization and deployment of cruise missiles. Furthermore, every effort should be made to overcome verification problems and to bring SLCMs into an arms control regime which would parallel a START treaty.

START and Stability

The underlying aim of the negotiations on limiting strategic nuclear weapons is to avoid nuclear war. Both superpowers are therefore very interested in strengthening crisis (or first-strike) stability. This means reducing the chances of any direct military conflict between the superpowers by strengthening the retaliatory (or second-strike) forces, and reducing any incentives on either side to launch a nuclear first-strike.

The NST aim to establish both structural and operational arms control measures. The former include reductions in strategic offensive forces and the strengthening of deterrent capabilities. The latter include the establishment of procedures and mechanisms to create military transparency by such means as information exchanges, crisis control centres, on-site monitoring, and advance notification of strategic exercises.

In addition, the superpowers have a common interest in slowing down the arms race and achieving stability at lower levels of armaments. Negotiated, verifiable arms control agreements are essential instruments for this purpose.

Finally, the overall political relationship between the United States and the Soviet Union plays an important role in creating an environment conducive to arms limitation and an increase in the level of mutual trust. Recent changes in the Soviet Union under the leadership of Mikhail Gorbachev, such as *glasnost*, *perestroika*, the acceptance of intrusive, on-site verification, renunciation of the use of force, and the de-ideologization of foreign policy have all contributed to a radical change in the East-West political atmosphere.

The Bush administration, in contrast to its predecessor, has adopted a more cooperative and sober approach toward relations with the East. The prospects for achieving a START treaty, therefore, seem encouraging, but numerous technical details and some major policy differences will have to be sorted out soon if a treaty is to be ready for signature by late 1990.

Conclusions

The emerging East-West détente raises the possibility of further reductions beyond those to be achieved under a START agreement. Such possibilities have given rise to some new literature on the concept of minimum deterrence, which postulates that a situation of zero nuclear weapons would lead to instability and that therefore some minimum number of nuclear weapons would have to be retained (Committee of Soviet Scientists 1987: 32; and Michael May, et. al. 1988).

The rapid change in East-West relations signified by the end of the Cold War, the acceptance of intrusive on-site verification by the Soviet Union, major political developments in Eastern Europe, and the tearing down of the Iron Curtain, have combined to create pressure on governments to find ways of making further reductions in both strategic and conventional armaments as a means of reducing the defence burden.

A consensus seems to be emerging that improved East-West relations, resulting in arms control agreements, can lead to savings of billions of dollars—the so-called "peace dividend" (*Financial Post* 1989; *Toronto Star* 1989a; *New York Times* 1989d). The expectation is that this money could be spent on much needed civilian projects, such as education, health, and economic infrastructure. Others, however, warn that actual reductions might be small since any savings resulting from arms control will likely be used up for verification and monitoring, and funds left over from these operations will go to reduce government deficits.

Despite the breath-taking changes underway in Eastern Europe and the Soviet Union, and rapid progress in arms control talks, it is important to note that no U.S.-U.S.S.R. strategic arms control agreement has been signed since 1979. However, as 1990 opened, both sides were hopeful that a START treaty could be concluded later in the year. With a new leadership in Washington, unprecedented high-level support in Moscow for radical arms reductions, a START treaty might, if the appropriate political will is present, be ratified before the next American presidential election campaign begins; such a step would clearly contribute to the security of both superpowers. Post-START forces on both sides would have substantially similar configurations, and this would enhance both crisis and arms race stability, and consequently reduce the risk of nuclear war.

Finally, given its proven expertise in the area of verification, Canada could help to develop methodologies to facilitate some of the complex verification tasks involved in the implementation of a START treaty. In order to do this, however, Canada must continue to devote the necessary resources to arms control.

Notes

[1] The opinions presented in this paper are purely personal, and should not be taken as representing the views of the Canadian Centre for Arms Control and Disarmament.

References

Arms Control Association. 1989. *Arms Control and International Security: An Introduction.* Washington, D.C.

The Arms Control Reporter: A Chronicle of Treaties, Negotiations, Proposals. 1985 and 1989. Brookline, Mass.: Institute for Defense and Disarmament Studies.

Arms Control Today. 1989. "Arms Control in Jackson Hole: Baker/ Shevardnadze and Beyond." 19, no. 8: 9-14.

Barometer. 1989. "Open Skies: Prospects for International Aerial Surveillance." no. 1 (Fall).

Barton, John H. 1976. *International Arms Control: Issues and Agreements.* Stanford, Cal.: Stanford University Press.

Bulletin of the Atomic Scientists. 1989. "Nunn's SDI Two Step." 45, no. 10 (December).

Canadian Centre for Arms Control and Disarmament (CCAD). 1987. "Canada is on the 'Front Line' for Strategic Arms Reduction." *Arms Control Communique* no. 42 (December 8). Ottawa.

———. 1989a. "Strategic Nuclear Forces of the Soviet Union/United States." *Arms Control Communique* no. 63 (November 30). Ottawa.

_____. 1989b. "Canadian Perspectives on U.S.-U.S.S.R. Arms Control in the Context of U.S. President Bush's Visit to Canada." *Arms Control Communique* no. 59. Ottawa.

Committee of Soviet Scientists for Peace and Against the Nuclear Threat. 1987. "Strategic Stability Under the Conditions of Radical Nuclear Arms Reductions." Report of a Study (Abridged). Moscow.

Canada. 1987. Office of the Prime Minister. Notes for a Speech by the Right Honourable Brian Mulroney, Prime Minister of Canada, to the North Atlantic Assembly, Quebec City, May 23. Ottawa.

_____. 1988a. Department of External Affairs *Annual Report 1987/ 88*. Ottawa: Supply and Services Canada.

_____. 1988b. Office of the Secretary of State for External Affairs. "Sovereignty in an Interdependent World." Notes for a Speech by the Right Honourable Joe Clark, Secretary of State for External Affairs, at Carleton University, October 18. Ottawa.

_____. 1989a. Department of External Affairs and International Trade. "Canada to Host Open Skies Conference." *The Disarmament Bulletin* 11 (Fall 1989).

_____. 1989b. Office of the Prime Minister. Notes for a Statement by the Right Honourable Brian Mulroney, Prime Minister of Canada, November 27. Ottawa.

_____. 1989c. Office of the Prime Minister. Canada and the U.S.S.R. Sign Political Declaration: Canada-Soviet Political Declaration. *Release.* November 22. Ottawa.

Financial Post. 1989. "Eastern Europe's Transition is Shaking U.S. Defence Firms: Less Tension between U.S., Soviets will Shrink Military Budgets." (Rod McQueen) December 6: 4.

May, Michael M., George F. Bing and John D. Steinbrunner. 1988. *Strategic Arms Reductions.* Washington, D.C.: The Brookings Institution.

Natural Resources Defense Council (NRDC). 1987. Natural Resources Defense Council, "START and Strategic Modernization," Washington, D.C.: NWD 87-2.

New York Times. 1989a. "Choose: MX, Midgetman, Other." October 19: A6.

_____. 1989b. "Arms Negotiators, Friendly and Confident, Announce Agreements." December 9: 10.

_____. 1989c. "Arms Makers Gird for Peace." (Leslie Wayne) December 17.

————. 1989d. "The Peace Dividend: What to do with the Cold War Money?" (Seymour Melman) December 17.

Union of Concerned Scientists. 1989. "The Black Sea Experiment: A Breakthrough for Verification." In *Nucleus* (Fall). Cambridge, Mass.

Ottawa Citizen. 1989. "Nuclear talks end with little progress." (Frances Williams) December 9: 7.

Roche, Douglas. 1988. Opening Statement by Ambassador Douglas Roche, Chairman First Committee United Nations General Assembly 43, October 17.

Stockholm International Peace Research Institute (SIPRI). 1988. *World Armaments and Disarmament*, SIPRI Yearbook 1988. New York: Oxford University Press.

Talbott, Strobe. 1988. "Why START Stopped." *Foreign Affairs.* Fall: 49-69.

Toronto Star. 1989a. "U.S. Eyes 'Dividends' of Peace: Billions Spent on Defence Could Aid Social Programmes." (Bob Hepburn) December 7.

————. 1989b. "Shift in U.S. Nuclear Forces Puts Missiles on our Doorstep." (Olivia Ward) December 10: A1, A26.

U.S. Congress. 1988. "Breakout, Verification and Force Structure: Dealing with the Full Implications of START," Report of the Defense Policy Panel, H.A.S.C., May 24, 1988. Washington, D.C.: United States Government Printing Office: 21-23.

United States Information Service. 1989a. *Wireless File.* "Baker: Soviets End 'Stumbling Block' to START Talks." Transcript: *Face the Nation.* SUF 721. September 28. Ottawa: United States Embassy.

————. 1989b. "U.S., Soviet Scientists Conduct SLCM Experiment," by Michael Saks. EUR 508. July 28.

6 Conventional Arms Control

Roger Hill

L ast year political developments took centre stage in European affairs as further changes swept the Eastern part of the continent and the world witnessed such previously unimaginable happenings as the installation of a Solidarity government in Poland, the exodus of tens of thousands of East Germans to the West, the overthrow of the Ceaucescu regime in Romania and shifts towards multi-party democracy in Czechoslovakia and elsewhere. No one who witnessed the spectacle of young Germans joyfully celebrating on the Berlin Wall or watched the demonstrations by half a million people in Prague could fail to grasp the message that fundamental changes were underway in the field of European security, driven by the new policies emanating from Moscow and by rising expectations across the length and breadth of Eastern Europe.

But it must be remembered that equally important for the hopes of lasting peace and co-operation between East and West were the negotiations on Conventional Armed Forces in Europe (CFE) in progress in Vienna. After major developments early in the year, these dropped temporarily out of the limelight. But that was only because the diplomats, military experts and other officials of the NATO and Warsaw Pact states were feverishly scrambling to meet the deadlines imposed by political leaderships and by the evident need to move very fast on the arms control front in order to keep abreast of the headlong process of political change. East and West were aiming at an initial agreement on conventional force reductions in Europe by the middle of 1990, and there was no question that this was a very demanding proposition, considering the sheer breadth and complexity of the technical and related issues as well as the enormous political and military implications of a possible CFE agreement.

Background

Five years ago the question of conventional force reductions in Europe was on the back-burner. Although negotiations had been underway since 1973 in the talks on Mutual and Balanced Force Reductions (MBFR) in Vienna, these had never succeeded in arriving at any concrete agreement. They had helped to clarify key issues of conventional arms control and to develop an understanding of the underlying military relationships between East and West in Europe, but they had bogged down over such issues as data and verification and, in any case, the general international atmosphere had not been conducive to the conclusion of an accord.

This situation changed radically following Mikhail Gorbachev's rise to leadership of the Soviet Union in the mid-1980s. Soon the Warsaw Pact was advancing new proposals on conventional force reductions in Europe which offered hope of breaking through the old log-jam. In Budapest, on June 11, 1986, the Soviet Union and its allies proposed major reductions in land and tactical air forces, and also in theatre nuclear weapons, in an area extending across the whole of Europe from the Atlantic to the Urals, and mentioned, as the kind of sweeping cuts they had in mind, 100,000 to 150,000 troops on each side within a year or two, and half a million on each side by the early 1990s.

The Reykjavik summit of October 11-12, 1986 also had a major impact on the conventional forces issue. At this meeting, President Reagan and General Secretary Gorbachev changed the whole tone of East-West relations and set in train new efforts to promote far-reaching measures of arms control and disarmament. The first two objectives emerging from the summit were treaties on strategic nuclear weapons and intermediate-range nuclear forces, but it soon became clear that the control of conventional forces would also be a priority item. The issue did, in fact, quickly return to the centre of the international agenda, and one of the most important reasons was the concern felt by America's allies at the prospect of being left, after deep nuclear cuts, at the mercy of a Warsaw Pact alliance with a perceived superiority in conventional forces.

NATO was interested in conventional arms stability, no matter whether it might be attained by asymmetrical reductions to a new and more secure balance, or by an increase in its own forces. It had been working intensively on this question throughout 1986, and on December 11 and 12 held a meeting in Brussels which issued an important new declaration; it offered to open up a new East-West dialogue with a view to establishing a mandate for negotiations on conventional arms control which would cover the whole of Europe from the Atlantic to the Urals. A set of objectives were listed, indicating the indispensable criteria for an East-West agreement. Another important aspect of this meeting was that for the first time France and Spain participated fully in working out major NATO policies on conventional arms control.

During 1987 and 1988 there were further major developments in conventional arms control. In February 1987, the NATO and Warsaw Pact states opened Conventional Mandate Talks (CMT) in an effort to develop the terms for new negotiations intended to supersede MBFR. On May 29, 1987, the Warsaw Pact recognized the existence of asymmetries, and expressed readiness to "rectify in the course of reductions the disbalance that has emerged in some elements by way of corresponding cuts on the side that is ahead" (Government of the U.S.S.R. 1987). On March 2-3, 1988, NATO held a summit meeting in Brussels which issued a new, tough statement calling on the Warsaw Pact to make highly asymmetrical reductions, focusing on tanks, artillery and other conventional systems that would be especially useful in launching surprise attacks or initiating large-scale offensive action. Warsaw Pact foreign ministers responded on March 30 by indicating readiness to make substantial asymmetrical cuts in military manpower and various conventional armaments. Further statements by Warsaw Pact leaders, later in 1988, reiterated willingness to remove asymmetries, scale down offensive capabilities, and exchange data. At the United Nations on December 8, Mr. Gorbachev took a further major step by announcing unilateral cuts in the Soviet armed forces, amounting to 500,000 men and including reductions of 10,000 tanks, 8,500 artillery systems and 800 combat aircraft in Eastern Europe including the European parts of the U.S.S.R. NATO Foreign Ministers, who were at the time meeting in Brussels, noted Mr. Gorbachev's announcement, and called for further reductions until a new balance could be achieved at lower levels of forces, including ceilings of 40,000 tanks for the whole of Europe.

As 1988 drew to a close, however, the two sides, despite improvements in the international atmosphere and some remarkable statements of position, still seemed to have a long way to go in the quest for a conventional force reductions agreement. The world wondered if the Soviet Union would effectively implement the unilateral cuts announced by Mr. Gorbachev and whether the stated readiness to discuss further asymmetrical cuts would lead to serious negotiations or only to rounds of fruitless bargaining over details. People speculated about the policies that Mr. Bush, the President-elect of the United States, would pursue on arms control issues and questioned whether NATO would go part way to meet the other side and show more flexibility in its approach to the CFE issue.

Developments in 1989

The New Year opened with some further remarkable developments. Before the end of January, the German Democratic Republic announced that it would also make unilateral cuts in its armed forces, demobilizing 10,000 men and reducing defence expenditures by 10 percent by the end of 1990. Six tank regiments would be dissolved, the GDR government stated, 600 tanks would be scrapped or re-equipped for civil purposes, and one aircraft squadron with 50 fighter planes would be disbanded. Shortly afterwards Czechoslovakia, Hungary, Poland and Bulgaria also announced significant unilateral reductions in their conventional forces.

On January 10 the mandate talks finally ended. Participating states agreed on the terms for new negotiations on Conventional Armed Forces in Europe—subsequently designated the CFE talks—which were to include the 23 members of NATO and the Warsaw Pact. The aim would be to strengthen stability and security in Europe by moving to a new balance at lower levels, by eliminating disparities, and by removing the capability for launching surprise attack and for initiating large-scale offensive action. This was to be done by the application of militarily significant measures such as reductions, limitations, redeployment provisions, and equal ceilings. The area of coverage would be the Atlantic to the Urals, but with provisions for regional differentiation to address particular disparities. There would be strict and effective verification, including on-site inspection. Nuclear, naval and chemical weapons or forces would be excluded. An annex spelled out means of informing all the states participating in the Conference on Security and Cooperation in Europe (CSCE)—including the European neutrals and non-aligned countries—about the progress of the new CFE negotiations.

Now NATO and the Warsaw Pact wound up the old MBFR negotiations, and moved forward to the new CFE talks. Just before these opened, however, the Soviet Union once again made a notable announcement. On March 6, Foreign Minister Eduard Shevardnadze proposed to eliminate imbalances in the troops and main armaments of the two sides by cutting them to 10-15 percent below the current lowest numbers within two or three years and then to reduce by a further 25 percent on each side within an additional two to three years. All battlefield nuclear weapons should be eliminated, he said, and the forces of the two sides should as soon as possible assume a strictly defensive character.

The most noteworthy element of this statement was that it confirmed readiness to make massive cuts in Soviet tanks and other equipment in the European parts of the U.S.S.R. as well as in Eastern Europe. The Warsaw Pact was informing NATO that it was ready to make major concessions by moving towards the tough positions outlined by NATO Foreign Ministers the previous December.

The West's own proposals on conventional force reductions were tabled in the CFE talks in Vienna by David Peel, Canada's Representative, on March 9, 1989. They were in line with earlier NATO thinking, and contained such items as ceilings of 40,000 tanks, 33,000 artillery pieces and 56,000 armoured personnel carriers for the two sides for the whole of Europe. No one country would be entitled to more than 30 percent of the total of any type of armament, and stationed forces would be limited on each side to 3,200 main battle tanks, 1,700 artillery pieces and 6,000 armoured personnel carriers.

Negotiations now proceeded in Vienna, but meanwhile world attention shifted to the question of short-range nuclear weapons, which presented particular difficulties for the West. The Federal German government was keen for NATO to delay modernization of existing systems while engaging immediately in negotiations, whereas the United States and Britain felt that modernization should go ahead and that negotiations should be postponed to an indefinite future. The other allies were divided; there was a great deal of press comment about a perceived failure of American leadership and about the risk that the dissension might bring about the collapse of NATO as the alliance approached a new Western summit meeting scheduled for the end of May.

New thinking about the short-range nuclear issue and conventional arms control was reported in Washington in the last week of May. Meanwhile the Warsaw Pact produced further proposals which again narrowed the gap between East and West on the CFE question. The Soviet Union and its allies now advocated dividing Europe into three regions—contact zones, rear zones and Central Europe—with sub-limits of equipment and forces for each. They accepted the basic Western approach to reductions in tanks, artillery and armoured troop carriers. Nevertheless, outstanding differences remained over the East's call for the establishment of limits on troop levels and aircraft.

Meanwhile, Western leaders were gathering in Brussels. The summit meeting of May 29-30 did not, as some had predicted, see the collapse of the Alliance. Instead, it resulted in a diplomatic triumph for Mr. Bush and produced a sense of achievement among the other Western leaders. The problem of short-range nuclear weapons was resolved by an agreement to authorize U.S.-Soviet talks on partial reductions once CFE cuts had begun. The conventional forces issue was covered in the main Declaration of the conference and in a major statement entitled: "A Comprehensive Concept of Arms Control and Dis-armament" (NATO 1989a, 1989b). Allied leaders agreed rapidly to U.S. proposals to include the pursuit of new ceilings on heli-copters and land-based combat aircraft in the negotiations. They also proposed "a 20 percent cut in combat manpower in U.S. stationed forces, and a resulting ceiling on U.S. and Soviet ground and air force personnel stationed outside of national territory in the Atlantic-to-the-Urals zone at approximately 275,000." This would require the Soviet Union to "reduce its forces in Eastern Europe by some 325,000" (NATO 1989b). To maintain momentum the Allies stated that an initial CFE agreement should be sought within a period of six months to a year, and that the reductions it would stipulate should be carried out by 1992 or 1993. Accordingly, they directed that work on their new proposals should be given high priority and completed in time for the third round of the CFE negotiations, due to open on September 7, 1989.

Working out the details of a new allied position within three months was a tall order but it was indeed accomplished. Now negotiations in Vienna are moving rapidly ahead. Latest reports indicate that good progress is being made, with attention being concentrated on such issues as zones of reduction, verification provisions, inclusion or non-inclusion of various types of aircraft, and the treatment of such equipment as light tanks and heavy armoured personnel carriers. Draft treaties were tabled by both sides in mid-December shortly after President Bush and President Gorbachev met at the Malta summit. The points made by the two leaders included expressions of hope for an early first agreement on the conventional forces issue.

Future Prospects and Implications

There now appears to be good prospects for agreement by East and West on an initial treaty on conventional arms control in Europe sometime in 1990, or in the opening months of 1991 at the latest. Many difficult technical issues remain but the two sides are now very close on fundamentals and should be able to press on to an accord provided that the political will to do so remains strong.

The details of such an agreement still remain to be clarified. The main features will probably include ceilings for each side which would be approximately as follows: 20,000 tanks, with sub-limits in various regional zones; 28,000 armoured personnel carriers; and 1,900 helicopters. There will likely also be ceilings and sub-ceilings for artillery pieces, attack aircraft, other combat aircraft, overall ground forces manpower, overall air forces manpower, and U.S. and Soviet stationed forces. There will also be strong verification measures, including on-site inspection. Reaching these levels will require the removal and dismantling of tens of thousands of tanks and other types of military equipment, thereby making the first CFE agreement by far the most important arms control agreement ever achieved in human history.

The CFE negotiations are not likely to end with the establishment of an initial agreement. There will certainly be further rounds of discussions aimed at reducing still further force levels on the Central Front and elsewhere in Europe. Second and third levels of reduction may be agreed in due course, especially if confidence in East-West cooperation grows and the old confrontation gives way to a condition of mutual or common security.

Europe will be a different continent after the establishment of an initial agreement on conventional force reductions. A new arms control regime will be put in place and will become a key feature of the security landscape. It will incorporate not only the new conventional force levels resulting from the reductions, but also verification systems, consultative mechanisms, dispute-settlement provisions, and review procedures. As time passes, the countries involved in the arms control system will come to see it as a major contributor to their national security and to the stability of Europe as a whole. They will rely heavily on it, as well as on the balance of military power and existing or modified alliance connections, and will work to uphold it whenever it might be threatened by the behaviour of any of the members. The effective functioning of such a regime could assist East and West to develop the confidence needed to make second, third or even further cuts in their conventional forces in Europe.

The evolving political situation is also bound to have a major impact on the conventional arms control issue. In fact, it is no longer a question of arms control activities leading political change and maybe provoking instability, euphoria, excitement and upheaval. Political change and popular demands for democracy are already sweeping Eastern Europe. It is now the task of arms control to keep pace with the new, evolving situation. For example, the CFE negotiators may soon have to grapple with the problem of establishing a new status and reduced levels for the Soviet forces in East Germany in the event that the GDR moves towards a much closer association with the Federal Republic. Such a move would certainly pose the problem of making some compensatory force reductions on the NATO side, and this might not be easy to do without adversely affecting Western security.

The processes of political change now underway in Eastern Europe may even be so far-reaching that they will alter the whole security framework of the continent. In the 1990s we are likely to see the reunification of the two Germanies. Poland, Hungary, Czechoslovakia and other East European states may move into some form of association with the European Community. A new European confederation could emerge, associated with the Soviet Union on the one hand and the United States on the other. The U.S. Secretary of State, James Baker, evidently envisaged something along these lines in his speech about a new Atlanticism and a new Europe, delivered in West Berlin on December 12, 1989. Such a grouping would require new or modified defence and other relationships with the two present superpowers. Either the Soviet Union and the United States would withdraw their military forces entirely from the territories of this new confederation, or, through the CFE and CSCE processes, they would reduce them to much lower levels and change their roles. The remaining Soviet or American stationed divisions would no longer be parts of confronting armies poised against each other, but would take the form of guarantee forces intended to assure Germans, Poles, Czechs and others of continued interest in the various aspects of European stability, including the inviolability of existing borders. Their numbers would probably not need to be great and they could be located and managed in such a way that they would not become involved in, or have any impact on, the political life of the host states.

Because of all these current or potential political changes in Europe the CFE negotiations are likely to remain in the forefront of world affairs in the coming decade. Another reason for their importance is their potential economic impact, for they relate to a confrontation which accounts for well over fifty percent of all world military expenditures. Savings might be very limited if an initial reduction agreement were implemented but could become very extensive if further cuts went much deeper, in response, for example, to the emergence of a new European confederation.

The negotiations on conventional arms control in Europe also have implications for similar processes in other contexts. The Western countries have made it clear that they are not prepared to discuss the control or reduction of general Alliance naval forces in the CFE context, but such talks may eventually take place partly because the Soviets would favour such a procedure in a parallel forum. Also, negotiations on conventional arms control in Asia, Africa or other areas could be held in various regional fora or under United Nations auspices. The UN has been addressing regional arms control, the global reduction of conventional armaments, the arms trade, and similar issues, for many years, and possibly some of these efforts may bear fruit in the future, if there is serious interest in the Third World countries as well as a major, positive change in East-West relations.

Canadian Roles and Implications

Canada has a long-standing interest in the question of conventional arms control in Europe. This interest is likely to continue while the international community grapples with the problem of political change in Europe and tries to work out a new equilibrium and a new political structure for that continent. Having participated actively from the beginning in the MBFR, CFE and CSCE processes, Canada is not likely to drop out at a time when momentous developments are taking place that are likely to have a direct impact on the security of all members of the Western Alliance. Indeed, this country will probably have to pay more attention to European affairs in the next decade than it did in the 1980s, if it is not to find itself increasingly marginalized with respect to major international political, security and economic issues.

During 1989 Canada's contribution to the pursuit of conventional force reductions in Europe continued as previously. This country has a relatively small military presence in Europe, but it has always been a full participant in conventional arms control negotiations and has joined actively in the work of NATO in Brussels and in the efforts of the inter-allied caucuses in Vienna. The manpower committed full-time to this work in the Departments of External Affairs and National Defence is limited. Nevertheless, as a recent report by the Senate Special Committee on National Defence points out Canada has for the most part provided solid input for the negotiating and consultative process.

Two Canadian developments in 1989 are particularly worthy of note. The Government introduced a new national budget in April which had the effect of eliminating, cutting, or delaying some major defence equipment programs. However, troop levels in Europe were not cut. The Government seems anxious not to undermine NATO's diplomatic position as the Alliance heads into a period of intensive activity concerning the CFE question.

The second move had to do with Open Skies. President Bush called for a new initiative on this question at the NATO summit meeting in May 1989, the aim of which would be to develop aerial surveillance and confidence-building measures which would be related to the CFE process although they would not be directly incorporated into it. Canada encouraged and supported the President. The Canadian Government subsequently put forward the idea of hosting the first Open Skies meeting, to be held in early 1990, and this proposal was eventually accepted by the other NATO and Warsaw Pact countries.

If there is rapid progress on conventional arms control and other aspects of European security in the coming decade the world is likely to see the growth of an increasingly powerful European Community or confederation and the transformation of the Atlantic relationship into an essentially bipolar connection. Canada will have to work hard to make its views known in this new environment, using, for example, bilateral contacts with the United States and the European Community, and such vehicles as Atlantic consultations, the CSCE meetings and the new arms control systems. If Canadian diplomacy is not reshaped in this manner there is likely to be impairment of the country's long-standing interests in the maintenance of stability in Europe and the promotion of trade and other economic links with the European Community.

Conventional arms control agreements would also have direct implications for the Canadian armed forces in Germany. They will likely be maintained at existing levels until an initial accord is reached but will almost certainly undergo changes as a result of the CFE agreement, either immediately or in the very near future. Canadian public opinion and budgetary constraints may dictate cuts of some kind in the land or air forces in Europe, even though Canadians may remain committed to NATO itself or to whatever modified Atlantic structure develops from the present organization. Few people now believe that Canada will acquire the approximately 250 new tanks required for the armoured division envisaged in the 1987 Defence White Paper. Instead, the army in Germany may in due course be reduced to brigade group size, as is suggested in the report on the land forces issued by the Senate Special Committee on National Defence (Senate 1989), or it might be cut even further.

If Europe develops into the new Community or confederation discussed above, linked by security arrangements to both the United States and the Soviet Union, then Canadian armed forces will no longer be needed on the other side of the Atlantic for collective defence purposes, since the East-West confrontation will have largely disappeared. Some Canadian forces might conceivably remain in Europe to help guarantee the new security arrangements there, although they might be assigned duties such as border surveillance or general monitoring, which are by their nature closer to peacekeeping than to traditional Alliance roles.

With its long coastlines and extensive territorial waters, Canada also has a natural interest in the question of maritime arms control, and can be expected to participate actively in any negotiations on this issue that are organized on an East-West or a global basis. This country is also likely to join efforts within the United Nations or elsewhere to bring about global reductions in conventional land and air forces.

References

Canada. 1989. Department of External Affairs. "New Conventional Talks Underway." *Disarmament Bulletin* 10 (Spring/Summer): 1-17.

_____. 1989. The Senate. Canada's Land Forces. Report of the Special Committee on National Defence. Ottawa: Queen's Printer.

Government of the U.S.S.R. 1987. *Political Consultative Communiqué*. News Release 65 Press Office of the U.S.S.R. Embassy in Canada. Ottawa, June 1.

Hill, Roger. 1988. *Are Major Conventional Force Reductions in Europe Possible?* Aurora Paper 7, March. Ottawa: Canadian Centre for Arms Control and Disarmament.

NATO. 1986. *Brussels Declaration on Conventional Arms Control,* December 11. Brussels: NATO Information Service.

――――. 1988. *Conventional Arms Control.* Statement issued by the North Atlantic Council Meeting in Ministerial Session at NATO Headquarters. Press Communiqué M-3 (88) 75, December 8. Brussels: NATO Press Service.

――――. 1989. *Cutting Conventional Forces: an Analysis of the Official Mandate, Statistics and Proposals in the NATO-WTO Talks on Reducing Conventional Forces in Europe.* Brookline, Mass.

――――. 1989a. *A Comprehensive Concept of Arms Control and Disarmament.* Press Communiqué M-1 (89) 20, May 30. Brussels: NATO Press Service.

――――. 1989b. *Declaration of the Heads of Government Participating in the meeting of the North Atlantic Council in Brussels.* Press Communiqué M-1 (89) 21, May 30. Brussels: NATO Press Service.

――――. 1989c. *Conventional Arms Control: The Way Ahead.* Statement issued under the authority of the Heads of State and Government Participating in the Meeting of the North Atlantic Council in Brussels. Press Communiqué M-1 (89) 21, May 30. Brussels: NATO Press Service.

7   The North in Canada's International Relations

Ron Purver

Nineteen eighty-nine was an eventful year in Canada's Northern foreign policy. Noteworthy developments occurred in virtually every issue-area: defence, sovereignty, arms control, environmental relations, scientific cooperation, and cooperation among the indigenous peoples. In some respects, the government appeared to be living up to its earlier promise to accord greater attention to, and play a more significant role in, Arctic international relations. In other areas, however, performance fell far short of promise and expectation. Indeed, in certain respects, the government could justifiably be accused of reneging on past commitments and adopting a policy of retreat in flat contradiction to its earlier rhetoric.

Several years earlier the Conservative government of Brian Mulroney had proclaimed the Arctic as a new focus of Canadian foreign and security policy. In response to the public clamour arising from the voyage of the U.S. Coast Guard icebreaker *Polar Sea* through the Northwest Passage in August 1985, the government had announced a series of steps to reaffirm and strengthen Canadian sovereignty in the North. External Affairs Minister Clark declared in the House of Commons on September 10, 1985:

> Only with full sovereignty can we protect the entire range of Canadian interests. Full sovereignty is vital to Canada's security. It is vital to the Inuit people. And it is vital to Canada's national identity. The policy of this Government is to exercise full sovereignty in and on the waters of the Arctic archipelago and this applies to the airspace above as well. We will accept no substitutes (House of Commons 1985: 6463).

The specific measures announced by Mr. Clark included the establishment of straight baselines around the Arctic archipelago, effective January 1, 1986; the opening of Arctic cooperation talks with the United

States, "on the basis of full respect for Canadian sovereignty;" increased activities by the Canadian Forces in and over Arctic waters; and the construction of a Polar Class 8 icebreaker.

On the military side, the new focus on the Arctic arose even earlier, as the result of consultations with the United States on the modernization of the North American Aerospace Defence system. These had led to an agreement, signed at the Mulroney-Reagan "Quebec Summit" in March 1985, to replace the old Distant Early Warning (DEW) Line of radar stations across the North by a new North Warning System (NWS), and to upgrade several Northern airstrips to forward operating locations (FOLs) for NORAD interceptor aircraft. The Defence White Paper of June 1987 gave a further boost to Canadian military activities in the Arctic, promising an increase in the number of "sovereignty flights" by *Aurora* long-range patrol aircraft; the modernization of the *Tracker* medium-range aircraft; an expansion of the Canadian Ranger force; the establishment of a Northern Training Centre for the Canadian Forces; the deployment of fixed sonar systems for submarine detection in Arctic waters; and—most significant and controversial—the acquisition of ten to twelve nuclear-powered attack submarines (SSNs), justified partly on the basis of their under-ice capability.

Canada's Arctic foreign policy was highlighted in a series of governmental and non-governmental reports beginning in the mid-1980s. The June 1986 Report of the Special Joint Committee of the Senate and the House of Commons on Canada's International Relations (the Hockin-Simard Report), reflecting widespread public interest and concern, devoted an entire chapter to the subject of "A Northern Dimension for Canadian Foreign Policy" (*Independence and Internationalism* 1986a). A Working Group of the National Capital Branch of the Canadian Institute of International Affairs (CIIA) produced an influential report on "The North and Canada's International Relations" in March 1988 (CIIA 1988). Mr. Clark addressed the issue at length in a number of major speeches, including one in Tromso, Norway, in December 1987, and another at Carleton University, Ottawa, in October 1988. In Tromso, Mr. Clark declared that his government was "committed to intensifying its relations with Arctic neighbours" (Government of Canada 1987: 4). Indeed, only a month later he was able to announce the conclusion of a Canada-U.S. Arctic Cooperation Agreement, while negotiations continued with the U.S.S.R. on a Co-operation Agreement of a different kind.

In sum, the mid- to late 1980s witnessed a flurry of activity related to Canada's Arctic international relations. This has been the result of a number of factors: the growing strategic importance of the region, as a deployment area and a theatre of military operations; the parallel, and somewhat paradoxical, development of easier East-West relations and the opening up of new avenues of cooperation for the Soviet Union with the West; growing political awareness and activism among the indigenous peoples of the North; highly publicized challenges to Canadian sovereignty over its Arctic waters; and a greater appreciation of both threats to the Arctic physical environment and of the role of the Arctic in the global environment more generally. How Canada has responded to these challenges over the past year is the subject of this chapter, which will now deal with each of these issues individually.

Defence

The Defence White Paper of June 1987 had promised to upgrade considerably Canada's military capabilities in the Arctic. The modernization of the North American Aerospace Defence system continued more or less as planned in 1989, with some delays. However, the budget announced by the government in April 1989 came as a severe blow to those favouring increased military capabilities in the Arctic. The most dramatic move was the outright cancellation of the planned purchase of nuclear-powered attack submarines, which appeared to invalidate totally the new "three-ocean" maritime strategy proclaimed by the White Paper. Also cancelled were the plans to purchase additional *Aurora* long-range patrol aircraft, and to modernize the medium-range *Trackers* for Arctic patrols; at the same time the planned purchase of 820 all-terrain vehicles designed to operate in the Arctic was cut by over 50 percent (to 400), and will probably be delayed until at least 1995-1996. The new Defence Minister, Bill McKnight, was placed in the embarrassing position of having to admit that Canada would in the future have to rely more on its allies for the defence of the Canadian North. As he put it: "there are better ways of defending northern sovereignty," but "unfortunately we cannot afford those ways" (*Globe and Mail* 1989a).

The critics were not mollified by the defence minister's announcement in June that Canada would buy three Arctic and Maritime Surveillance Aircraft, to be known as the *Arcturus*, since these aircraft would not be equipped with weapons or anti-submarine warfare sensors. The government appeared to remain committed to building a network of fixed sonars for submarine detection in Canadian Arctic waters, but this was still in an experimental stage and it had previously argued strenuously that such a "tripwire" was insufficient for Canadian defence needs, requiring as it would the presence of a submarine to investigate contacts and actually enforce Canadian jurisdiction. In the wake of the SSN cancellation, defence planners were forced to fall back on measures which they had previously argued to be ineffective in the Arctic, such as exclusive reliance on a combination of fixed sensors, aircraft, and diesel-powered submarines, or investigation of technologies, as yet unproved, of air-independent propulsion for enhanced under-ice capability. Although the government insisted that the fundamental principles of the White Paper remained in force, the greater part of its Arctic component had been effectively gutted.

Sovereignty

The record of 1989 in respect to "sovereignty" issues was a more mixed one. United States Coast Guard icebreakers continued to abide by the terms of the January 1988 Canada-U.S. Arctic Cooperation Agreement, as interpreted by Canada. Critics of the agreement at the time had complained that it failed to ensure that Canadian permission for transits of the Northwest Passage would be requested on a case-by-case basis, thus leaving a loophole which the United States could exploit by seeking permission for multiple transits on a seasonal or other basis. So far, the critics appear to have been proven wrong on this point. The first test of the new agreement came in October 1988, when External Affairs Minister Clark was able to announce Canadian consent to a U.S. request for transit of the Northwest Passage by the U.S. Coast Guard icebreaker *Polar Star.*

Of course, Canada's success in gaining U.S. agreement to request permission for icebreaker transit through the Northwest Passage fell far short of the "full respect for Canada's sovereignty" that Mr. Clark had demanded in September 1985. The Arctic Cooperation Agreement contains a "non-prejudice clause" according to which "Nothing in this agreement of cooperative endeavour between Arctic neighbours and friends nor any practice thereunder affects the respective positions of the Governments of the United States and of Canada on the Law of the Sea in this or other maritime areas or their respective positions regarding third parties" (Department of External Affairs 1988). This reflects the continuing U.S. refusal to recognize Canada's claim to the Northwest Passage as part of its "internal waters," rather than an international strait. It also appears to render plausible the argument that the Arctic Cooperation Agreement has no effect at all, one way or the other, on the dispute over Canadian sovereignty.

Another shortcoming of the Agreement is that it applies only to government-owned icebreakers, and does not apply to other types of government-owned craft (including surface warships and submarines) and privately-owned vessels (used for commercial or other purposes). While Washington reportedly offered assurances to Ottawa that it would not support a commercial challenge to the Arctic Waters Pollution Prevention Act, the past, and presumably continuing, unannounced use of the Northwest Passage by American nuclear-powered submarines remains a sore point in Canada-U.S. relations.

Nevertheless, it is probably true, that the January 1988 agreement was the best that could be reached under the circumstances. Washington was not prepared to budge an inch on the basic sovereignty question; an agreement to disagree while removing the potential for future incidents of the *Polar Sea* variety may have been better than no agreement at all.

With regard to unilateral measures to strengthen Canadian sovereignty in the Arctic there is one key element of Mr. Clark's September 1985 package that has encountered rough seas indeed. This is the announcement that Canada would build a Polar Class 8 icebreaker to ply Arctic waters by 1990. The project has fallen years behind schedule for a variety of reasons (*Globe and Mail* 1989b). When only $1.6 million was earmarked for it in the government's budget for fiscal year 1989-90, and approval of a construction contract was pushed back until the spring of 1990, many supporters feared that the Polar 8 would suffer the same fate as the SSNs. On November 23, 1989 Canadian Coast Guard Commissioner Ran Quail revealed that the company chosen had yet to submit a firm price and building plan, but that one was expected before the end of the year. He assured the House of Commons Standing Committee on National Defence and Veterans Affairs that the vessel would be built, but acknowledged that it would not be going to sea until spring 1994 at the earliest—four years later than the date anticipated by Mr. Clark in 1985.

To sum up: in view of the delay in acquisition of the Polar 8 and the various defence cut-backs discussed in the previous section,

Canada's capacity to monitor and control its territorial claims effectively—a characteristic usually considered to be the hallmark of a
nation's sovereignty—appears highly questionable so far as the Arctic
is concerned.

Cooperation on the Environment, Science, and the Indigenous Peoples

Canada has enthusiastically supported, and actively participated in, the
so-called "Finnish Initiative," formally launched by the Finnish Government in January 1989 and aimed at the conclusion of an umbrella
agreement among the circumpolar states to promote environmental
protection in the North. At a preparatory meeting of the eight
circumpolar states in Rovaniemi, Finland, held from September 20
through 26, 1989, one of two working groups—on the use of
international legal mechanisms to promote cooperation on Arctic
environmental protection—was chaired by the head of the Canadian
delegation, Ambassador J. Alan Beesley. Canada joined Sweden and
Finland in a task force established to compile, analyze, and assess a
list of the principal international agreements relating to protection of
the Arctic ecology. The group intends to have a summary review
prepared in time for the next consultative meeting, which will be held
in Yellowknife, Northwest Territories, in mid-April 1990.

Canadian representatives have also played a leading role in multilateral efforts to coordinate scientific research in the Arctic (Roots
1988). A meeting of twenty-nine scientists and science administrators
from the eight circumpolar states, held at the premises of the Royal
Swedish Academy of Sciences in Stockholm March 24-26, 1988,
agreed that an International Arctic Science Committee (IASC) should
be established as a non-governmental body to promote international
cooperation and coordination of scientific research in the North
(International Cooperation in Arctic Science: 46). The basic structure
of the Committee was agreed at a meeting on Arctic Scientific
Cooperation in Leningrad in December 1988, and the founding meeting
was to take place in Northern Canada in the summer of 1989 (IASC
Drafting Group 1988). Unfortunately, subsequent disagreement over
the precise role of non-Arctic states in the Committee made it
impossible to meet this schedule, and discussions are continuing.

Canada has also been actively involved in various other scientific
bodies focusing on the Arctic, such as the Northern Science Network

of UNESCO's Man and the Biosphere Program. During a speech to the Arctic and Antarctic Institute in Leningrad on November 24, 1989, Prime Minister Mulroney announced the creation of a Canadian Polar Commission. The mandate of the Commission, to be established by Act of Parliament on April 1, 1990, will include the following objectives: to "enhance Canada's international polar profile by fostering and facilitating international and domestic liaison and cooperation in circumpolar research," and to "increase international focus on circumpolar concerns such as Arctic haze, the greenhouse effect, and air- and water-borne toxins in the food chain" (Office of the Prime Minister 1989a: 2). In the same speech, while noting Canada's "strong support" for the creation of an IASC, Mr. Mulroney hinted at the possibility of a circumpolar organization with a much broader mandate: "Eventually, we would like to see the nascent multilateral environmental and scientific cooperation become more broadly based to cover the full range of economic and social issues, just as Canada and the U.S.S.R. are doing bilaterally. And why not a council of Arctic countries eventually coming into existence to coordinate and promote cooperation among them?" (Office of the Prime Minister 1989b: 6).

The greatest progress in promoting scientific and other forms of cooperation in the Arctic so far has, however, been made in the bilateral sphere. In this regard the signing of a Canada-U.S.S.R. Agreement on Cooperation in the Arctic and the North during Prime Minister Mulroney's visit to Moscow in November 1989 marked a significant achievement. Until this time, Canadian-Soviet cooperation in Arctic science was governed by a Protocol of Canadian-Soviet Consultations on the Development of a Programme of Scientific and Technical Cooperation in the Arctic and the North, signed in April 1984. During the period leading up to renegotiation of this Protocol in February 1987, the Soviet Government presented Ottawa with the draft text of a full-scale Agreement on Arctic Cooperation, intended to raise the status of the program and expand its scope. Despite an unfortunate incident involving a Soviet leak of the text and unjustified complaints that Canada was stalling on the issue under pressure from the United States, the two countries were able to finalize the text of an agreement during a meeting in Moscow in November 1988 (Hannigan 1988: 3-4). Formal signature had to await the visit of Prime Minister Mulroney to the U.S.S.R. a year later.

Under the new "Canada-U.S.S.R. Agreement on Cooperation in the Arctic and the North," signed on November 20, 1989 by Prime

Ministers Mulroney and Ryzhkov, programs will be developed in three areas:

— scientific and technical cooperation, including geology, meteorology, climatology, construction, environmental protection, Arctic marine, land and air technology, and other agreed fields;
— economic cooperation, including the development of renewable and non-renewable resources; and
— cooperation on social and cultural questions, including ethnography, education, public health, the socio-economic problems of the native peoples of the North and Northern territories, cultural and academic exchanges, and contacts between native peoples. (Office of the Prime Minister 1989c: 3)

The agreement establishes a Canada-U.S.S.R. Mixed Commission to monitor its implementation. Chaired jointly by the Canadian Minister of Indian Affairs and Northern Development and a representative of the U.S.S.R. State Committee for Science and Technology, the Commission will meet at least once every two years, alternately in Canada and the U.S.S.R. (Office of the Prime Minister 1989c: 3). A number of other agreements signed during the Mulroney visit to Moscow also dealt with Arctic issues. A Memorandum of Understanding (MOU) on Arctic Marine Pollution to "prevent, reduce and control pollution of the Arctic marine environment resulting from commercial shipping" provides for cooperation in a number of areas: information-sharing; technology transfers; operations; and policy and legislation. Among other things, the two countries have agreed to assist each other in responding to specific pollution incidents through the shared use of ships, exchanges of icebreaker captains, helicopters, pollution equipment and trained personnel (Office of the Prime Minister 1989d). Two other MOUs coming under the framework of a more general Agreement Concerning Environmental Cooperation focus to a considerable extent on the Arctic. One of them deals with Cooperative Atmospheric Environmental Programs, and the other with Water Research (Department of External Affairs 1989e and 1989f).

Finally, the Canadian Government for many years has been urging the U.S.S.R. to permit representatives of its Arctic indigenous peoples to attend the triennial General Assemblies of the Inuit Circumpolar Conference (representing Inuit from Alaska, Canada, and Greenland). Soviet willingness to do so was finally confirmed during a visit to the Soviet Union, in mid-August 1988, of an ICC delegation led by its president, Mary Simon of Canada. Accordingly, for the first time in the history of the organization, a delegation of Soviet Inuit from the Chukchi Peninsula attended the Sixth General Assembly of the ICC in Sisimiut, Greenland in July 1989. The meeting also re-elected Mary Simon as President for a second term.

Arms Control

One aspect of its Arctic foreign policy which caused the Government to be criticized by increasing numbers of Canadians in 1989 was its continued rejection of any regional arms control measures for the Arctic. The Hockin-Simard Report of June 1986 had recommended "that Canada, in cooperation with other Arctic and nordic nations, seek the demilitarization of the Arctic region through pressure on the United States and the Soviet Union, as well as through a general regional approach to arms control and disarmament" (*Independence and Internationalism* 1986a: 135). In its response to the Report, the government had rejected outright demilitarization of the Arctic as impracticable, although it did pledge to "strive to limit excessive militarization of the Arctic in the interest of strategic stability and in the context of our associated arms control and disarmament effort, and [to] seek out new ways of building trust in the circumpolar North" (Department of External Affairs 1986b: 87).

Nevertheless, after Mikhail Gorbachev's Murmansk speech of October 1987, calling for an Arctic "Zone of Peace," Canadian officials were unremittingly negative in their appraisal of such proposals, from whatever source. Canadian ministers pointed to the heavy concentration of nuclear firepower on the Kola Peninsula as evidence of Soviet duplicity on this question. The Soviets argued in response that the ballistic missile submarines based on the Kola were already under negotiation at the Strategic Arms Reduction Talks (START) in Geneva (see Chapter 5). Nevertheless, they have unilaterally withdrawn shorter-range missiles from the area (even before the signing of the INF Treaty), and have also included Arctic-based units in various unilateral reductions of conventional forces announced since last December.

A consistent theme in the Canadian government's criticism of Arctic arms control proposals has been that the region cannot be artificially separated from the broader East-West context. As Mr. Clark put it in his December 1987 Troms speech: "... the nuclear-weapons threat is global, not regional.... Declaring the Arctic a nuclear-weapon-free zone or restricting certain naval movements there would do nothing to reduce the threat from these weapons. It would be destabilizing for other regions" (Office of the Secretary of State for External Affairs 1987: 7).

An independent, expert Panel on Arctic Arms Control was convened by the Canadian Centre for Arms Control and Disarmament in May 1989 to "develop a set of practical arms control proposals for the Arctic" (Cox and Rauf 1989: ii) in response to President Gorbachev's call for a dialogue on this question. The Panel's report, presented to a Canada-U.S.S.R. Conference on "Canadian-Soviet Arctic Co-operation" in Ottawa in late October 1989, made a number of quite specific proposals, including:

— establishment of a Central Arctic Demilitarized Zone in the Arctic Ocean beyond the 200-mile exclusive economic zones (EEZs) of the circumpolar states;
— extension of U.S. President Bush's "Open Skies" proposal for mutual aerial reconnaissance to the entire Arctic region;
— various aerial confidence-building measures, including a prohibition of simulated bombing missions or unannounced intrusions by military aircraft into each other's air defence identification zones, a ban on the carrying of nuclear weapons by aircraft in peacetime, and consideration of a common space-based surveillance radar system for all of the circumpolar states;
— strict limits or a ban on nuclear-tipped, sea-launched cruise missiles (SLCMs), as well as the elimination of tactical naval nuclear weapons;
— establishment of a Conference on Arctic Security and Co-operation (CASC), modelled after the successful European version;
— appointment of a Canadian Ambassador for Circumpolar Affairs; and
— two additional, unilateral gestures by the U.S.S.R.: first, to declare officially that its submarines do not transit the waters of the Canadian archipelago, and second, a cessation of nuclear weapons testing on the Arctic island of Novaya Zemlya (Cox and Rauf 1989: vi-vii).

The initial reaction of Canadian officials to the Report was categorically negative, but Soviet Foreign Minister Shevardnadze appeared to respond directly to two of the Panel's proposals when he announced a few weeks later that Soviet submarines "do not enter the waters of the Canadian Archipelago," and stated a willingness to "negotiate an agreement with the United States, and other countries that have strategic aircraft, on limiting the areas of test and combat flights by nuclear-capable aircraft" (U.S.S.R. Embassy 1989: 8).

The Canada-U.S.S.R. Arctic Cooperation Agreement signed in November 1989 made no reference whatsoever to security issues. Prime Minister Mulroney was widely criticized back home for having failed to use the opportunity afforded by his Soviet visit to launch a Canadian initiative on Arctic arms control. He did tell the House of Commons upon his return that he had raised the issue of the Murmansk proposals with President Gorbachev, reminded him of Mr. Clark's initial reactions, and stated "that we were quite prepared to discuss with the Soviets any refinements they might have to make to their original ideas." He also informed the Soviet president of his belief that "the best avenues for making progress on these issues" were the "current ongoing arms control negotiations between the two superpowers and the two alliances." According to the prime minister, President Gorbachev "understands fully our position and agreed that further review of this issue should be pursued by the Secretary of State for External Affairs (Mr. Clark) and Mr. Shevardnadze" (House of Commons 1989g: 6237).

Later in the same debate, External Affairs Minister Clark referred to President Gorbachev's desire to have "the matter ... be under more regular review between myself as Canadian foreign minister and Mr. Shevardnadze." Describing this as "one of the significant developments of the discussions in Moscow," Mr. Clark went on: "We agreed to that immediately because we think that will provide us with the opportunity to make proposals and provide the Soviets with the opportunity to make proposals, and as well provide an occasion for them to be looked at on a very high level" (House of Commons 1989g: 6261). However, he made clear that such discussions would proceed "always on the understanding that any negotiations would occur on an alliance basis because that is the way that negotiations lead to real reduction in weapons" (House of Commons 1989g: 6264).

Replying to Opposition calls for the appointment of an Ambassador for Circumpolar Affairs, Mr. Clark attributed the proposal to the Arctic Arms Control Panel's report, revealed that he had arranged to meet its co-chairman, and said that he "look[ed] forward to discussing the proposals of that conference, including the question of an ambassador who might be involved particularly in circumpolar affairs" (House of Commons 1989g: 6261-2).

Thus, at the time of writing, it was unclear whether Canadians could expect their government to make any counter-proposals in response to the various Soviet initiatives in the field of Arctic arms control. On the one hand officials had begun to discuss such issues actively with their Soviet counterparts, and appeared to be adopting a more positive attitude toward the question as a whole. On the other hand, as long as NATO was preoccupied with the conventional force reduction talks and the demand for Alliance unity was correspondingly high, it appeared unlikely that Canada, either alone or together with a few of its like-minded, smaller allies, would break ranks to press upon the United States a reconsideration of American policy with regard to Arctic arms control which, so far, had excluded any new, positive approach. At the very least 1990 promised greater attention to this issue.

Conclusion

In sum, Canada continued to play an active role in fostering bilateral and multilateral cooperation in several areas of Arctic international relations during 1989. On the security side government performance came under substantial attack from both ends of the political spectrum: from critics on the right and others, who decried the evisceration of the Defence White Paper's commitment to increasing Canadian military capabilities in the Arctic; and from those on the left, who charged that Ottawa was squandering unique opportunities for making progress in the area of Arctic arms control. Clearly, the government had fallen well short of the objectives it had proclaimed earlier (which may have been overly ambitious) of winning full recognition of Canada's sovereignty over its Arctic waters and substantially bolstering its ability to enforce those claims physically, while striving to limit the "excessive militarization" of the Arctic as a whole. Despite Canadian encouragement and some signs of progress, multilateral environmental and scientific cooperation in the Arctic was only beginning to take root. For Canada, the main achievements of the year lay in the further deepening of amicable relations with its two most important Arctic neighbours, the United States and Soviet Union. On the multilateral front much remained uncertain. What did seem clear was that Arctic issues of various kinds would continue to figure prominently on the Canadian foreign and security policy agenda for many years to come.

References

Canadian Institute of International Affairs. 1988. *The North and Canada's International Relations: The Report of a Working Group of the National Capital Branch of the Canadian Institute of International Affairs.* Ottawa: Canadian Arctic Resources Committee, March.

Cox, David and Tariq Rauf. 1989. *Security Co-operation in the Arctic: A Canadian Response to Murmansk (Report of the Panel on Arctic Arms Control).* Ottawa: Canadian Centre for Arms Control and Disarmament, October 24.

Canada. 1985. Parliament. House of Commons. *Debates,* September 10: 6463.

_____. 1986a. Parliament. *Independence and Internationalism.* Report of the Special Joint Committee of the Senate and of the House of Commons on Canada's International Relations. Ottawa, Queen's Printer.

_____. 1986b. Department of External Affairs. *Canada's International Relations.* Response of the Government of Canada to the Report of the Special Joint Committee of the Senate and the House of Commons. Ottawa.

_____. 1987. Office of the Secretary of State for External Affaris. Speech by the Right Honourable Joe Clark, Secretary of State for External Affairs, to the Norway-Canada Conference on Circumpolar Issues, Tromso, Norway, December 9. *Statement* 87/72.

_____. 1988. Department of External Affairs. "Agreement Between the Government of Canada and the Government of the United States of America on Arctic Cooperation." *News Release* no. 010, January 11.

_____. 1989a. Office of the Prime Minister. "Creation of the Canadian Polar Commission." *Release,* November 24.

_____. 1989b. Office of the Prime Minister. Notes for an Address by the Right Honourable Brian Mulroney, Prime Minister of Canada, Arctic and Antarctic Institute, Leningrad, November 24.

_____. 1989c. Office of the Prime Minister. "Canada and the U.S.S.R. Sign an Agreement on Cooperation in the Arctic and the North." *Release,* November 21.

_____. 1989d. Office of the Prime Minister. "Canada and the U.S.S.R. Take Steps to Limit Oil Spill Possibilities in the Arctic." *Release,* November 21.

118   Canada Among Nations 1989

——. 1989e. Department of External Affairs. "Canada and the
U.S.S.R. to Cooperate on Atmospheric Environmental Programs."
News Release, November 20.
——. 1989f. Department of External Affairs."Water Research
Agreement Signed with U.S.S.R." *News Release*, November 20.
——. 1989g. Parliament. House of Commons. *Debates*, November
27.
Globe and Mail. 1989a. "Defence of Arctic left to allies by budget
cuts." (Paul Koring) April 28: A2.
——. 1989b. "Bouchard delays plans for Polar 8 as cost rises." (Paul
Koring) May 8: A1.
Hannigan, John. 1988. *New Dimensions in Canadian-Soviet Arctic
Relations. Points of View.* Ottawa: Canadian Institute for Interna-
tional Peace and Security, November 6.
International Arctic Science Committee (IASC) Drafting Group. 1988.
"Status Report: Founding Articles for an International Arctic
Science Committee (A Review of Proposal and Next Steps),"
December 30.
"International Cooperation in Arctic Science." 1988 *Arctic Research
of the United States*, 2 (Spring).
Roots, E. F. 1988. "Cooperation in Arctic Science—Background and
Prospects". Keynote Address to the Meeting on International
Cooperation in Arctic Science held at The Royal Swedish Academy
of Sciences, Stockholm, March 24-26.
U.S.S.R. Embassy. 1989. "Common Concerns—Close Partnership"
(Interview with Foreign Minister Eduard Shevardnadze in *Izvestia*,
November 23). Ottawa: Press Office of the U.S.S.R. Embassy in
Canada, *News Release* no. 90, November 30.

8 Canadian Defence Policy: An Uncertain Transition

Dan W. Middlemiss

Historically, peacetime Canadian governments have displayed a marked reluctance to provide sufficient funds to enable the Canadian Forces (CF) to carry out their assigned commitments and roles effectively. Despite its earlier pledge to depart from this tradition the Mulroney government has proved to be no exception. The April 1989 budget undermined the central premises of the 1987 White Paper. Although the announced cuts in defence spending were solely a response to the government's attack on the mounting federal deficit, by year's end the prospective political and military changes in Eastern Europe had raised important questions about the validity of Canada's traditional defence role in Europe (see chapter 2). As a result the year was marked by growing uncertainty about what direction Canadian defence policy should take to meet Canada's security requirements at home and abroad.

The Legacy of the 1987 White Paper on Defence

After much delay the Conservatives finally produced their promised White Paper on defence in June 1987. At the heart of *Challenge and Commitment: A Defence Policy for Canada* was the government's pledge to redirect, rebuild, and revitalize the armed forces in order to close the widening commitment-capability gap caused by decades of neglect. Virtually every aspect of the deteriorating posture of the CF was targeted for significant improvement (Hampson 1988).

Overall, the 1987 White Paper represented a major commitment by the Mulroney government to restore the capabilities of the CF. While the focus was clearly on the means to achieve the traditional ends of Canadian defence policy, the measures outlined in the White Paper entailed an implicit reorientation of the European emphasis of previous policy towards North American roles. But above all else, the implementation of this bold blueprint for change would depend on the determination of the Conservatives to honour their funding promises.

Despite widespread support, including that of the two main opposition parties in Parliament, for the three-ocean concept of the White Paper, the nuclear submarine (SSN) program quickly became the symbolic focal point of vociferous public criticism of the White Paper. This single program rapidly overshadowed the other programs in the government's defence agenda which were less contentious, and many of the latter were put on hold pending a resolution of the SSN debate.

Defence and the 1988 Federal Election

Because both the Liberals and the New Democrats were firmly opposed to the SSN purchase, there was good reason to expect that defence issues, and especially the SSN question, would figure prominently in the fall 1988 federal election campaign (Keating 1988). However, despite some public lobbying for and against the SSN project by a few interest groups, it became evident, as the election approached that all three major political parties preferred to avoid making defence a prominent feature of their respective campaigns (*Defence Newsletter* 1988a: 1-3). By September, the government had postponed its decision on the choice between the British and French SSN designs until after the election, and this despite the fact that the navy's evaluation of the contenders had been completed. This led to speculation that the Mulroney cabinet was becoming increasingly concerned that waning public support for the program, as reflected in opinion polls, had made the SSN issue a political liability for the government.

During the election itself, defence policy was completely overshadowed by the free trade issue. Consequently, when the Mulroney Conservatives returned with another majority, it appeared that the path was clear for an early decision on the SSN program and the other items in the White Paper's equipment shopping list.

The Election Aftermath: Waiting For Decisions

As 1988 drew to a close the constraints on the ability of Canada's defence policymakers' to implement the 1987 White Paper had become increasingly evident. Mikhail Gorbachev's dramatic December 1988 promise of substantial unilateral reductions in Soviet conventional forces struck a resonant chord among Western peoples (Hampson 1989: 48-49). Subsequent plans to re-orient the Soviet armed forces in accordance with a new doctrine of "reasonable sufficiency" and a "defensive defence" structure further served to undermine the White Paper's cold war rhetoric, which seemingly provided the essential justification for Canada's force modernization program (Armstrong 1989; Manson 1989).

At the same time, as a long-standing member of the Western Alliance, Canada had to reassure its NATO allies that it was not letting down its guard at a time when so many uncertainties remained concerning both the degree of Gorbachev's commitment to real military reform and his ability to carry it out. Canada's poor track record in fulfilling its previous NATO obligations made the allies suspicious (NATO 1988: 11-18, 48).

It was not immediately clear in early 1989 how the Mulroney government intended to reconcile these apparently contradictory pressures on Canadian defence policy. Some observers saw the prime minister's January 30 cabinet shuffle—in which Perrin Beatty, the driving force behind the 1987 White Paper, was replaced by a relatively unknown minister, William McKnight—in the defence portfolio, as a sign that the SSN program was in serious trouble. Mr. Mulroney denied the shuffle signalled any substantive change in defence policy, and underscored the government's commitment to the White Paper. He added, however, that the policy would have to be reviewed, along with all programs and initiatives, by a new Cabinet Expenditure Review Committee, "in the light of the fiscal realities" (*Defence Newsletter* 1989a: 8, 17).

As the spectre of the government's attack on the federal deficit loomed over DND new opinion polls confirmed that a growing majority of Canadians were now more opposed than ever to the SSN program. SSNs were clearly becoming a political embarrassment for the Mulroney government and this fact was readily apparent to many anti-defence groups. Some, citing "psychic numbness," decided not to stage their usual protests against the annual series of U.S. tests of the air-launched cruise missile over Canadian territory; instead, groups like Greenpeace decided to concentrate their attention on Canada's overall military policy, including the planned purchase of SSNs (*Ottawa Citizen* 1989a).

Despite the growing unpopularity of the SSN program, Prime Minister Mulroney indicated that he and his cabinet colleagues were still committed to it. He stated that cancellation would not be an effective option for tackling the federal deficit for two reasons: the monies required for the program would be spent over more than two decades and conventionally-powered submarines would be almost as expensive as nuclear-powered ones. The prime minister concluded, "so you'll see that if you're trying to deal with billion-dollar deficits, you'd better find other ways of doing it" (*Ottawa Citizen* 1989b).

Although the fate of this program dominated the government's defence policy agenda there were other significant developments during the early months of 1989. In one of his last acts as Minister of National Defence, Perrin Beatty announced steps to improve Soviet-Canadian military relations and to decrease international tension. These measures included: a DND invitation to Soviet officials to visit the Defence Research Establishment at Suffield for the purpose of observing Canada's chemical agent destruction facilities and sharing technical information, in the hope of advancing negotiations for a ban on chemical weapons; the initiation of senior-level military staff talks between the two countries, and regular National Defence College visits to the Soviet Union, combined with the encouragement of reciprocal visits by the Soviets. An additional step was the renewal of reciprocal port visits with the Soviet Union following the completion of the Soviet withdrawal from Afghanistan (Beatty 1989). Canada was evidently prepared to countenance some Soviet-style "glasnost" of its own.

At the same time, the government remained steadfast in its support for two traditional mainstays of its defence policy. On February 1 the new defence minister, Bill McKnight, announced that the government had agreed to a U.S. request to test the unarmed, advanced cruise missile (ACM) over Canadian territory, under the terms of the Canada-U.S. Test and Evaluation Program signed in February 1983 and renewed (for five years) in 1988. McKnight justified the test as "an important Canadian contribution to the effectiveness of NATO's strategic deterrent" (Department of National Defence 1989a). Some spokesmen for the peace movement derided the decision as "starting down a slippery slope" towards endorsing a U.S. first-strike, nuclear warfighting strategy which would increase the risk of nuclear conflict, without the benefit of any informed public debate in Canada (CCACD 1989; Rosenblum and Robinson 1989).

The government also demonstrated that it was stepping up its commitment to peacekeeping. Canada was preparing to send twelve soldiers to Pakistan under the terms of a four-month "Mine Awareness and Clearing Training Program" to teach Afghan refugees how to dispose of mines left behind by the Soviet army. In February, Canada agreed to a request from Nicaragua, Honduras, Guatemala, El Salvador, and Costa Rica to the United Nations to send Canadian, West German, and Spanish inspectors to their countries to prevent armed forces and weapons from crossing their borders. Canada also agreed to provide logistics personnel from the CF to the United Nations Transition Assistance Group in Namibia (*Defence Newsletter* 1989b: 6).

The 1989 Federal Budget: Full Retreat on Defence

The April 27 budget finally ended the many months of speculation about the government's plans regarding its 1987 White Paper promises, but merely replaced them with additional uncertainties about the future direction of Canadian defence policy and the roles and posture of the armed forces.

Planned Defence Spending Levels

As part of its overall fiscal restraint package the government slashed planned DND expenditures. Although there was a discrepancy in the figures provided in the Budget Papers and those in the Main Estimates, according to the former defence funding would be $11.2 billion for 1989-90; this, according to the *Public Accounts of Canada*, represented a 0.2 percent increase over actual expenditures of $11.18 billion for 1988-89. Planned increases in defence spending would then rise by about 5 percent annually to 1993-94. As a result defence spending would average more than 11 percent as a share of total federal program expenditures over the 1989-90 to 1993-94 period, approximately the same percentage share as for the period 1985-86 to 1988-89.

The Budget Papers noted that:

> The basic parameters of the White Paper remain the defence policy of the Government although, in the current fiscal context, that policy will need to be implemented more slowly. It is expected that real growth in defence spending in the ten year period beyond 1993-94 will be able to increase compared to the real growth over the next five years, as the fiscal situation is brought under better control (Department of Finance 1989b: 23-24).

Over the next five years, however, the government expected to save $2.74 billion through cuts to previously planned spending. DND's share of the Conservatives' deficit reduction program for 1989-90 was to be $575 million, or 37.2 percent of the total expenditure reductions of $1.545 billion; for 1990-91, DND's share was to be $611 million, or 29.4 percent of the $2.079 billion total.

Impact on Defence Programs

To achieve these savings DND was forced to make significant adjustments in its internal budgetary allocations. Based on hurried preliminary planning DND proposed to effect the $575 million in savings for 1989-90 by reducing its spending on personnel by $25 million, on operations and maintenance by $100 million, and on capital outlays by $450 million. Most of the reductions would therefore come from equipment programs which were cancelled, scaled back, or rescheduled.

The projects cancelled were: the ten to twelve SSNs; the six long-range patrol aircraft; the upgrading of the fleet of *Tracker* medium-range patrol aircraft; the thirteen to twenty-eight additional CF-18A fighter aircraft; and the unmanned airborne surveillance and target acquisition systems.

A number of projects were scaled back or rescheduled as follows: the purchase of 197 long-range night observation devices (in addition to the 233 already planned), was cancelled; the upgrade of fifty-six CF-5 aircraft as lead-in trainers for the CF-18 was limited to the replacement of essential flight safety avionics; the planned acquisition of 250 main battle tanks was reduced in scope to apply only to the replacement of the tanks currently stationed in Europe, and even this replacement was placed on hold pending a future decision to proceed; the July 1988 order for 820 northern terrain vehicles was reduced to approximately 400 vehicles and implementation was postponed until at least 1995-96; the plan to equip up to seven *Challenger* aircraft with electronic warfare systems was reduced to a maximum of three; and the plan to replace both combat radios and area communication systems was scaled back to cover only radios for Canadian troops in Europe; the plan to acquire some 221 light armoured vehicles for the militia was delayed until at least 1990-91; finally, other equipment projects— such as the light observation helicopter and the ERYX short-range anti-armour weapon system—were also put on hold (CIIPS 1989: 123-125).

DND hoped to make further savings by closing nine military bases and stations in Canada, and by reducing operations at five others. DND initially estimated the cost of closing, reducing, and relocating these installations to be at least $153.5 million, while savings in personnel, operations, and maintenance costs could amount to $3.3 billion over a fifteen-year period. Additional savings would come from reductions of at least 2,200 regular and 1,200 civilian personnel in the CF.

Process

According to most reports, the decision to eliminate, reduce, and re-schedule many of DND's planned defence programs was made shortly before the budget announcement by a small group of senior military and civilian insiders without consulting their headquarters staff or the heads of the various commands. In particular, the cancellation of the SSN program appears to have resulted from a "last minute" change of heart by the Prime Minister who was anxious to avoid the inevitable political backlash that would come from forging ahead with a large, expensive—and unpopular—defence project while at the same time extolling the virtues of reducing social programs (*Financial Post* 1989a).

That these budgetary decisions were made hastily, at the eleventh hour, is supported by the fact that the DND Estimates still included $20 million earmarked for the project definition phase of the SSN program; similarly, allocations for many other defence equipment programs, later cancelled or delayed in the budget, were still included in these Estimates (*Globe and Mail* 1989a). The Estimates for DND acknowledged that the amended summary of the proposed cuts represented only "the initial assessment of how the reduction will be absorbed. It is based on preliminary planning carried out within a constrained period of time" (Department of Finance 1989b: 23-24). Admiral Charles Thomas, the head of Maritime Command, admitted that navy officials were "disappointed" by the cuts, and gave further credibility to the "eleventh hour" hypothesis when he said that his staff began examining alternatives to the submarine program the morning *after* the budget announcement (*Ottawa Citizen* 1989c). Finally, Wilson's budget itself noted that the government would "undertake an immediate examination of alternatives for the continued rebuilding of an effective navy," a statement which further suggests that the SSN decision was taken just prior to the budget announcement without warning to senior navy officials.

Nevertheless, the fact that DND immediately released detailed estimates of the planned savings from the base closures and reductions indicates that DND officials had played a role in determining where some of the expenditure cutbacks would fall, and were thus forewarned that some reductions in defence spending were coming. Perhaps DND had not anticipated that its share of the government's overall deficit reduction plan would be as large as it turned out to be. However, DND might have been luckier than some department officials thought. Reports indicated that the Finance Department had initially sought $6 billion or more in spending cuts over the next five-year period (*Financial Post* 1989b), and that the Prime Minister's Chief of Staff had "been gunning for the defence department's budgets for nearly three years" because of his belief that "defence spending was threatening to get out of control" (*Financial Post* 1989c).

What emerges most clearly from post-mortems of the 1989 defence budget process is that the cuts resulted solely from domestic financial considerations rather than from any fundamental government reassessment of the external strategic environment. Kenneth Calder, DND's Director General for Policy Planning, explained the government's position succinctly when he said:

> Programmes have been delayed and cut not for policy reasons, not because the objectives have changed, but because the money is not there—simple as that, the money is not there (Calder 1989: 9).

Parliamentary Response

In general, neither the Liberals nor the New Democrats opposed the decision to reduce defence spending, but both criticized the rationale for the reductions as well as choice of items to receive the axe. The NDP in particular scorned the government's repeated claim that the basic parameters of the 1987 White Paper remained intact as Canada's defence policy. Derek Blackburn charged that the defence "White Paper is in disgrace. The Defence Department is without direction. . . . We owe it to those in our Armed Forces to produce a new White Paper" (House of Commons 1989d: 1127).

Both parties questioned the policy rationale for the proposed cutbacks. The NDP would have preferred savings to come from reductions of Canadian troops stationed in Europe rather than from base closures in Canada which threatened to sabotage local economies. The Liberals also indicated that the government should have considered withdrawing land forces from Europe and directing the monies saved into maritime defence, Arctic disarmament, and peacekeeping. Liberal leader John Turner, noting that nine of the fourteen bases to be closed or reduced were in Liberal ridings, charged that the Conservative Government had scrapped its 1987 White Paper solely on the basis of partisan politics and had ignored military priorities or alliance commitments.

Although the parliamentary opposition expressed concern about the apparent lack of clear-cut priorities in cutbacks, it was clear that it was more interested in cashing in on the media's almost exclusive concern about the closure of military bases. Expressing outrage at the job losses and local economic repercussions entailed in the bases decision critics ignored the government's arguments that these bases no longer were justified from a military standpoint. Furthermore, the opposition refused to credit the government for reversing its stand on the SSNs, although both Liberals and the NDP had opposed this procurement program. In the heat of the debate the SSN decision was scarcely mentioned and, for that matter, no attention was paid to any of the other major procurement programs cancelled or deferred in the budget announcement; jobs, not the substance of defence policy, was the dominant defence issue arising from the wake of the April budget.

Domestic Political Reaction

Canadian peace groups claimed the cancellation of the SSN program as a victory. As one speaker noted:

> ... the government couldn't afford the political cost of the program. The Conservatives couldn't sell large cuts in unemployment insurance, day care or other social programs if they were going to spend billions on submarines. Defending the subs just wasn't worth risking the whole program of deficit reduction (*Globe and Mail* 1989b).

Elation at this outcome was nevertheless tempered by concern about the government's contention that the basic policy framework of the 1987 White Paper remained intact. In response, the Canadian Peace Alliance (CPA) argued that the 1987 document had been "gutted" by the April budget and therefore had to be redrafted to reflect the relaxation of East-West tensions. Moreover, in an apparent attempt to demonstrate that it was not wholly anti-defence, the CPA indicated that it would lobby the government to preserve jobs at the military bases scheduled for closure. Peter Davison, the CPA's Atlantic Canada spokesperson, said, "We're not here to put people out of work. We are here to challenge capital-intensive projects that don't further disarmament" (*Chronicle-Herald* 1989: 19).

Most pro-defence groups expressed dismay at the defence cuts and agreed that the budget had undermined the basic tenets of the 1987 White Paper. Canada's defence industry was clearly worried about the ultimate fate of the programs postponed in the April budget and foresaw grim times ahead for the industry as a whole.

Both anti- and pro-White Paper groups agreed that the April cuts had been made solely out of financial considerations and not because of any fundamental re-assessment of the underlying principles of Canadian defence policy. Both groups therefore urged the government to begin immediately the process of producing a new White Paper on defence.

Canadian academics specializing in military affairs agreed that a new White Paper was urgently required. To most of these experts the government's evisceration of its own defence White Paper less than two years after it had been issued demonstrated the Conservatives' lack of political commitment to defence and the tenuousness of their supposedly firm financial pledges to restore Canada's armed forces (Critchley 1989; Halstead 1989). In particular, these academics derided Mr. McKnight's remark that in the future Canada might have to rely more on its allies to protect its Arctic sovereignty; to many, this represented a contradiction in terms because it implied that Canadians would depend increasingly on the United States for information about what was happening on their own territory. Others believed that the budget cuts would weaken Canada's international position, particularly within NATO.

Editorial opinion, while noting that the Conservatives had broken many of their defence promises by cutting the defence budget, tended to focus far more on the headline-grabbing hysteria surrounding the base closures. In the weeks immediately following the budget the media engaged in a travelling circus treatment of the base closures as one local community after another was visited by television crews and prospective economic disaster highlighted in graphic and heart-rending detail. In contrast, the media paid scant attention to problems facing the Canadian Forces, still burdened with a wide range of commitments and shackled by a continuing decrease in the resources needed to carry them out.

The Future of Canadian Defence Policy

The April budget raised questions about both the short-and the long-term future of Canadian defence policy. Of immediate concern to DND and the CF was the issue of what equipment, if any, the navy and the army—the two services hardest hit by the budget cuts—were to receive. Linked to this was the broader question of whether DND could still regard the 1987 White Paper as an authoritative guide for equipment planning purposes, or whether the government would produce a new, revised White Paper which would reflect more accurately changes in the international environment, and the new fiscal priorities of the Mulroney government.

As the year progressed, there were a number of ambiguous and sometimes conflicting signals emanating from the cabinet and DND regarding these issues. To ease the shock of the SSN cancellation for the navy the government announced that it was immediately examining "alternatives for the continued rebuilding of an effective navy" (Department of Finance 1989b). Admiral Thomas himself added that recommendations to this end would be forthcoming in "a matter of days or weeks, not months" (*Ottawa Citizen* 1989c).

With respect to the army the Chief of the Defence Staff, General Manson, made it clear that DND would not proceed with its earlier plans to establish a land division in Central Europe; according to Manson, this plan was no longer affordable. Manson added that, because of the cancelled purchase of extra CF-18s, it was virtually inevitable that, by the mid-1990s, Canada would not have enough of these aircraft to meet current commitments. Despite growing signs that Canada might contemplate a change in its NATO commitments both Defence Minister McKnight and Prime Minister Mulroney hastened to assure Canadians and the NATO allies that the government's resolve to maintain existing contributions to Europe was unwavering.

In the months following the budget announcement, however, it became apparent that DND had embarked on a much broader planning process for the CF and that few equipment "quick-fixes" for *any* of the services would be forthcoming. General Manson indicated that an entirely new equipment planning and priority-setting exercise was underway and that DND was "not starting off with any assumptions about what money is in what envelopes—land, sea versus air. We've got to make the whole thing fit together" (*Financial Post* 1989b).

Nonetheless some interim measures were announced. On June 30 the Defence Minister announced the purchase of three *Arcturus* Arctic and maritime surveillance aircraft to supplement the *Aurora* fleet, although they were not equipped with the latter's sophisticated anti-submarine warfare equipment. In August DND announced the purchase of a Royal Navy *Oberon*-class, conventionally-powered submarine for permanent dockside basic training; this acquisition would relieve some of the training time required of the existing three-boat *Oberon* fleet.

Defence Minister McKnight remained evasive about what the navy's new fleet-mix might contain. In June he told a Parliamentary committee that he did not see how his department could afford a full, six-ship, third batch of frigates, while in October he stated that the navy would acquire some conventionally-powered submarines although he was uncertain of the exact number. However, he was sure of one thing: "we won't be able to spend the money we had anticipated. The fleet mix has to be planned with a much lower dollar figure than we'd planned" (*Defence Newsletter* 1989c: 7).

To many observers the long delay in producing the new acquisition plan, and all the attendant talk about affordability, merely confirmed their impressions that DND planners were finding it very difficult to reconcile the competing equipment demands of the three services with the preference of the cabinet for cutting the defence budget still further. For example, in September Mr. McKnight acknowledged that an additional $500 million in defence cuts still had to be identified to meet the five-year $2.74 billion target outlined in the April budget. Earlier the Vice Chief of the Defence Staff revealed that:

> Not only are we to receive $2.74 billion less than we had expected in the first five years, but we have had to make serious revisions to our expectations for funding in the outer ten years (Senate Special Committee 1989c: 6).

In the House, Mr. McKnight added that the total reductions would amount to some $22 billion over fifteen years. Significantly, in September the new CDS, General de Chastelain, indicated DND's new approach to dealing with the Forces' commitment-capability gap when he said, "The important point will be to tailor our commitments to our resources" (*Defence Newsletter* 1989d: 8).

The hint that some of Canada's existing defence commitments might have to be altered in the face of continuing budgetary constraints clearly pointed to the need for the government to produce a new White Paper to explain the rationale behind such changes. But in July Mr. McKnight reiterated that the broad parameters of the 1987 White Paper were intact and that no new priority planning exercise was warranted.

Nevertheless, by early September, he had apparently changed his mind for he said he expected to have cabinet approval of a new weapons acquisition plan for the CF by the end of the year—a plan which would place equal emphasis on all three services and would be set out in an "updated" White Paper.

By year's end McKnight's expectations had been overtaken by events both at home and abroad. The Mulroney government displayed continuing unwillingness to provide firm direction on defence policy, and repeatedly claimed that the 1987 policy framework was still valid, despite mounting evidence of thawing East-West relations. Accordingly, senior DND planners, so it is reported, gave the defence minister their analysis of what the forces would look like in fifteen years. According to one account, McKnight was "disturbed" by this analysis, which in effect put the ball back in the politicians' court; it asked them to determine which defence roles had to be discarded because of funding constraints (*Financial Post* 1989d).

Moreover, the wave of political reform sweeping over the Eastern bloc countries—most graphically exemplified by the crumbling of the infamous Berlin Wall—was clearly making it impossible for Canada's political leadership to maintain the fiction that the international political environment of late 1989 was still faithfully captured in the 1987 White Paper's strategic assessment. Momentous political-military changes were underway in the Soviet bloc, but it was less clear what this meant for Canadian defence policy. The Mulroney government was determined not to be out of step with its NATO allies at a moment when the international political situation was in such a state of flux. Ironically, despite the evident westward and northern re-orientation of Canadian defence policy embodied in the 1987 White Paper, and the incipient demise of Canada's Central Front NATO commitment entailed in the April 1989 budget cuts, Canada's political leaders had, by the close of 1989, decided that the prudent response to the political revolution underway in Eastern Europe was to close ranks with the allies and make no radical, unilateral changes to Canada's existing NATO contributions.

Thus, by the end of 1989, Mr. McKnight found himself with very little room to manoeuvre in adjusting Canada's basic military roles to generate the cost savings expected by the cabinet. On the one hand he admitted that the geopolitical changes in Eastern Europe were forcing DND to re-evaluate its European roles and equipment requirements on an "hourly" basis. At the same time his senior military advisors, the Department of External Affairs, and even the prime minister, were all urging caution with respect to the unsettled political climate in Europe. On the other hand, in the face of a virtual undeclared fishing war off the East and West coasts involving Canada, several European nations, and the United States, both the opposition parties were urging the government to adopt a more militant stance, to resolve the issue, including increased fisheries patrols by DND aircraft and ships. In addition, the opposition and other groups were calling for the increased use of the Canadian military to stop drug trafficking into Canada and to protect the maritime environment from polluters. Finally, the Canadian military were becoming further involved in international peacekeeping operations—the November 30 agreement by Canada to participate in the Central American United Nations Observer Group being only the latest example of this trend.

Conclusion

With all of these conflicting pressures acting simultaneously upon a dwindling budgetary base it was not clear how DND and the Mulroney government would be able to maintain Canada's existing defence commitments or devise a new, balanced equipment program for the CF within politically acceptable funding limits.

The time is obviously ripe for a serious re-examination of the traditional pillars of Canadian defence policy, especially the nature and extent of Canada's commitment to NATO. The central premises of the 1987 White Paper—the divisional re-structuring of Canadian Forces Europe, the three-ocean concept and the 2 percent-plus increments funding formula—have all been overtaken by a combination of domestic and external events. Recent surveys indicate that public opinion in Canada provides no clear guidance to the government on the future direction of Canadian defence policy: a majority still support the stationing of Canadian troops in Europe, but an increasing percentage favour further reductions in defence spending, and a large majority rank economic and environmental concerns much higher than military ones (Munton 1989).

Much political and strategic uncertainty surrounds this policy area. It is currently reflected in DND's long delay in formulating a new statement of priorities and equipment requirements. Past practice has been for Canadian defence planning to be governed by ad hoc, incremental decision-making rather than by firm, clear political direction from the top. Whether or not this pattern continues into the 1990s remains to be seen, as those responsible for policy-making wrestle with the implications of an increasingly uncertain domestic and international political climate.

References

Armstrong, G.P. 1989. "Reasonable Sufficiency: The New Soviet Military Doctrine." *Canadian Defence Quarterly* 19, no. 2 (Autumn): 22-26.

Beatty, Honourable Perrin. 1989. Address to the Conference of Defence Associations, Ottawa, Ontario, January 27.

Calder, Kenneth. 1989. "The Federal Budget: Defence and Foreign Policy—A Media Roundtable." *Peace & Security* 4, no. 2 (Summer): 9.

Canada. 1989a. Department of National Defence (DND). "Government Announces Approval For Unarmed Advanced Cruise Missile Testing." *News Release*, AFN: 06/89. Ottawa, February 1.

_____. 1989b. Department of Finance *Budget Papers*, April 27.

_____. 1989c. Parliament. Senate Special Committee on National Defence. *Proceedings*. Ottawa, May 16.

_____. 1989d. Parliament. House of Commons. *Debates*. May 1: 1127.

Canadian Centre for Arms Control and Disarmament (CCACD). 1989. "Testing the Advanced Cruise Missile: Starting Down a Slippery Slope." *Arms Control Communiqué No. 60*, February 2.

Canadian Institute for International Peace and Security (CIIPS). 1989. *The Guide to Canadian Policies on Arms Control, Disarmament, Defence and Conflict Resolution 1989*. Ottawa.

Centre for Foreign Policy Studies. 1988a. *Defence Newsletter*. No. 10 (October). Halifax: Dalhousie University.

_____. 1989a. *Defence Newsletter*. No. 1 (January). Halifax: Dalhousie University.

_____. 1989b. *Defence Newsletter*. No. 2 (February). Halifax: Dalhousie University.

_____. 1989c. *Defence Newsletter*. No. 10 (October). Halifax: Dalhousie University.

_____. 1989d. *Defence Newsletter*. No. 9 (September). Halifax: Dalhousie University.

Chronicle-Herald. 1989. "Peace alliance takes new approach to defence cuts." (Randy Jones) April 29: 19.

Critchley, W. Harriet. 1989. "Does Canada Have a Defence Policy?" *Canadian Defence Quarterly* 19, no. 2 (Autumn).

Financial Post. 1989a. "PM's last-minute decision may have scuttled sub plan." (James Bagnall) April 28: 33.

_____. 1989b. "Fierce budget attack makes Armed Forces scramble to regroup." (James Bagnall) May 8: 8.

_____. 1989c. "Cabinet defect leaves Defence on budget hook." (James Bagnall) September 4: 15.

_____. 1989d. "Armed forces lost sight of our future defence targets." (James Bagnall) November 13: 22.

Globe and Mail. 1989a. "Defence estimates overtaken by cuts." April 30: A8.

_____. 1989b. "What sank the nuclear subs." (David Langille) May 2: A7.

Halstead, J.G.H.. 1989. "A Defence Policy for Canada: the White Paper Two Years On." *Behind the Headlines* 47, no. 2 (Winter).

Hampson, Fen Osler. 1989. "A Post-Modernist World: The Changing International Politico-Security System." In *Canada Among Nations 1988: The Tory Record*, edited by Brian W. Tomlin and Maureen Appel Molot. Toronto: James Lorimer & Co.: 41-59

Hampson, Fen Osler. 1988. "Call to Arms: Canadian National Security Policy." In *Canada Among Nations 1987: A World of Conflict*, edited by Maureen Appel Molot and Brian W. Tomlin. Toronto: James Lorimer & Co.: 68-91

Keating, Tom. 1988. "Defence and Canadian political parties." *International Perspectives*, July/August: 11-14.

Manson, General P.D. 1989. "Glasnost and its Impact on the Canadian Forces." *Canadian Defence Quarterly* 18, no. 2 (June): 9-12.

Munton, Don. 1989. "Uncommon Threats and Common Security." *Peace & Security* 4, no. 4 (Winter).

North Atlantic Treaty Organization (NATO). Defence Planning Committee. 1988. *Enhancing Alliance Collective Security: Shared Roles, Risks and Responsibilities in the Alliance.* Brussels.

Ottawa Citizen. 1989a. "Peace movement quiet as cruise tests resume." (Richard Hoffman) January 23.

_____. 1989b. "PM hints nuclear submarine plans still afloat." (Greg Weston) March 8.

_____. 1989c. "Navy seeks quick solution to budget cuts." (Julian Beltrame) May 2: A5.

Rosenblum, Simon and Bill Robinson. 1989. "Modernizing the cruise." *International Perspectives*, July/August: 13-15.

9 Two Steps Forward, One Step Back: Into the 1990s[1]

Lorraine Eden

The image of the year has to be one of thousands of East and West Germans on the Berlin Wall, symbolizing the major relaxation of Communist domination of Eastern Europe in October 1989. Germans pouring through the wall, the removal of party officials, free elections in several East European countries, increased ethnic tensions within the U.S.S.R., Gorbachev meeting the new non-Communist leader in Poland: these events confounded Western spectators and kept us glued to our television sets. Each night the television brings more news of reforms in Eastern Europe, reforms that most commentators a month earlier denied could ever happen.

More sobering, and in direct contrast to the relaxation of East-West tensions, was the Chinese military massacre of thousands of students in Tiananmen Square in June. The brutal repression in the People's Republic of China reminds us that rapid movements of the general population toward democracy can easily be derailed by the return of authoritarianism.

The easing of tensions between Eastern and Western Europe, the self-marginalization and retrenchment of the Soviet Union, the looming spectre of German reunification, the clampdown in China, all will have spillovers into the international economy in the 1990s. It is too early to conclude that the Cold War is forever ended, or that China has permanently closed its doors. The challenge of these political changes for trade and finance, as well as diplomacy and strategy, will keep policymakers busy for years.

It was already clear at the end of 1989 that an economic slowdown of the U.S. and Canadian economies had started. The landing appears to be a soft one, but the length and depth of the slowdown are uncertain. The global economy may face only a one-to-two year slowdown before growth resumes. However, there still are significant financial imbalances within the developed market economies (DMEs) and continuing debt problems face the less developed countries (LDCs). A failure to contain the U.S. "terrible twins", the budget and balance of payments deficits, could lead to significantly higher U.S. interest rates and increased protectionism, adversely affecting DMEs and LDCs.

A more encouraging factor is the strong potential for a global upswing. The combination of rapid technological change, coupled with lower trade and regulatory barriers and the increased globalization of production, could result in a marked increase in potential world income and welfare in the 1990s. However, if the imbalances noted above actually result in a hard landing in 1990-91, the subsequent recession will likely derail this potential long-run upswing. The problem facing policymakers is that of steering a tight course by reducing deficits and debt levels without unduly slowing a global economy already in the midst of significant political and structural change.

Political events colour our analysis of the economic changes that face the global economy as it moves into the last decade of this century. The purpose of this chapter is to examine key changes in the international economy in the 1980s and to flag likely routes into the 1990s. The analytical framework of the chapter is based on the concept of tension between the state and the market, as policy changes impact on market forces and vice versa. The first section looks at the health of the global economy from 1985 to forecasts for 1990, concentrating on macroeconomic variables and policies for the G-7 and the net debtor developing countries, and the growth in trade. The second section highlights the tension between state and market with an analysis of three key market forces that are changing the role of states in the global economy. First is the ongoing shift to multipolarity among the developed market economies; second is the growing importance of technology in the production process; and third is the increased globalization of firms and markets. The next section examines three key policy changes in the process of implementation by states that will profoundly affect domestic and international markets: one is multilateral (the Uruguay Round), one regional (1992 in Western Europe) and one unilateral (the 1988 trade bill in the United States). The last section of the chapter looks at implications for Canada.

The Global Economy in 1989

The Developed Market Economies

(a) 1985-88 for the DMEs in Review

The year 1985 was a key year in macroeconomic policy terms. After President Reagan assumed office in 1981, he introduced an economic package of tax cuts, increased defence spending and deregulation, designed to increase economic efficiency and spur supply-side growth (Eden 1989). As a result, in 1980-85 the U.S. gross domestic product (GDP) grew, the dollar rose, and the U.S. balance of payments and fiscal budgetary (FB) deficits widened. A large FB deficit crowded out private domestic investment spending, which coupled with high interest rates, caused large foreign portfolio capital inflows and put upward pressure on the dollar. As the dollar rose, U.S. products became less competitive on world markets and the U.S. current account (CA) went even further into deficit, increasing domestic calls for protectionism.

In 1985, for the first time in forty years, the U.S. capital account moved into surplus as capital inflows exceeded outflows. Domestic public reaction to the United States becoming an international debtor forced the Congress to face the terrible deficit twins and to acknowledge that the FB deficit could be affecting the CA deficit. Congress passed the Gramm-Rudman Act, setting budgetary limits on government spending. The Federal Reserve Board relaxed its control over the money supply, helping the dollar to fall in the hope that devaluation would lessen the CA deficit. The U.S. government was forced to recognize that the dollar was overvalued, due, at least in part, to the FB deficit, and that international coordination of monetary and fiscal policies would be necessary to solve the budgetary and payments imbalances.

As a result, 1985 marked an historic turning point in U.S. domestic policy management when the G-5 countries (the United States, West Germany, Japan, the United Kingdom and France) signed the Plaza Accord. The G-5 agreed to coordinate their macroeconomic policies and, in particular, to use central bank intervention to push the dollar down in foreign exchange markets. By the fall of 1986, the U.S. trade deficit had started to improve.

In 1987 the G-7 countries (the G-5 plus Canada and Italy) signed the Louvre Accord. Fourteen years of floating exchange rates effectively ended when the G-7 agreed to hold the dollar at its current level, by central bank intervention if necessary. However, rising U.S. interest rates widened the gap between the returns on equities and bonds, tipping stock markets into the October 1987 crash. The G-7 central banks were forced to intervene heavily in foreign exchange markets to support the dollar. A global recession in 1988 was avoided by this quick action, albeit at substantial cost to the G-7 treasuries. The dollar was then allowed to drift downwards, and the U.S. economy continued to grow.

In 1988, the increased domestic demands for protectionism resulted in the passage of the U.S. Omnibus Trade and Competitiveness Act. While the Act in its final form, was scaled down in relation to the initial draft proposals, it still represented a major shift towards unilateral neoprotectionism. In November 1988, when George Bush was elected President, U.S. economists asserted the economy had reached full employment. Since Bush had promised not to raise taxes, the fiscal policy apparatus in the United States was stalemated; the Republican executive branch refused to raise taxes while the Democratic House refused to cut expenditures.

Tables 9-1 and 9-2 provide some statistics on the performance of the G-7 countries between 1985 and (forecasted) 1990, based on statistics from the International Monetary Fund (IMF 1989). The first row in Table 9-1 for each country is the general government FB deficit or surplus, taxes (T) minus government spending (G) as a percent of GNP. A minus (plus) sign indicates a budgetary deficit (surplus). The second row is the current account (CA) deficit or surplus, exports (X) minus imports (M) as a percent of GNP. A minus (plus) sign indicates a CA deficit (surplus). Row three is the short-term nominal interest rate (i), from which the expected inflation rate for the year (P^e) is subtracted to give the real interest rate (r) in the fourth row.[2] The fifth row is the unemployment rate. Sixth is the foreign exchange rate; what it costs in Canadian dollars to buy one unit of foreign currency.

The statistics show clearly how large U.S. and Canadian FB and CA deficits are in comparison to those of to Japan, West Germany and the United Kingdom, although by 1988 the U.S. FB deficit had dropped to 1.8 percent, and the CA deficit to 2.8 percent, of GNP. Throughout 1985-88 real interest rates and unemployment rates were highest in Canada and the United Kingdom. Note the marked increase in the yen, mark and pound over the period.

Table 9-1
Indicators of Economic Performance for the G-7 Countries, 1985-90

	1985	1986	1987	1988	Forecast 1989	Forecast 1990
CANADA						
FB as % GNP	-7.0%	-5.5%	-4.6%	-3.1%	-4.4%	-3.8%
CA as % GNP	-0.4	-2.1	-1.9	-1.9	-2.6	-2.9
Interest rate	9.6	9.2	8.4	9.6	11.7	NA
$r = i - P^e$	6.7	6.7	4.1	5.4	7.4	NA
Unemployment rate	10.5	9.5	8.8	7.8	8.0	8.0
UNITED STATES						
FB as % GNP	-3.3	-3.4	-2.3	-1.8	-2.2	-1.7
CA as % GNP	-2.9	-3.3	-3.4	-2.8	-2.7	-2.8
Interest rate	8.0	6.5	6.9	7.7	9.5	NA
$r = i - P^e$	5.0	3.8	3.6	4.3	4.8	NA
Unemployment rate	7.2	7.0	6.2	5.5	5.3	5.3
Exch. Rate ($Cdn)	1.37	1.39	1.33	1.23	1.19	NA
JAPAN						
FB as % GNP	-0.8	-0.9	0.6	1.1	1.6	2.0
CA as % GNP	3.7	4.3	3.6	2.8	2.7	2.8
Interest rate	6.7	5.1	3.9	4.1	4.6	NA
$r = i - P^e$	5.1	3.3	4.1	3.6	3.2	NA
Unemployment rate	2.6	2.8	2.8	2.5	2.4	2.4
Exch. Rate ($Cdn)	0.0058	0.0083	0.0092	0.0096	0.0087	NA
WEST GERMANY						
FB as % GNP	-1.1	-1.3	-1.8	-2.0	-0.6	-1.2
CA as % GNP	2.6	4.4	4.0	4.0	4.1	3.9
Interest rate	5.4	4.6	4.0	4.3	6.4	NA
$r = i - P^e$	3.2	1.5	2.0	2.8	3.9	NA
Unemployment rate	8.2	7.9	7.9	7.7	7.5	7.3
Exch. Rate ($ Cdn)	0.47	0.64	0.74	0.70	0.63	NA
UNITED KINGDOM						
FB as % GNP	-2.9	-2.4	-1.4	0.5	1.7	1.9
CA as % GNP	0.9	0.0	-0.6	-3.2	-3.4	-2.7
Interest rate	12.2	10.9	9.6	10.3	13.0	NA
$r = i - P^e$	6.3	7.3	4.7	4.3	6.4	NA
Unemployment rate	11.2	11.3	10.2	8.2	7.3	7.5
Exch. Rate ($ Cdn)	1.77	2.04	2.17	2.19	1.95	NA
ALL G-7 COUNTRIES						
FB as % GNP	-3.3	-3.3	-2.3	-1.7	-1.5	- 1.2
CA as % GNP	-0.6	-0.2	-0.4	-0.4	-0.5	-0.5
Interest rate	10.0	6.9	6.6	7.1	8.5	NA
$r = i - P^e$	6.6	3.8	3.9	4.2	4.7	NA
Unemployment rate	7.4	7.3	7.0	6.4	6.1	6.1

Sources: Calculations based on IMF (1989: 129, 134, 140, 142 and 157), and *Report on the Nation* (1989: 80).

Table 9-2
Growth Rates for the G-7 Countries, 1985-90

	1985	1986	1987	1988	Forecast 1989	Forecast 1990
	(in percentages)					
CANADA						
Real GNP growth	4.6	3.2	4.0	4.5	2.9	2.5
% chg.real GNP/POP	3.8	2.4	2.9	3.6	2.0	1.6
Real I Impulse	3.6	1.8	5.6	8.0	3.0	2.6
Fiscal Impulse	1.5	-1.1	-0.7	-0.7	1.3	-0.7
Monetary Impulse	1.9	3.0	1.8	1.4	NA	NA
UNITED STATES						
Real GNP growth	3.4	2.8	3.4	3.9	3.1	2.5
% chg.real GNP/POP	2.4	1.9	2.4	2.9	2.2	1.5
Real I Impulse	2.0	-2.8	-1.5	2.1	0.7	1.4
Fiscal Impulse	0.7	0.2	-0.8	-0.1	0.6	-0.6
Monetary Impulse	2.5	2.8	-0.1	-2.2	NA	NA
JAPAN						
Real GNP growth	4.8	2.5	4.5	5.7	4.5	4.4
% chg.real GNP/POP	4.3	1.8	3.9	5.1	3.9	3.8
Real I Impulse	3.3	0.5	5.8	7.6	2.2	1.3
Fiscal Impulse	-0.9	-0.3	-1.4	-0.1	-0.4	-0.2
Monetary Impulse	2.0	4.4	6.1	5.0	NA	NA
WEST GERMANY						
Real GNP growth	1.9	2.3	1.8	3.4	2.4	2.9
% chg.real GNP/POP	2.2	2.3	1.6	3.1	2.0	2.6
Real I Impulse	-1.8	1.0	0.7	2.4	0.3	1.0
Fiscal Impulse	-0.9	0.3	0.1	0.6	-1.6	0.8
Monetary Impulse	0.8	0.4	3.3	1.5	NA	NA
UNITED KINGDOM						
Real GNP growth	3.7	3.2	4.6	4.4	3.3	2.1
% chg.real GNP/POP	3.3	3.0	4.1	4.2	3.3	1.7
Real I Impulse	-0.7	-2.3	1.0	7.0	3.9	-0.9
Fiscal Impulse	-0.5	-0.1	-0.1	-0.7	-0.7	-0.4
Monetary Impulse	4.3	11.7	11.6	10.2	NA	NA
ALL G-7 COUNTRIES						
Real GNP growth	3.4	2.7	3.4	4.2	3.4	3.0
% chg.real GNP/POP	2.7	2.0	2.8	3.5	2.7	2.3
Real I Impulse	1.1	-0.8	1.0	4.0	1.4	1.4
Fiscal Impulse	0.2	0.0	-0.7	0.0	0.0	-0.3
Monetary Impulse	2.0	2.9	2.2	0.5	NA	NA

Sources: Calculations based on and taken from IMF (1989: 126, 127, 129, 134, 139, 142).

In Table 9-2 we look at macroeconomic performance in terms of growth rates. The first two lines in Table 9-2 for each country show the percentage change in real GNP (i.e. nominal GNP divided by the GNP price deflator), and real GNP per capita (GNP/POP). The third line is the real investment impulse, defined as the gap between the percentage change in real private investment expenditures and the percentage change in real GNP. Investment impulse gives some indication of the extent to which the private sector in each economy is productively investing in future growth. Real GNP and GNP per capita rose steadily over the 1985-88 period for the G-7 members. The investment impulse, however, is uneven and occasionally negative, suggesting that something, perhaps the fiscal budget deficit (see Table 9-1), was crowding out private investment in this period.

Lines four and five show the mismatch between the macroeconomic policies of the G-7 as measured by the "fiscal impulse" and "monetary impulse" of their government policies. Fiscal impulse is defined as the gap between the percentage change in FB and the percentage change in nominal GNP. If the gap is positive (negative), the budget deficit is growing faster (slower) than GNP and has an expansionary (contractionary) impact on the economy. Monetary impulse is similarly defined as the gap between the percentage change in broad money supply and the percentage change in nominal GNP. If the money supply is growing faster (slower) than GNP, the monetary impulse is positive (negative) and expansionary (contractionary). Therefore negative numbers in the table are contractionary; positive ones, expansionary. Throughout the period most G-7 governments ran conflicting policies: contractionary fiscal policies, as governments tried to reduce the size of their fiscal deficits, but expansionary monetary policies (note especially the United Kingdom), partly as a consequence of having to prop up the U.S. dollar under the Louvre Accord.

(b) 1989: a Soft Landing?

U.S. real interest rates have risen slightly over the year, with a forecasted 1989 real rate of 4.8 percent. Rising interest rates probably reflect targeting of inflation by the Federal Reserve Board, along with G-7 coordination of macroeconomic policies. The positive impact of the 1987-88 falling dollar has petered out and the forecasted current account deficit as a percent of GNP is basically unchanged from 1988. The FB deficit is expected to increase from 1.8 to 2.2 percent of GNP.

(See Table 9-1.) In Canada, both the FB and CA deficits are expected to rise as a percent of GNP. As a group the G-7 members are expected to have both FB and CA deficits. Real interest rates are higher in all member countries except Japan. Unemployment and inflation rates are expected to hold steady, except in Canada where both are rising.

As Table 9-2 shows, real GNP growth slowed in the G-7 from 4.2 percent in 1988 to an estimated 3.4 percent in 1989. The large investment impulse recorded in 1988 in Canada, Japan and the United Kingdom is also subsiding, with a forecasted real investment impulse for the G-7 of 1.4 percent. The enormous monetary increases in the United Kingdom (and their probable inflationary impact) should be noted. The U.S. economy is apparently headed for a soft landing, as output growth, auto sales and industrial production continue to slow (*Business Review* 1989). Unemployment and inflation are, however, holding steady at 5.3 and 4.5 percent, respectively.

Canada ran a moderately expansionary fiscal policy in 1989, as is shown by its larger FB deficit in Table 9-1. However, the only fiscal growth was in debt servicing due to high interest rates. Discretionary tax and expenditure changes in the April 1989 budget combined to take the steam out of the economy. The Wilson budget contained several tax increases and some spending cuts, notably cuts to defence and official development aid. The major tax increase was expected to come from the Goods and Services Tax (GST) which is to be in place by January 1991. Monetary policy was tight, with Bank Governor John Crow holding interest rates several points above those in the United States. As a result, the Canadian dollar rose steadily over the year.

Due to strong opposition to the Goods and Services Tax from business, labour and provincial government groups, the Finance Department has been forced to concentrate its resources on selling the tax to Canadians. External Affairs has been preoccupied with implementation of the Canada-U.S. free trade agreement and negotiations under the Uruguay Round. In 1989, large numbers of mergers and acquisitions made the headlines, along with their accompanying layoffs and movements either north or south across the Canada-U.S. border. Since big gains in investment and jobs were predicted to occur after free trade, their absence has been used by the media to condemn the agreement. Job losses, high interest rates and the expected GST made the Conservative government's job in 1989 a difficult one.

(c) Forecast for 1990: Uncertainties Ahead

The forecast for 1990 very much depends on events in the United States. If the U.S. economy continues its moderate slowdown, unemployment should rise and pressure on inflation ease. Improvements in the U.S. CA depend on changes in the FB deficit and the value of the dollar. If it remains at the present level and nothing substantial is done about the FB deficit by the U.S. Congress, portfolio capital inflows are likely to continue, because of the relatively high U.S. real interest rates. As a result, the CA deficit may again start to rise.

In addition, the U.S. CA deficit may also rise in 1990 due to lags between national business cycles. Since the North American economy is already slowing down, while the European economies are still growing, American exports are being pulled abroad by strong demand overseas while import growth is depressed by our slowing economies. If the European and Japanese economies move into this slowdown over the next year, the North American CA and balance of payments (BOP) deficits should widen further.

The IMF (see Tables 9-1 and 9-2) is forecasting smaller FB and CA deficits, slower growth, and unchanged inflation and unemployment rates for most G-7 countries. However, there are still reasons to fear a hard landing for the United States in 1990-91 (Feldstein 1989). Since the positive impact on the U.S. CA deficit has stopped now that the dollar is no longer falling, further reductions in the CA deficit must come from reduced domestic expenditure or increased saving (i.e. from cutting the FB deficit). With the Congressional election in 1990 and the Presidential one in 1992, it is unlikely that the political will exists to make substantial cuts in the FB deficit. The attempts to shift the savings and loan bailout to off-budget items so that the Gramm-Rudman targets would be officially met does not suggest any real commitment to deal with the problem. The potential peace dividend associated with relaxation of Cold War tensions is also an unlikely solution since it is seen by many in Congress as a way to finance and expand social programs rather than as a means to deal with the FB deficit problem. The most likely scenario is that the United States will continue to muddle through until after the 1992 Presidential election.

The Less Developed Countries

The 1980s have not been a good decade for the less developed countries, particularly since the onset of the debt crisis in 1982.[3] However, the economic effects have varied sharply between the newly industrializing economies (NIEs) which experienced substantial growth increases, the oil-exporting countries with fortunes tied to stagnant oil prices, and the net debtor LDCs which suffered from high interest rates and slow domestic growth. In addition, there are substantial regional variations, e.g. between Africa and Latin America. We concentrate our attention in this chapter on the net debtor LDCs (ND-LDCs).

Table 9-3
Indicators of Economic Performance, Net Debtor Developing Countries, 1985-90

	1985	1986	1987	1988	Forecast 1989	Forecast 1990
(in percentages)						
% chg. real GDP	4.6	4.6	4.0	4.5	3.3	4.3
% chg. real GDP/POP	2.7	2.5	2.0	2.9	1.1	2.5
Inflation (wt.avg)	46.4	34.4	45.3	77.1	51.7	19.5
% chg. broad money	51.6	39.1	55.9	81.3	NA	NA
Central FB as % GDP	-3.9	-4.8	-5.0	-4.6	-3.7	NA
% chg. terms of trade	-2.1	-12.8	0.1	-1.7	-0.6	-0.7
Debt service as % of exports	26.0	27.2	24.0	22.9	22.2	20.6
External debt as % of GDP	39.8	41.5	41.1	38.7	36.6	35.2
% chg. priv. lending	1.6	0.7	-0.9	1.5	1.5	2.7
% chg. offic.lending	12.1	10.8	10.9	5.2	7.1	6.0

Note: Net debtor countries include 126 developing countries which are net debtors in terms of their stocks of external assets and liabilities. The net debtors category can be further subdivided according to predominant type of creditor (market, official, diversified) and/or by experience with respect to debt servicing (with or without difficulty). For more information see IMF 1989:117-22.
Sources: IMF (1989: 47, 131, 136, 143, 144, 154, 186, 193).

Some statistics on the ND-LDCs, taken from IMF (1989), are provided in Table 9-3 for the period 1985 to forecasted 1990. Real growth rates since 1985 have hovered around 4 percent per year, with real GNP per capita growing about 2 percent per year. Inflation rates have been much higher than in the DMEs, averaging between 34 and 77 percent, about the same rate of increase as that of broad monetary aggregates in these economies. Average central government FB deficits have stabilized around 4 percent of GDP. The terms of trade of the ND-LDCs fell steadily throughout the period, with a large drop in 1986 as natural resource prices fell. The cost of servicing their external debt as a percent of exports has fallen slowly over the period from 26 percent in 1985 to 22 percent in 1989. The stock of external debt has also fallen slowly as a percent of GDP, from 40 to 37 percent. Private lending has hardly grown at all over the period, while official lending has slowed markedly from a 12 percent annual growth rate to 7 percent.

Sustained growth over the 1980s in the DMEs has had a positive impact on exports from the ND-LDCs. However, the unwillingness of private lenders to finance more debt relief has meant increasing reliance by the ND-LDCs on official lending sources. At the same time there has been a move towards structural adjustment and liberalization of domestic economies, as part of the conditions attached to official funding. In some countries, like Mexico, the reforms have been moderately successful in lowering inflation and encouraging growth and trade. Others, Brazil and Argentina for example, are enduring hyperinflation, capital flight and severe recession. The average inflation rate for Latin America in 1989 is expected to be 1,200 percent (*Business Review* 1989: 7).

Given the apparent failure of the U.S. Brady Plan as a solution to the debt crisis, due to the unwillingness of private banks to finance more loans to the ND-LDCs, the situation in the early 1990s depends very much on conditions in the DMEs. As they move into a slowdown, growth in the ND-LDCs should also slow. If interest rates start rising as central banks try to contain domestic inflationary pressures and prop up domestic currencies, the effect will be felt most negatively by the ND-LDCs. Their best hope is for a mild global slowdown, falling interest rates and substantial liberalization of trade under the Uruguay Round.

The Growth of International Trade

World merchandise trade volume grew 8.5 percent in 1988 and is expected to continue to grow by 7 percent in 1989. Trade growth is outstripping world output growth by almost two to one. There are at least nine possible explanations for this rapid trade growth, according to the Secretariat of the General Agreement on Trade and Tariffs (GATT 1989: 1,4), four of which are due to basic economic forces and five due to policy changes:

- technological innovations are widening the scope of traded goods and services;
- the real cost of petroleum has fallen by half since its peak in 1980;

- the share of manufactures in world trade in value terms has risen by one third since the 1980s and is now 73 percent of the value of world merchandise trade and half of the value of the exports of LDCs;
- the numbers of international joint ventures and mergers have been growing rapidly, along with the increasing interdependence of financial markets;
- market improvements have resulted from deregulation and denationalization;
- investors and consumers have shown confidence in the ability and willingness of the DME central banks to prevent inflation;
- capital flows have been liberalized;
- economic reforms are taking place in Eastern Europe and the U.S.S.R.; and
- the Uruguay Round, together with regional and bilateral trade policy reforms, implies a commitment to a new liberalized trade policy.

This list offers a basis for a positive perception of a global economy moving towards more open markets and liberalized economies. This trend should lead to an expansion of the global capital stock, faster economic growth and more employment in the 1990s. However, the road to good times is not an easy one, and for every two steps forward, there is one step back. The global economy is in the midst of state and market changes that will have significant long-run impacts on current global trade and investment patterns and on economic growth. Three key market forces are the diffusion of economic power, rapid technological change and the globalization of markets. Three key state policy changes, one multilateral (the Uruguay Round), one regional (1992 in Western Europe) and one unilateral (the 1988 U.S. trade bill), also pose their own challenges and suggest opportunities for the 1990s. The next two sections of this chapter examine the tensions between these state and market forces.

Two Steps Forward, One Step Back: Markets in the Global Economy

The Diffusion of Economic Power

In 1945, the United States stood alone as the undisputed hegemon, due to its commanding share of the world's economic and military resources. International institutions were weak or new, and nonstate actors such as multinational enterprises (MNEs) were just beginning to reach across international borders to set up affiliates.

Today, the situation is very different. As Gilpin (1987) and Hoffman (1989b) argue, most countries at the end of the 1980s are closely linked and interdependent, through their reliance on trade, investment, finance and production flows. The per capita income of the Triad countries (North America, the EC and Japan) is now roughly equivalent (Morris 1989). As Ohmae (1985, 1989) argues, these Triadic consumers represent a new democratization of consumer tastes on a global basis. The EC now has 320 million people in one market, compared to 250 million in the United States (Lees 1989). Small countries with regional influence, the so-called regional influentials such as Indonesia, are also more important in political economy terms (Thornton 1989). International institutions such as the GATT, IMF and World Bank have more political and economic power (although perhaps less so than in the 1960s and early 1970s). Plans are underway to form a new organization of the Pacific Rim economies. MNEs now straddle the globe and many have sales and assets several times larger than national incomes of the smaller LDCs (United Nations 1988).

The United States still remains a hegemon in terms of economic size. In 1988, its per capita GDP was the largest in terms of purchasing power parities; although in terms of current exchange rates, per capita incomes in several countries, such as Switzerland, Japan and Sweden were higher than in the United States (*Economist* 1989: 123). In 1986, at $4,444 billion, the U.S. GNP was the largest share, approximately 23 percent, of world GNP (Japan 1988). As several authors have argued (Gilpin 1987; Hoffman 1989b; Tonelson 1989), the increased diffusion of economic power, in some sense, was inevitable once the Western allies regained their economic strength after the Second World War. There are grounds for arguing that the current diffusion of power is simply a return to the historical norm, and that the 1945-80 period was an abberation in history.

However, even if the United States is still "the only 'complete' great power" (Hoffman 1989b: 88), its ability to lead the Western alliance is now severely constrained by market forces, in particular by the U.S. reliance on foreign borrowing, and the rise of regional blocs with markets larger than that of the U.S. Deficits make it less likely that the United States can afford to defend the Alliance (this may be a dated concept), and more likely that U.S. contributions to foreign aid and international institutions will be reduced in order to fund domestic programs. Multipolarity is a much-used word, but it does describe the market forces which are reducing the United States to the status of first among equals, a leader instead of a ruler (Eden 1989; Hampson 1989).

Japan remains the enigmatic power behind the U.S. throne. The top twenty-five banks are headquartered in Japan, which now has one-tenth of world GNP (Japan 1988). Japan now holds 50 percent of global patents, finances the bulk of the U.S. budget deficit, and in 1989 became the world's largest aid donor (McMillan 1989). Its present foreign policy is designed to ensure a continuation of postwar strategic and economic relationships between itself and the United States (Japan 1988; Okita 1989). Faced with a hostile U.S. Congress, a wary group of Pacific Rim neighbours and a eager crowd of ND-LDC borrowers, Japan contemplates its "quiet strength" in the 1990s.

As events in 1989 demonstrate, the Soviet Union's empire is apparently collapsing. The ability of the United States to exercise economic clout in Eastern Europe is uncertain. As Stern (1989) clearly shows, the use of economic leverage through threats of sanctions has had little effect on the U.S.S.R. Its economic fortunes are driven more by oil and gold prices and the success or failure of the wheat crop. Given the enormous short-run dislocation costs of *perestroika*, the U.S.S.R., like the U.S. is losing economic clout relative to other nations. As the two Germanies move closer together, there is the potential in the 1990s for a four-sided hegemonic power game: the United States, Russia, Germany and Japan, each with its own sphere of interests.

The Importance of Knowledge-Based Production

The global economy is in the midst of a third technological revolution based on microelectronics (Eden 1989). Through such new technology tools as CAD-CAM, microsoftware, flexible automation and information networking systems, a firm can be linked with its key operations, customers, suppliers and procurement officers worldwide. The start-up costs of this automation are extremely high, necessitating external markets so that the firm can reap economies of scale and scope (Levitt 1983). Product innovations have a higher knowledge content, and new processing methods such as just-in-time inventories and flexible automation have led to reduced wastage and substitution among materials (Fleck and D'Cruz 1987; van Tulder and Junne 1989).

Information technology is also being used as a tool to downsize and flatten the corporation. U.S. firms have shed more than one million managers and professional staff since 1979 (Applegate et al. 1988). Information technology can also be used to relocate production back from developing countries to the DMEs. The 1970s and 1980s shift to offshore processing as a way to cut costs may no longer be necessary with rapid automation at home. The ability of the NIEs to retain their offshore platforms in the 1990s will depend on their labour costs, political stability and the speed at which they can automate relative to the DMEs.[4]

Globalization of Markets and Firms

The joining of computers and telecommunications has revolutionized communications, changing the concept of a market from a geographic location to a network of computers linked by telephone lines. Just as the railroad revolutionized transportation of goods within and between national markets by lowering transportation costs to its downstream industries, so too is the computer revolutionizing transportation of services within and between markets. The railroad affected transportation in terms of both carriage and content, carriage through the use of freight cars and content in terms of bulk freight goods. The computer is changing transportation again in terms of carriage (airways, telephone lines, cables) and content (voice, data and video services).[5] Just as lower transport costs overcame tariff barriers, linking markets and increasing trade in goods, so also are lower communications costs overcoming regulatory and other non-tariff barriers, making previously untraded goods and services tradeable. By 1990, there will be one billion telephones in the world, all able to dial each other directly (Hax 1989). Trade in commercial services grew faster than in trade in goods between 1980 and 1988. World exports of commercial services in 1988 were estimated at U.S. $560 billion or about 20 percent of total world exports (GATT 1989).

Technology affects not only the globalization of trade in services, but also the overall volume of trade, since many goods have a high service content. GATT (1989: 3) concludes that the "greater the availability and the lower the costs of the needed services, the faster [is] the pace of globalization of markets," and that access to competitively priced producer services is a key determinant of a firm's ability to complete in global markets.

Almost all industries now have global markets, competitors, customers and suppliers. Ohmae (1985, 1989) argues that the Triad is the critical framework for MNEs thinking about global competition. Each multinational should have a position in each of the three leading blocs in order to be a "true insider" in that market. At the same time, each firm should develop "lead country models", products tailored to the dominant markets, which can be minimally tailored for smaller markets.

The globalization of markets is forcing multinationals to juggle simultaneously the goals of economic efficiency, national responsiveness and world-wide learning, according to Bartlett and Ghoshal (1987a, 1987b). They argue that three important intrafirm trade flows are at the centre of the emerging new global corporation: (1) product interdependence: flows of components and finished goods; (2) resource interdependence: flows of funds, skills and other scarce resources; and (3) knowledge interdependence: flows of intelligence, ideas and knowledge personnel. At the same time, MNEs are turning to partnerships, joint ventures and other co-operative arrangements as a way of spreading the high overhead costs of technological innovation; they are linking with firms with complementary skills and resources, and achieving "insider" status (United Nations 1988).

Implications of Market Changes for State Policies

The diffusion of economic power, the technological revolution and the globalization of firms and markets have faced governments with a major policy problem: how to ensure that their firms remain competitive in an increasingly competitive world. Globalization of markets is also encouraged by state policies such as deregulation, the liberalization of trade and the integration of financial and capital markets through the G-7 and the European Monetary System. The perception that technology is key to good trade performance and economic competitiveness has led governments to subsidize and protect their high-tech industries, and to encourage the production of high-skilled labour (van Tulder and Junne 1989; McMillan 1989).

What is international competitiveness? The World Competitiveness Report summarized in *European Affairs* (1989: 116) defines competitiveness as: "the ability of entrepreneurs to design, produce and market goods and services, the price and non-price qualities of which form a more attractive package than that of competitors." Competitiveness comes from two sources: the internal efficiency of the firm and the national environment. The report focuses on the impact of national environments on firms operating within domestic borders.

Of the twenty-two DMEs surveyed in the report the leader this year, as last year, was Japan, followed by Switzerland. Canada's position improved from sixth to fourth place, due mostly to the implementation of the free trade agreement. The ranking of the G-7 countries is summarized in Table 9-4. Japan has the current lead in process technology while the United States leads in product technology (McMillan 1989). Since product innovations can be rapidly duplicated, while process innovations are difficult to transfer, Japan's advantage may be more sustainable in the long run than that of the U.S. Canada's worrisome performance in terms of financial dynamism, and outward and innovative forward orientation should be noted.

Table 9-4
Competitiveness of the G-7 Countries, 1989
(rank out of 22 developed market economies)

	CAN	U.S.	JAPAN	F.R.G.	U.K.	FRANCE	ITALY
Dynamism of economy	3	2	1	4	11	13	19
Industrial efficiency	4	3	1	5	10	12	13
Market orientation	4	1	3	5	12	11	17
Financial dynamism	11	6	2	3	8	10	17
Human resources	2	1	3	12	15	11	19
State interference	3	2	5	7	8	17	20
Natural endowments	2	9	13	10	5	8	19
Outward orientation	14	9	2	4	6	12	17
Innovative forward Orientation	15	6	1	3	12	8	18
Socio-political stability	6	3	2	5	15	17	16

Source: "The World Competitiveness Report", *European Affairs* (1989: 117).

Two Steps Forward, One Step Back: States in the Global Economy

Multilateral State Initiatives: the Uruguay Round

The GATT is now forty-two years old. Its membership includes 96 countries that account for over 85 percent of world trade (Kelly et al. 1988: 29). In September 1986 the Uruguay Round of Multilateral Trade Negotiations (MTN) was launched at Punta del Este, Uruguay. The purpose of this round is broader than earlier MTN rounds because it includes both trade in goods and services. However services are being treated separately and any services accord is unlikely to be binding on all members. The goods negotiations are divided into fourteen negotiating groups covering tariffs, non-tariff barriers (NTBs), safeguards, various product categories, subsidies and countervailing duties, trade-related intellectual property rights (TRIPS) and trade-related investment measures (TRIMS) (Kelly et al. 1988; *Canada Export* 1989).

Since the negotiations were launched, individual countries have been discussing the breadth of issues that can be covered by each committee and tabling position papers. In December 1988, the mid-term review of the Uruguay Round was held in Montreal. At this meeting, the so-called "Montreal principles" of national treatment, nondiscrimination, market access, progressive liberalization and transparency were proposed for services, TRIMs and TRIPs. Eleven negotiating papers were tabled and tentatively approved. The mid-term review process reached an impasse, however, largely due to U.S.-European Community conflicts over agricultural reform, and reconvened in Geneva in April 1989.

The April 1989 meeting tabled draft negotiating papers setting out the objectives and timetables for completion of the Uruguay Round by the end of 1990. More than 100 countries ratified these papers, along with the ones passed at the 1988 Montreal meeting. The major points agreed upon at the April 1989 meeting, including those agreed upon in Montreal, were the following:

- agreement on an overall cut of 30-40 percent in tariffs;
- reductions, to begin in 1991, of support (read: EC) and protection (read: U.S.) to agriculture;
- the initiation of negotiations to bring textiles trade into the GATT after the Multi-Fibre Agreement expires in 1991;
- agreement to negotiate standards, rules and dispute settlement mechanisms for TRIPS;
- agreement to liberalize NTBs, trade in natural resources; and
- agreement to bring trade in business services into the GATT.

By August 1990, the delegations are to have reached broad agreement in each group so that, by November, the agreements can be finalized and legal documents prepared. The final meeting is to be held at Brussels in December 1990.

If the Round is successful it will substantially broaden the issues covered by the GATT and address the new realities of the global economy. As Preeg has recently argued: "The great irony in world trade is that just as actual trade relations are becoming truly globalized, the credibility of the GATT multilateral trading system has been in decline" (1989: 201). The growth of regional and bilateral trade, the increasing use of non-tariff barriers, the omission of major traded commodities such as agriculture, textiles and services, have all damaged the GATT's ability to manage the international trading system. The outcome will depend on the success of the Uruguay Round in broadening the issues covered by the GATT, as evidenced by the number of serious policy measures passed, the number of signatories to those measures and the speed with which the measures are implemented.

Regional State Initiatives: On the Road to 1992

The GATT needs a broadening both of issues and geography. Preferential trading arrangements fall under Article 24 of the GATT and were, in 1947, expected to represent exceptions to the rule of multilateral trade. However, the exception has become the rule, as preferential trading areas exist in all corners of the world. The most prominent of these, of course, have been the European Community, the Canada-U.S. free trade agreement and COMECON.[6]

In March 1985, the European Council passed a resolution to move to a single market ending the current maze of border controls, subsidies, regulations and preferential procurement policies. In June the Commission, the executive branch of the EC, published a White Paper listing three hundred areas where controls on capital, labour, goods and services flows needed to be liberalized, and setting a deadline of 1992 for passing the necessary legislation (Hoffman 1989a).

The EC Commission has estimated a once-and-for-all gain of 2 to 3 percent in Community GDP from the removal of border controls alone, and another 2 to 3 percent from improvements in competitiveness (Giersch 1989; Kelly et al. 1988: 88-105). Thus there could be a one-time gain of 5 percent in actual GDP due to liberalization under 1992. However, Giersch argues that this may underestimate the true gain if increased productivity due to decontrol and liberalization raises the potential level of GDP. A gain in potential GDP is a permanent gain, as compared to a one-time gain. Giersch observes that inflation in the EC is low, oil prices and wage demands are stable, investment is high and rising as is foreign direct investment. In addition, faster technological innovation, increased knowledge-intensity of production, and the spread of Europe-wide sourcing by EC multinationals is accelerating growth within the Community.

While the output gain to the EC may be clear, the impact on nonmembers is more worrisome. The 1992 liberalization is a regional initiative and, as such, can be a "building bloc" or catalyst for further multilateral liberalization, or an inward-looking bloc and a force for protectionism. Under Jacques Delors, head of the EC Commission, the pressure has been to harmonize legislation and set common standards across the twelve member countries. U.K. Prime Minister Margaret Thatcher, however, has been pressing for mutual recognition of each member's standards, allowing harmonization to come from competition rather than bureaucrats. (This conflict between upper-and-lower tier governments is a tension that Canadians know well). It is clear that the easiest harmonization has already occurred and that the 1992 deadline will not be met for all 300 directives. However, the hundreds of mergers and acquisitions taking place as firms position themselves within the Community suggest that economic restructuring is sufficiently advanced that it would be difficult to stop.

Schmieding (1989) argues that the trade diversion effects of 1992, particularly for the COMECON countries, may be larger than expected. Not only will outsiders will be at a disadvantage, since suppliers from member states enjoy easier access to partners' markets than do third country suppliers, but harmonization can accentuate this trade diversion. Over 70 percent of the 130 directives passed so far provide for harmonization. These uniform norms set by the EC bureaucracy can be misused as barriers to entry. For example, the new local content rule to the effect that any European good must not embody more than a fixed share of imported inputs is clearly discriminatory. In addition, Schmieding asserts that harmonizing social systems and labour laws will generate cost-push pressures of such a kind that the EC will increase its common external tariff.

As a result of the move to 1992, the members of the European Free Trade Area (EFTA) are deciding whether to apply for membership in the EC or, if they remain in EFTA, how to restructure the EC-EFTA relationship after 1992. The EFTA members generally are high-income, liberalized economies, and have their own long-run, preferential access to the EC. The key problem is the European neutrals in EFTA which would have to give up their neutrality to join the EC: Austria, Switzerland and Finland. If some of the members of EFTA join the EC, the longevity of EFTA may be problematic. A possible solution may be found in a new arrangement between the EC and EFTA that takes account of the changed political and economic situation in Europe.

An additional challenge and opportunity is the opening of Eastern Europe, which now looks to Western Europe for investment, goods and aid. The talk is of a new Marshall Plan for Eastern Europe and of a "common European home" in which the Community would be the centrepiece. The potential hegemonic dominance of Germany within Europe is unmistakable, and reflected in the booming West German stock market at the end of 1989. West German economic strength is likely to grow significantly in 1990s, as the country reaps the largest share of the gains from 1992.

The recent political and economic upheavals in Eastern Europe and the Soviet Union may well lead to requests from that quarter to join the GATT and/or the EC. The lack of convertible currencies and markets, and the low per capita incomes, will make it difficult to accept these countries into the GATT, and yet their omission has been one of its major holes. It is perhaps more likely that the East Europeans will turn first to the EC and seek preferential access. The Community, in the middle of 1992 reforms, is likely to agree to short-term limited access and to negotiations for a long-term permanent relationship.

Unilateral State Initiatives: U.S. Punitive Reciprocity

William Niskanen recently labelled the United States as the "new bully of international trade" (1989). While the increasing protectionism of the U.S. government may simply be a return to its pre-1935 hostility to free trade (see Gilpin 1987), it is clear that successive trade bills since the 1984 Trade and Tariff Act have become more and more protectionist. Over the 1980-87 period, the U.S. government initiated 411 antidumping, 283 countervailing and 60 safeguard investigations, according to Kelly et al. (1988: 11). The United States has unilaterally moved away from its postwar position of supporting multilateral trade access under generally agreed upon rules to a new (or renewed) position of permanent bilateral negotiation over market access.

This shift is most clearly spelled out in the 1988 Omnibus Trade and Competitiveness Act. As Ludlow notes, "If the act does not guarantee illiberal behaviour, it will certainly facilitate it." (1989: 157) Section 301 or "Super 301" of the Act requires the U.S. Trade Representative (USTR) to identify which countries and practices most limit U.S. exports and to demand negotiations with those countries to open their markets. If negotiations fail, the USTR can impose punitive tariffs on imports from the offending country.

The 1988 Act also authorizes private litigation that was impossible under the old U.S. trading rules. Super 301 allows any U.S. firm to claim as an unfair trade practice any foreign country's policies that do not correspond to U.S. trade, labour relations and antitrust legislation. Under the GATT unfair trade is defined as a trade practice inconsistent with the rules to which each affected party has agreed. Super 301, however, ignores international rules in its definition of unfair trade. Even if the United States already engages in the same offending practice, this fact can be ignored by the USTR if the practice is perceived as harming U.S. interests. American economic clout can be used to harass foreign governments with the threat of heavy tariffs on their exports unless they open their markets to U.S. exports. Because any firm, large or small, that wants to bring an action can do so, and claim it is justified under section 301, there is enormous potential for harassment of foreign firms. The president or the USTR can reject the suits, but any firm still has the right to bring one forward. It may well be that, as Feldstein (1989) has argued, that private 301 cases will be the dominant protectionist force in the 1990s.

In May 1989, the USTR, Carla Hills, cited Japan, Brazil and India under Super 301 as three countries which have erected significant barriers to U.S. exports (Niskanen 1989). While the average level of tariffs in Japan is about 2 percent, it is 37 percent in Brazil and 138 percent in India. The USTR claimed Japan discriminated against foreign-manufactured space satellites, supercomputers and lumber (through its building and fire codes). All three practices have their U.S. counterparts, and under the GATT would not be considered unfair trade. Although both parties are discussing these issues at the so-called "structural impediments initiatives" talks, no resolution had been achieved by the end of 1989.[7]

Milner and Yoffie (1989) argue that the U.S. shift to forcing foreign governments to open their markets to U.S. goods, and to retaliating by closing the U.S. door in the event that negotiations prove unsatisfactory, is a new form of strategic trade policy. The use of U.S. rules and definitions to mount a unilateral threat on perceived unfair trade practices abroad is also a perverse form of reciprocity. Reciprocity normally refers to the mutual lowering of trade barriers and increased market access that occurs during multilateral, regional or bilateral trade negotiations. The new U.S. tack is "punitive reciprocity" which threatens to raise U.S. barriers if other countries do not lower their barriers (as defined by the USTR, despite the fact that often similar barriers exist in the United States).

States and Markets: Implications for Canada

The ongoing changes in states and markets outlined in the sections above are both an opportunity and a worry for Canada, a small economy, highly dependent on access to the U.S. markets for Canadian raw material and automotive exports. Its fiscal budget and current account deficits are proportionately larger than those of the U.S., and inflation and unemployment rates are higher. The need to "get our house in order" is clear. Further expenditure cuts in the February 1990 budget are widely anticipated. Coupled with implementation of the Goods and Services Tax in 1991, these cuts should lessen the FB deficit. Continuing high interest rates, however, suggest that the current account deficit will persist in the near future.

The shift of economic power away from the United States, and the subsequent use by that country of neoprotectionism to shift the adjustment costs to outsiders, were major reasons for the Canadian government's push for the free trade agreement (to get in "before the doors closed"). As a result of spending our policy energies tying our economy to the United States, we have done little to encourage links with the emerging power centres of Western Europe and the Pacific Rim. Our firms have been slower to adapt to, and diffuse, the new product and process technologies. The impact of globalization on the Canadian market and firms has perhaps been stronger than in the United States, due to the more open nature of our economy. Some greenfield foreign investments have occurred due to the free trade agreement, but most Canadians have focused on the rash of mergers, plant closures and layoffs.

The international policy shift to comparative advantage engineered by nation states jockeying for competitiveness is also a worrisome trend for a small country like Canada. In an era of fiscal restraint there will be few tax dollars to spend on engineering our own comparative advantage. UNCTAD (1989) argues that the successful countries in the 1980s, in terms of international competitiveness, were those countries which moved into sectors of high demand, especially those with high R&D content, and/or applied advanced technological processes to generate increased exports in less dynamic sectors. Given Canada's poor rating in terms of outward orientation and innovative forward orientation policies (see Table 9-4), it is critically important that Canadian policymakers devise a long-run strategy that addresses these deficiencies.

Given our small number of domestic high-tech firms, one way to do this could be to encourage technological diffusion to the more numerous medium-tech and low-tech firms. Technological spillovers from foreign investments in Canada could also be a significant factor. Human resource development, particularly in the scientific and technical areas, should also be a priority, given Canada's poor standing in worldwide mathematics competitions and the high dropout rate from our schools. This is not a call for an activist industrial strategy, but rather a reflection of the need to assess and remedy areas of long-run weakness in Canada's human and technological resources.

Conclusions

The end of the 1980s has been a time of rapid technological, economic, political, strategic and institutional change. Uncertainty offers both opportunities and potential pitfalls for the global economy. As the Soviet Union and Eastern Europe move towards a new rapprochement with the West, and the United States and Japan sort out their relative positions in a world of diffused power, new strategies will be needed.

The tension between state and market is the crucial dynamic of which policymakers must take account. Our analysis of key market forces and state policy initiatives leads us to conclude that state and market have become more intertwined in the late 1980s. How countries handle the tension between political sovereignty and global interdependence will determine their relative national positions in the international competitiveness sweepstakes. Canada will need to step carefully to ensure it does not get left behind as we move two steps forward, one step backward into the 1990s.

Notes

1. I thank Judith van Walsum for her research assistance. Helpful comments were provided by David Malone at External Affairs, Christopher Maule and the editors. The responsibility for all views and any remaining errors is mine.
2. The implicit assumption is that the expected rate can be proxied by the actual inflation rate.
3. For a short summary of the debt crisis see IMF (1989, 49-57 and 61-7). An excellent compendium of papers on the debt crisis can be found in Sachs (1989).
4. For opposing views on offshore processing, see UNCTAD 1989, Grunwald and Flamm 1985, and Markides and Berg 1988.
5. I am indebted to Christopher Maule for this analogy.
6. See Curtis and McMillan in this volume. The free trade agreement includes a schedule for bilateral removal of tariffs, new rules of origin, freer cross-border movement for services, investment flows and professionals, binational dispute settlement, and new institutions (a trade commission, secretariat and ad hoc working groups on subsidies, antidumping and others). See *Canada Export* (1988: 1,6) for a brief outline.
7. Interestingly, the USTR argued that the EC also had unfair trade barriers. However, the United States did not launch an aggressive attack on the Europeans, perhaps because the EC refused to negotiate in response to a Super 301 charge whereas the Japanese were willing to discuss the issue.

References

Applegate, Lynda, James Cash and D. Quinn Mills. 1988. "Information Technology and Tomorrow's Manager." *Harvard Business Review* (Nov.-Dec.):128-36.

Bartlett, Christopher and Sumantra Ghoshal. 1987a. "Managing Across Borders: New Strategic Requirements." *Sloan Management Review* 28 (Summer): 7-17.

Bartlett, Christopher and Sumantra Ghoshal. 1987b. "Managing Across Borders: New Organizational Responses." *Sloan Management Review* 29 (Fall): 43-53.

Business Review. 1989. No. 89/3 (July-Aug.-Sept.) Toronto: Bank of Montreal.

Canada Export. 1989 (May 15). Ottawa: External Affairs Canada.

Economist. 1989. New York: The Economist Newspaper, NA, Inc.: Nov. 4-10.

Eden, Lorraine. 1989. "Choices for the Global Economy." In *Canada Among Nations, 1988: The Tory Record,* edited by Brian W. Tomlin and Maureen Appel Molot. Toronto: James Lorimer and Co.: 83-106.

Feldstein, Martin. 1989. "US Protectionism on the Rise." *European Affairs* 3 (Autumn):108-13.

Financial Post, 1989. *Report on the Nation: The 1990s: Gloom or Glory?* (Winter).

Fleck, James and Joseph D'Cruz. 1987. "The Globalization of Manufacturing." *Business Quarterly* (Winter): 42-51.

General Agreement on Tariffs and Trade. 1989. *Focus: GATT Newsletter* 65 (October): 1, 4.

Giersch, Herbert. 1989. "EC 1992: Competition is the Clue." *European Affairs* 3 (Autumn): 10-17.

Gilpin, Robert. 1987. *The Political Economy of International Relations.* Princeton, N.J.: Princeton University Press.

Grunwald, Joseph and Kenneth Flamm. 1985. *The Global Factory: Foreign Assembly in International Trade.* Washington, D.C.: The Brookings Institution.

Hampson, Fen. 1989. "A Post-Modernist World: The Changing International Politico-Security System." In *Canada Among Nations, 1988: The Tory Record*, edited by Brian W. Tomlin and Maureen Appel Molot. Toronto: James Lorimer and Co.: 41-59.

Hax, Arnoldo C. 1989. "Building the Firm of the Future." *Sloan Management Review 30* (Spring): 75-82.

Hoffmann, Stanley. 1989a. "The European Community and 1992." *Foreign Affairs* 68, no.4 (Fall): 27-47.

Hoffman, Stanley. 1989b. "What Should We Do in the World?" *The Atlantic Monthly* (Oct.): 84-96.

International Monetary Fund. 1989. *World Economic Outlook* April 1989. Washington, D.C.: IMF.

Japan. 1988. *Diplomatic Bluebook: 1988 Japan's Diplomatic Activities.* Tokyo: Ministry of Foreign Affairs.

Kelly, Margaret et al. 1988. *Issues and Developments in International Trade Policy.* Washington, D.C.: IMF.

Kirkland, Richard I. Jr. 1989. "Entering a New Age of Boundless Competition." *Fortune* (March 14): 40-47.

Lees, Martin. 1989. "The Impact of Europe 1992 on the Atlantic Partnership." *The Washington Quarterly* 12, no.4 (Autumn): 171-82.

Levitt, Theodore. 1983. "The Globalization of Markets." *Harvard Business Review* (May/June): 92-102.

Ludlow, Peter. 1989. "The Future of the International Trading System." *The Washington Quarterly* 12, no.4 (Autumn): 157-69.

Markides, Constantinos and Norman Berg. 1988. "Manufacturing Offshore Is Bad Business." *Harvard Business Review* (Sept./Oct.): 113-20.

McMillan, Charles J. 1989. *Investing in Tomorrow: Japan's Science and Technology Organization and Strategies.* Ottawa: Canada-Japan Trade Council.

Milner, Helen and David Yoffie. 1989. "Between Free Trade and Protectionism: Strategic Trade Policy and a Theory of Corporate Trade Demands". *International Organization* 43, no.2 (Spring): 239-72.

Morris, Charles R. 1989. "The Coming Global Boom." *The Atlantic Monthly* (Oct.): 51-64.

Niskanen, William A. 1989. "The Bully of World Trade." *Orbis* 33, no.4 (Fall): 531-38.

Ohmae, Kenichi. 1985. *Triad Power: The Coming Shape of Global Competition.* New York: The Free Press, Macmillan.

Ohmae, Kenichi. 1989. "Managing in a Borderless World." *Harvard Business Review* (May-June): 152-61.

Okita, Saburo. 1989. "Japan's Quiet Strength." *Foreign Policy* 75 (Summer): 128-45.

Preeg, Ernest H. 1989. "The GATT Trading System in Transition: An Analytic Survey of Recent Literature." *The Washington Quarterly* 12, no.4 (Autumn): 201-13.

Sachs, Jeffrey, ed. 1989. *Developing Country Debt and the World Economy.* National Bureau of Economic Research. Chicago: University of Chicago Press.

Schmieding, Holger. 1989. "A Concept for a Pan-European Economic Integration." *European Affairs* 3 (Autumn): 33-8.

Stern, Paula. 1989. "U.S.-Soviet Trade: The Question of Leverage." *The Washington Quarterly* 12, no.4 (Autumn): 183-97.

Thornton, Thomas Perry. 1989. "The Regional Influentials: Perception and Reality." *SAIS Review* 9, no.2 (Summer-Fall): 247- 60.

Tonelson, Alan. 1989. "America in a Multipolar World—Whatever That Is." *SAIS Review* 9, no.2 (Summer-Fall): 45-59.

United Nations. 1988. *Transnational Corporations in World Development.* New York: United Nations.

UNCTAD. 1989. "The Impact of Technological Change on World Trade Patterns." *UNCTAD Bulletin* 252 (May): 3-6.

"World Competitiveness Report 1989." 1989 *European Affairs* 3 (Autumn): 114-26.

Van Tulder, Rob and Gerd Junne. 1989. *European Multinationals in Core Technologies.* New York and Toronto: John Wiley and Sons.

10 The Trade Policy Response: Negotiating with the United States and the World

John M. Curtis

Faced with a rapidly changing and uncertain international economy, as well as with the worst domestic economic performance since the Great Depression, in the early 1980s Canada set out to actively explore and to implement new structural economic policies. These policies, which were to include deregulation, privatization, and tax reform, also involved new policy initiatives in the area of trade. The process of economic policy change took many forms: political debate, often highly-charged, academic and related research, industry and trade association advocacy, internal governmental studies and ultimately a Royal Commission in whose proceedings trade policy came to occupy a central place.

The outcome of all the study, debate and discussion resulted in two major complementary trade policy initiatives: the negotiation and implementation of a comprehensive bilateral free trade agreement (FTA) with Canada's major trade partner, the United States, and active participation in the largest multilateral trade negotiations (MTN) ever undertaken, the Uruguay Round, a major world-wide effort to set the rules of the road for global trade, including trade between the various regional economic groupings, into the 1990s and beyond. While the political economy underlying these two major trade policy initiatives might be viewed by some as different, the economic, legal and institutional underpinnings of the two trade agreements are largely the same. They form part of a single policy framework, the ongoing deregulation of the Canadian economy within a framework of mutually agreed international laws and institutions which themselves reflect the steady liberalization of the world economy. They were also key elements of the Canadian government's broader program of structural economic reform, intended to improve the market orientation and the competitiveness of the Canadian economy (Department of Finance 1984).

The Policy Link

The fundamental economic policy premise underlying the trade and economic policy framework, and therefore both sets of trade negotiations was that the competitiveness of Canada's economy and its long-term economic development would be advanced through trade liberalization. The FTA was designed to create the basis for industries and related economic activities located in Canada to become fully competitive on a North American basis by taking advantage of economies of scale and scope; the MTN was to provide these industries with the opportunity to be more competitive against American and offshore imports in the Canadian market, and to compete more effectively in foreign markets.

Another important objective of Canada's two-track trade liberalizing policy of the 1980s was to fight protectionist forces in foreign markets. Such protectionist pressures and the resulting uncertainties, coming from both inside and outside the United States, made the status quo an unrealistic and a non-viable option for a relatively small, trade-dependent economy such as Canada. New trade rules and acceptable rules of behaviour were required which would better protect Canada from unilateralism, and from exclusive bilateral or plurilateral trade arrangements set up by other countries.

Although seven post-war rounds of trade negotiations under the General Agreement on Tariffs and Trade (GATT), conducted prior to the 1980s, had succeeded in reducing foreign barriers to Canadian goods and services significantly, many such barriers still remained. Access to some markets was not always secure because of a lack of tariff bindings or because of the actual or threatened use of trade laws, largely American, to impede Canadian exports. Further, for historic reasons, entire sectors of interest to Canada, such as agriculture, operated almost entirely outside existing GATT rules.[1] There were other areas of increasing interest to Canada, including high technology and services, which were not covered by existing GATT rules; these, together with the long-standing unresolved issues of agriculture and textiles, became important negotiating issues in the Uruguay Round.

The three major elements which underlay a renewed emphasis by Canada on trade liberalizing negotiations during the middle and late 1980s were reflected in Canada's objectives for both sets of negotiations: to expand access abroad for Canadian agriculture, for resource-based products, and for a range of manufacturing and high technology products and services. In addition, an important Canadian objective was to update, improve and expand trade rules in a number of areas involving non-tariff measures, particularly government procurement, technical barriers, import safeguards, subsidies and countervail, and dispute settlement procedures. This was also a major motivation in developing new, mutually acceptable standards for the conduct and expansion of international trade in services, trade-related intellectual property (TRIPs) and investment matters (Department of External Affairs 1987). Many of these objectives were to a greater or lesser extent achieved in the FTA and found expression in many of the FTA provisions that are drawn directly out of the GATT, or provide for a bilateral interpretation of GATT provisions, or build on such provisions by going further. The legal links between the FTA and the MTN are elucidated in the section immediately below. Those portions of the objectives that were not fully achieved in the FTA form part of the ongoing negotiations now underway under the FTA implementation process, and often are issues for negotiation in the Uruguay Round. This interwoven and unfinished agenda is elaborated below.

The Legal Connection

At the most general level, the FTA and the GATT are directly related, in that the FTA technically constitutes an international agreement within the terms of Article XXIV of the GATT. There are, in addition, a number of specific provisions within Chapters 3 to 13 of the Free Trade Agreement that concentrate on goods.

FTA Articles 407 and 409 (as well as 902 and 904 concerning energy products) reaffirm, clarify and interpret existing GATT rights and obligations with respect to import and export restrictions and prohibitions as these apply to Canada-U.S. bilateral trade.

FTA Article 602 re-affirms the rights and obligations of the FTA participants under the GATT Agreement on Technical Barriers to Trade reached during the Tokyo Round, particularly those provisions stating that technical regulations and standards, including packaging and labelling requirements and methods for certifying conformity, should not create unnecessary barriers to trade. FTA Article 710 re-affirms existing rights and obligations under GATT Article XI which deals with supply management measures for agricultural products. Chapter 8 of the FTA extends national treatment to U.S. wines and spirits by provincial liquor boards, with respect to listing, pricing, and distribution practices. These privileges have also had to be accorded to European and to other foreign products—with some variations—as a result of an almost concurrent GATT Panel report in 1988.

FTA Articles 1301 through 1305 modestly broaden and deepen the obligations that both countries have assumed in the GATT Agreement on Government Procurement, reached during the Tokyo Round, by lowering to US$ 25,000 the threshold for the amount of procurement open to competition between Canadian and U.S. suppliers in each other's market and by improving transparency procedures relating to the bidding process.

The FTA provisions with respect to emergency safeguard actions are built on both a bilateral track (Article 1101) and a global track (Article 1103). The global track exempts each of the two signatory countries from global actions under GATT Article XIX, except where the producers in one country contribute significantly to the injury caused to the other by a surge of imports from all countries; in such a case the exports of that country will be protected against reductions below the trend line of previous bilateral trade, subject to an allowance for growth.

Article 2001 incorporates the exception clauses of GATT Article XX, while Articles 2002 and 2003 cover GATT balance of payments and national security situations.

In the important area of government subsidies and countervailing duties the FTA established an innovative mandatory binational dispute settlement process to handle anti-dumping and countervailing duty cases after the final determinations are available, but existing GATT rules and the national body of unfair trade remedy laws will continue to apply to bilateral trade between Canada and the United States until a new system is successfully negotiated to replace existing regimes (See Department of External Affairs 1988 [Article 1906]). Indeed, one protection against unjustified recourse to countervail built into the FTA-Article 1902.2 d) i) is that amendments to national countervailing duty laws need to be consistent with the GATT.

The Common Unfinished Agenda

The FTA and the MTN, are not only linked in a number of areas of economic policy and law; there are also a number of major issues which appear on both the current Uruguay Round agenda and on the agenda of negotiations called for under the Free Trade Agreement itself. Some of these issues, such as procurement, TRIPs and subsidies and countervail have explicitly been put on the MTN agenda by the two countries because they could not be resolved during the FTA negotiations. In this regard, the FTA negotiations provided the opportunity for much useful homework in understanding the issues and developing practical approaches to negotiating them in a trade context. In these areas and in others, a successful MTN outcome will impact upon the trade and investment environment within North America, because of the way the FTA and other international trade arrangements affect competitive conditions.

A central driving force behind both global and regional trade agreements has always been the need to further improve conditions of access to principal export markets. Although the reduction of traditional tariff barriers is relatively less critical today, because tariff barriers generally are lower than they were in the immediate post-war era, and because non-tariff barriers and trade remedy measures can affect the certainty or predictability of market access conditions, the tariff has continued to play a major role in trade negotiations both bilaterally and multilaterally. In many ways, the tariff remains the underlying issue of any trade negotiation.

Canada has been pressing the European Community, for example, to extend to Canadian exporters of resource-based products, such as fishery and forest products and non-ferrous metals, competitive opportunities which would approximate more closely those enjoyed by Scandinavian suppliers who now benefit from preferential status with the Community. In turn, foreign suppliers are interested in seeking reductions, within the Uruguay Round, in Canadian and American most-favoured-nation tariffs, so as to restore competitive conditions that are closer to those facing domestic suppliers within North America. As a result of the FTA, Canada is in this bargaining position for the first time since its success in bargaining away Commonwealth preferential margins in the early post-war period. Market access therefore remains a high priority for Canada in the MTN, in which forum it has been pressing for the largest possible result in terms of liberalization.

Another important crosswalk between the FTA and the MTN, closely related to market access, is in the area of government procurement of goods and services. The objectives set out in the FTA in this respect were put in the context of a "further step toward multilateral liberalization and improvement of the GATT Agreement on Government

Procurement" (Article 1301.2). Further bilateral negotiations will take place after the conclusion of the Uruguay Round (Article 1307).

On this subject, Article 1301 stipulates that:

> In the interest of expanding mutually beneficial trade opportunities in government procurement based on the principles of non-discrimination and fair and open competition for the supply of goods and services, the Parties shall actively strive to achieve as quickly as possible the multilateral liberalization of international procurement policies to provide balanced and equitable opportunities.

This crosswalk, or linkage, between bilateral and multilateral government procurement negotiations is likely to be intensified; it is recognized there is a need to enlarge and deepen the scope and coverage of the GATT Procurement Code as the most effective way to ensure that Europe 1992 does not result in the imposition of procurement practices discriminating against foreign-based suppliers of goods and services.

A multilateral negotiating framework for addressing subsidies and countervail issues, as well as dispute settlement procedures, in a balanced, comprehensive and integrated manner was agreed to at the Ministerial Mid-Term Review of the MTN in Montreal in December 1988 (GATT 1989). This negotiation will likely proceed in parallel with the FTA's bilateral 5 to 7 year track as set out in that agreement. The multilateral track will include the matter of appropriate disciplines on export and other trade-distorting subsidies, including those which apply to agricultural products. Other major elements will cover the conditions and criteria under which foreign government subsidies could be legitimately actionable as unfair trade practices, whether on the domestic market (countervail), in the export market (import substitution) or in third country markets (export displacement). These complex and difficult questions—how actionable subsidies should be defined, how the injury criteria should be applied, and how investigation procedures should be handled—may eventually be brought into the FTA framework. In addition, the MTN framework for addressing subsidies and countervail issues will as far as possible be used to strengthen multilateral dispute settlement procedures, thus reducing the scope for unilateralism in interpreting, enforcing or redefining international rights and obligations.

Agricultural protectionism and trade-distorting subsidies around the world clearly constitute one of the most difficult and formidable

challenges currently facing international trade policy and trade relations. Agricultural trade is plagued both with extensive exceptions to
existing trade rules and with a devastating international subsidy
competition between major agricultural producers and exporters. In
the FTA, Canada and the United States agreed to consult more closely
with each other and to take account of each other's export interests
with a view to preventing prejudicial effects due to export subsidies
on sales to third markets. However, the FTA recognizes that the
problems of agricultural subsidies are global in scope and therefore
require global solutions under the GATT. Article 701 states that the
"primary goal" of FTA participants with respect to agricultural
subsidies is to deal with these issues in the MTN.

Substantial international agricultural trade reform may be achieved
for the first time in the post-war era as part of the overall outcome
of the MTN. Such a result would be based on the MTN negotiating
framework agreed to in April 1989 with respect to agriculture (GATT
1989). This framework provides for a substantial and progressive
reduction of market access barriers and of trade distorting subsidies.
It also provides for the development of new trade rules which should
be equally applicable to all GATT members. This could mean that
the U.S. GATT waiver, which was only slightly modified by the FTA,
may finally be removed at the end of the Uruguay Round. Canada
has worked actively within the Cairns Group of smaller agricultural
exporting countries, and also on its own, to ensure that agriculture is
brought fully within the GATT in the course of the current negotiations.

With respect to TRIPs, Article 2004 of the FTA embodies a
commitment to seek the development of multilateral solutions in the
Uruguay Round in light of the fact that an agreement on this subject
was not possible in the course of negotiating the FTA. The strategic
importance of state-of-the-art technologies as factors in competitive
strength, the increasing share of advanced technology embodied in
goods and services crossing national borders, as well as concerns over
extensive counterfeiting practices, all necessitate—notably for the U.S.,
Japan and the European Community—an effective set of international
rules covering adequate standards, effective, non-discriminatory enforcement, and multilateral dispute settlement within the GATT.

Any new GATT agreement on intellectual property matters will bear
directly on the problems related to the use of Section 337 of U.S. trade
law as a means of dealing with cases of alleged infringement of patents
in that country.[2] It will also necessarily affect those unilateralist features

of section 301 of existing U.S. trade legislation which substitute at times for the multilateral dispute resolution mechanism. Neither of these elements proved to be negotiable in the course of the FTA. Since then, however, the United States has accepted a GATT Panel report which found section 337 to be in violation of the GATT national treatment principle and committed itself to implement the finding in the context of the overall result of the Uruguay Round.

The FTA negotiations provided lessons in the determination of adequate intellectual property standards and the definition of reasonable provisions for their application and use, including compulsory licensing conditions and access to technology more generally; this experience will also be valuable in the TRIPs negotiations in the Uruguay Round. It also shows that GATT involvement in TRIPs need not be seen as a threat to the World Intellectual Property Organization (WIPO) and to other international institutions dealing with intellectual property matters.

In the areas of investment and services, including financial services and business travel, the FTA went well beyond the GATT. Agreement in these areas filled a major gap in Canada-U.S. bilateral economic relations and broke new ground with respect to international agreements in these areas. Before the implementation of the FTA, services were subject to limited international rules and procedures such as air agreements. In the case of Canada-U.S. trade, the movement of services across the borders was not even covered by a treaty of friendship, commerce and navigation, which is common practice among most industrial countries.[3]

The FTA, together with provisions relating to services that will be handled within the framework of the single European market (Europe 1992) and that are included in the 1988 expansion of the Closer Economic Relations Agreement between Australia and New Zealand, have provided impetus and direction to the drive for a possible multilateral services agreement, either under the GATT or drawing on its principles in a separate, but parallel, organization. As a practical matter, the need to head off threats of narrow reciprocity requirements in the context of Europe 1992 will be a highly important influence on the shape of an MTN deal on trade in services.

The FTA experience shows that services can be effectively brought within the scope of a comprehensive trade agreement. A precedent has been set by the inclusion of this category in an agreement such as the FTA, which is intended to open markets. Nevertheless, its significance must not be over-stated; the application of the basic rules and principles of the agreement is prospective, and it relates to a specific list of services, rather than the global category. More importantly, the significance of the services elements of the FTA comes from the useful conceptual and legal drafting and the homework done on key concepts such as the application of national treatment to trade in services, and from the inclusion of services within the general dispute settlement procedures. The example set for dealing with rights of establishment and commercial presence granted to service suppliers and with temporary entry for service providers similarly provides a good beginning for possible multilateral agreement.

The FTA's experience in dealing with some particularly difficult sectoral issues in the services area could prove to be salutary for the MTN process. For example, the distinction introduced between access to basic telecommunications networks and access to enhanced services is proving useful for the MTN. (On the other hand, the experience with respect to shipping services may not augur well for the Uruguay Round.) Although it is not yet possible to say what an MTN deal on services might realistically cover, it is interesting to note that the Montreal negotiating framework envisaged a comprehensive body of rules to govern multilateral international trade in services with no sector initially excluded from its potential coverage. It also incorporated possible rollbacks of specific impediments to services trade. The basic two-part structure of the FTA in services—framework and sectors might thus prove to be a "model" for an agreement on services forming part of the final outcome of the Uruguay Round.

While the FTA rules with respect to Investment (Chapter 16) have been widely perceived as setting a useful precedent for the Uruguay Round, it should be noted that the MTN deals only with trade-related investment measures (TRIMs) as opposed to investment policies themselves. The FTA/MTN link is therefore of most direct significance with respect to Article 1603 of the FTA, which prohibits the imposition of investment-related performance requirements (such as local content, import substitution, domestic sources or export targeting on investors), including those of a third country where such a requirement would have a significant impact on bilateral trade. Article 1610 of the FTA commits both Canada and the U.S. to endeavour in the Uruguay Round to improve multilateral arrangements and agreements related to investment.

Efforts to improve and to streamline the GATT dispute settlement system were made both as part of the FTA (Chapters 18 and 19) and within the MTN. They were brought, in part, to a successful conclusion at the Montreal Ministerial Meeting. More automatic establishment of GATT panels, voluntary arbitration procedures, and tighter time frames for the completion of panel proceedings (normally 6 months but no longer than 15 months from the beginning of bilateral consultations to the adoption of panel reports) were all agreed to. The improvements introduced in the general dispute settlement process, both bilaterally and multilaterally, are therefore going in the same direction. The next and final steps in the Uruguay Round will have to address the difficult issues of adoption and implementation of panel reports, including those connected with unilateral practices under Section 301 of the U.S. Omnibus Trade and Competitiveness Act.

The Canadian trade negotiations agenda developed and implemented during the 1980s reflected the underlying and shifting economic, technological, trade and investment developments that shaped the past decade and are already influencing the new one. Successive Canadian governments, as well as many analysts and commentators, appear to have recognized that the early post-war world trading system no longer exists, as a result of developments occurring on this continent, in Europe, in the Asia-Pacific region, and in other parts of the world. To ensure that the forces working for a more open and predictable trading environment will succeed in warding off the threat of protectionism—thereby reinforcing a domestic economic program of privatization, deregulation and tax reform—a stronger, revitalized and extended GATT is required, the FTA must be implemented effectively, and events must unfold in the Asia-Pacific region in an onward-looking, non-discriminatory fashion. These elements will play a major role in shaping Canadian trade policy in the 1990s.

A successful MTN, building on the FTA and other regional and sectoral trade arrangements, will ensure that trade initiatives around the world, over the next decade and beyond, are mutually supportive in fostering open and more secure markets and sustainable growth world-wide.

Notes

1 The United States, for example, asked for and received a waiver or exemption from GATT rules and obligations for its agricultural sector (Section 22) in 1955.
2 Section 337 of the U.S. Tariff Act of 1930, as amended, is commonly used in intellectual property cases, particularly to enforce patent rights in the United States. The provisions give the American intellectual property owner a major advantage against any foreign competitors.
3 These Treaties of Friendship, Commerce and Navigation (or variants thereof) were entered into by the United States between 1946 and 1966. Among the countries with which such treaties were negotiated and remain in force are the Federal Republic of Germany, Israel, Italy, Japan, The Netherlands, Belgium, and France, all of which were and are significant investors in the United States as well as hosts to substantial amounts of investment by United States investors. Since 1981, these treaties have been replaced by Bilateral Investment Treaties (BITs).

References

Canada. 1984. Department of Finance. *Economic and Fiscal Statement.* Ottawa: November 8.

———. 1987. Department of External Affairs. *The World Our Market: Canada, GATT and the Uruguay Round.* Ottawa: Supply and Services.

———. 1988. Department of External Affairs. *The Canada-U.S. Free Trade Agreement.* Ottawa: External Affairs Canada.

General Agreement on Tariffs and Trade (GATT). 1989. *Multilateral Trade Negotiations: The Uruguay Round Mid-Term Meeting.* Geneva: The General Agreement on Tariffs and Trade, Trade Negotiations Committee. April 21.

11 Pollution Across Borders: Canada's International Environmental Agenda[1]

Fen Osler Hampson

The summer of 1988 marked a turning point in public consciousness of the looming dangers of environmental catastrophe from human pollution of the biosphere. The fear that man's own actions somehow lay behind the hottest recorded summer of this century—a summer that brought searing droughts to the American and Canadian midwest and violent cyclonic storms in Asia, the Pacific, and the Caribbean—galvanized public demands for national and international action to address the problems of global warming, ozone depletion, and toxic pollution. In January 1989 a major oil spill from a barge off the Washington coast, which drifted onto Vancouver Island, polluting hundreds of beaches and killing wildlife, further dramatized the threat for Canadians; it was followed a few months later by another catastrophic oil spill in Alaska. Canadians themselves began to see the destruction of the environment as the number-one challenge to their own security and survival. This growing national sentiment was summed up by John Fraser, Speaker of the House of Commons: "For the first time in human history we are looking down the coming decades with the certain reality that if we do not change our ways we are not going to survive." But, while politicians struggled to outdo each other with their rhetoric, a year later the federal government had still not delivered its much-promised national policy on the environment. In spite of a lot of tough talk about the need to make hard choices that "will have heavy consequences on the behaviour of Canadians," Environment Minister Lucien Bouchard was at the same time warning Canadians to accept the competitive facts of life: "A country acting alone would have to be very cautious. No country would want to risk disrupting its economy and its chances of doing well in foreign markets" (Quoted in *Vancouver Sun* 1989: A19).

Of course, Canada was not alone in avoiding tough choices between economic growth and action to clean up the environment—action which might prove politically unpalatable and therefore difficult to implement. To the south, George Bush, who had been elected as "the environment president," was also shirking the issue. At the year's end he had still not delivered on his election promise to hold a White House conference on the environment and his much-ballyhooed "Clean Air Bill" was still awaiting Congressional approval.

At the same time, the situation was not altogether bleak. Although the pace of change might be too glacial for some, there were several important international initiatives in 1989 which began to set gears in motion to cope with the complex problems of global warming, ozone depletion, and toxic pollution. Canada was an active player in international efforts to grapple with these issues, and while it had yet to define a national policy for itself on the environment, the key elements of its international strategy were beginning to emerge. These reflected a strong commitment to international initiatives and agreements on the environment, in particular through the machinery of the United Nations (UN); but they also included the pursuit of independent bilateral and regional cooperative approaches to the environment in areas affecting vital Canadian interests, such as the Arctic.

Some Alarming Facts and Figures

The range of environmental concerns affecting Canadians is vast. Human activity is affecting our planet's future in a host of ways and we are only just beginning to understand the complex interdependence between human development and the environment. Substantial changes are occurring in the environment as a direct consequence of human activity. We are also learning that no nation is immune to these changes because most forms of pollution do not respect national boundaries. Many problems will therefore have to be addressed multilaterally or bilaterally through jointly undertaken cooperative measures. The environmentally sensitive nature of Canada's own natural resource base makes these problems of paramount concern to Canadians.

Ozone depletion and the "greenhouse effect"

There is widespread consensus within the scientific community that the burning of fossil fuels, the destruction of tropical forests (particularly in tropical regions like the Amazon basin), and the addition of man-made chemicals to the atmosphere are threatening the earth's ozone layer and leading to a dangerous build-up of carbon dioxide and other greenhouse gases such as nitrous oxide, methane, and surface ozone. The destruction of the ozone shield in the upper reaches of the atmosphere, resulting from the release of man-made chlorofluorocarbons (CFCs) and halons, will increase the amount of ultraviolet radiation that reaches the earth's surface. This radiation can cause skin cancer, reduce crop yields, and damage aquatic life. Each one percent decline in the ozone layer may mean a four to six percent increase in certain skin cancers. Ozone layer depletion has also been linked to eye diseases and suppression of the immune system.

The build-up of carbon dioxide and other greenhouse gases that keep heat from escaping into outer space will lead to a rapid and unprecedented rise in global mean temperatures. Worldwide temperatures are expected to rise between 1.5 and 4.5 degrees Celsius in the next fifty years or so. The rise in temperatures would be greater in higher latitudes than in the tropics, perhaps by a factor of two or three. Warming would affect global precipitation and weather circulation patterns and would be accompanied by rising sea levels of up to a metre or more (Flavin 1989; Graedel and Crutzen 1989; Schneider 1989; Mintzer 1987).

In Canada these climatic changes would lead to a longer growing season, the northward expansion of agriculture, lower home-heating costs, and ice-free navigation for ships. At the same time, water resources necessary for farming, hydro-electric generation, and industrial and household use would be reduced because of increased evaporation and reduced summer rainfall. Droughts would occur with increased frequency in the Prairies and lower water levels in the Great Lakes might limit shipping. Rising sea levels would threaten low-lying areas in Prince Edward Island, Hudson Bay, and river deltas in British Columbia and the Yukon. Melting permafrost in the north would threaten the foundations of buildings, roads, and pipelines (Environment Canada 1989a).

Scientists believe that the warming trend can be slowed by cutting carbon dioxide and other greenhouse gas emissions and ongoing forest conservation and reforestation, because trees store carbon dioxide in their tissues and wood fibre and "breathe" oxygen.

Forests

Tropical rain forests are being destroyed at the rate of 110,000 square kilometres a year through burning and clearing for agriculture. In addition to releasing into the atmosphere vast quantities of carbon dioxide stored in trees (which contributes to the greenhouse effect), the destruction of these forests is driving thousands of the earth's species to extinction each year. Scientists are in widespread agreement that more than half of the global total of 30 million species live in tropical rainforests which occupy only 6 percent of the land surface (Wilson 1989: 108). This biological stock represents a largely untapped source of material wealth in the form of food, medicine, and other commercial substances. But it is being destroyed at an alarming rate because of human-induced extinctions.

Temperate forests cover about 45 percent of the land in Canada. High-quality trees are being lost in large-scale logging operations which cut and strip-mine whole forests. The annual forest harvest has increased by 50 percent since the 1950s and most experts are in agreement that forests are being overharvested. Only one-fifth of the area harvested between 1975 and 1980 was seeded or replanted. The forest industry and related manufacturing constitute the largest single industry in Canada, accounting for 1 in 10 Canadian jobs.

Acid rain

Acid rain in the form of rainfall, snow, fog, or dust, contaminated with sulphur dioxide and nitrogen oxides, kills fish, slows the growth of trees, and weakens their resistance to disease and drought. It also destroys buildings and contributes to respiratory problems among children. More than 80 percent of the most productive agricultural land in Canada annually receives acid deposition exceeding the acceptable level (20 kilograms per hectare). In over 14,000 Canadian lakes fish have been completely wiped out and another 150,000 lakes are threatened. Acid rain causes over $1 billion in damage to Canada per year.

The major sources of airborne sulphur dioxide and nitrogen oxides are coal-fired electric generating plants in the U.S. midwest and smelters in central and western Canada. Prevailing winds carry acid rain to much of eastern Canada and New England. U.S. emissions account for half the acid rain depositions in Canada, while Canadian emissions account for 10 percent of the acid rain in the northeastern United States.

Toxic chemicals

Dioxins and furans are by-products of the manufacture of other chemicals (notably pesticides), the burning of solid waste and sewage sludge, and some pulp and paper processes. They enter the food chain when they are absorbed by microscopic organisms in contaminated wastes and, once absorbed, build up in animal tissue. The health effects on animals include cancerous tumors and lowered resistance to disease. Dioxins pose a threat to humans as well and are among the 44 substances which will be the first to be subjected to regulatory control under the Canadian Environmental Protection Act.

PCBs (polychlorinated biphenyls, which are synthetic compounds with a range of uses in coolants and insulators in electrical capacitors and transformers) pose another health hazard to humans and may cause cancer. Although the manufacture of PCBs has been banned in North America since 1977, large amounts remain in use and in stored wastes. They pose a major challenge because Canada lacks sufficient hazardous waste disposal facilities. Until recently Canada shipped its PCBs to the United Kingdom for destruction there, until British dock workers made it clear that they would no longer unload Canadian PCBs. Canada is now committed to phasing out the use of PCBs by 1993.

There are now more than 100,000 chemicals in commercial use, some of which are dangerous to health and the environment. More than 3 million tonnes of hazardous wastes are produced in Canada every year—enough to fill the CN tower 50 times over.

Water resources

Canada has nine percent of the world's total volume of renewable fresh water and the longest coastline of any nation in the world. Water issues are central to the health of the Canadian economy and the health of Canadians. Supplies of clean water for household, industrial, and agricultural use are already strained and there may soon be acute shortages due to the greenhouse effect. In 1986 agricultural use of water had risen 300 percent since 1951 and municipal use was up 200 percent in the same period. Increased water consumption may already be a partial consequence of the greenhouse effect.

Up to 60 percent of prairie wetlands in Canada have been drained for agricultural use as well as 70 percent of the wetlands in southern Ontario. This has destroyed key habitats for waterfowl and other animals.

Chemicals from industrial and municipal wastes and pesticides in agriculture are destroying fisheries and threatening human health. About 800 of the 30,000 compounds in use in the Great Lakes basin are known toxins. The Federation of Canadian Municipalities estimates that it will cost at least $7.5 billion to repair or replace outdated sewer and water treatment systems. Accidental spills of toxic and hazardous wastes pose another major threat to freshwater supplies (Environment Canada 1989a). A recent major international study, conducted by a joint project team of the Conservation Foundation in the United States and the Institute for Research on Public Policy in Canada, concluded that the five Great Lakes, and 80,000 lesser lakes in the region, continue to be threatened by airborne and water-borne toxins and organic chemicals. The adverse consequences of toxic pollution are being experienced almost everywhere up and down the animal and plant food chain. Fish-eating birds and animals are suffering major reproductive problems and population declines, some fish species can no longer reproduce naturally, and many are suffering from serious genetic damage. The weakened ecosystem of the Great Lakes region may be less able to cope with weather fluctuations and may threrefore be more vulnerable to the consequences of global warming. The study concluded that it will cost tens of billions of dollars to restore affected regions to acceptable levels of environmental health (Davidson and Hodge 1989).

Recent International Initiatives on the Environment

A comprehensive and meaningful policy response to the problems of global warming, ozone depletion, toxic pollution, and other environmental issues will require coordinated and concerted international, regional, and national action. Atmospheric change, for example, is the consequence of toxic pollution from many countries, including Canada, and no single country can address this problem on its own. Recent initiatives are therefore based on a recognized need for greater levels of international cooperation on both East-West and North-South axes. Canada has been extremely active in advancing international cooperation to devise global solutions to these problems, though it has done little as yet to match its activity on the international front by cleaning up its own front yard.

The elements of an international strategy to address the problems of global warming and climatic change were hammered out at the conference on "The Changing Atmosphere: Implications for Global Security," held in Toronto in 1988 and involving more than 300 policymakers from 46 countries. The conference, which was sponsored by Environment Canada, the World Meteorological Organization (WMO), and the United Nations Environment Programme (UNEP), underscored the growing urgency of addressing the problems of climate change and set out the following elements for a comprehensive global strategy:

- an international framework convention that would encourage other standard-setting agreements and national legislation to provide for the protection of the global atmosphere;
- a comprehensive global energy policy to reduce emissions of carbon dioxide and other trace gases in order to reduce the risks of future global warming (such reductions would be achieved through fulfilment of national commitments to greater energy efficiency, conservation, and modifications in supplies);
- establishment of a world atmosphere fund, financed perhaps through a tax on fossil fuel consumption, to mobilize the resources necessary to achieve energy efficiency improvements;
- establishment of continuing assessments of scientific results and government-to-government discussion of responses and strategies; and
- a worldwide plan to reduce deforestation and increase afforestation by establishing an international trust fund to provide adequate incentives to developing nations to manage their tropical forests and achieve sustainable development (Environment Canada 1988: 5-6).

These are enormously ambitious objectives and achieving them will not be easy because of major economic, social, and political barriers to change. Developed countries are currently responsible for most of the carbon dioxide emissions and will therefore have to make the biggest reductions in fossil fuel energy consumption. However, there are obvious economic and political obstacles to achieving greater energy efficiency, such as lack of finance, information, and low fuel prices. Thorny questions such as the desirability of raising fuel prices, promoting energy conservation and efficiency, and relying more heavily on alternative energy sources (like solar and/or nuclear power) have yet to be confronted in a serious way by the policymakers and the public alike.

Since the poor nations of the world are likely to sustain the heaviest losses arising from the interaction of population growth with atmospheric and ecosystem deterioration, special attention will have to be paid to their needs and resources will have to be transferred from rich to poor. For developing countries, to forego the use of fossil fuels in their industrial development or the use of wood for domestic purposes will be politically sensitive measures. They will resist policies that make them bear the burden of adjustment and thwart industrial and economic development. Efforts to halt deforestation and soil degradation will require a major transfer of resources to the Third World. There is no sign yet that the industrialized world is willing to make such a commitment. Many countries, including Canada, are in the process of cutting overseas development assistance to developing countries in response to domestic budgetary and fiscal pressures (see chapter 12).

Many LDCs are worried that the countries of the North will manipulate concerns about the environment in order to continue denying Third World countries the resources they need for economic growth and development. The failed legacy of international efforts to negotiate a new international economic order (NIEO) in the 1970s already bedevils current efforts to address the problems of climate change and global warming. There is a growing danger that efforts to forge a new international approach to the problems of global warming will be derailed by competing agendas, interests, and misperceptions in North-South relations.

Nevertheless, a number of steps have been taken in developing international law and practices to address pollution of the air, along with other measures and initiatives to handle the problems of climate change, global warming, and related environmental issues.

In February 1989 Canada hosted a ground-breaking Meeting of Legal and Policy Experts on Protection of the Atmosphere, at which participants from twenty-five countries and eight international bodies sought agreement on the principles that would lay the foundations for a convention on climate change. The conference examined a variety of different frameworks for, and approaches to, devising a convention on climate change, recommending that an international convention, or conventions, with appropriate protocols should be adopted as a means of ensuring rapid international action to protect the atmosphere and limit the rate of climate change. The conference also urged that protocols to limit carbon dioxide and other greenhouse gas concentrations in the atmosphere are required, either within the framework of a convention on climate change or a convention on the protection of the atmosphere. It concluded by adopting the Ottawa Declaration, which recognizes the atmosphere is a "common resource of vital interest to mankind" that should be protected by all states (Statement of Legal and Policy Experts 1989). This declaration will be presented for approval at the Second World Climate Conference in 1990.

Canada put the environment on the agenda for the first time at the 1988 annual economic summit of the seven leading industrialized countries (G-7) held in Toronto. The summit leaders endorsed the concept of sustainable development. At the G-7 summit in July 1989 in Paris the environment and the twin problems of ozone depletion and global warming were major items of discussion. In the final communiqué, the leaders strongly advocated "common efforts to limit emissions of carbon dioxide and other greenhouse gases, which threaten to induce climate change, endangering the environment and the economy." The leaders emphasized the need to "help developing countries deal with past damage and to encourage them to environmentally desirable action." They also called for the speedy "conclusion of a framework or umbrella convention on climate change to set out general principles or guidelines" (*New York Times* 1989a).

At the Paris Summit Canada also proposed the novel idea of the development of a series of "environmental indicators" modelled on the familiar economic indicators (e.g. cost of living indexes) to measure environmental change. The seven leaders asked the OECD (Organization for Economic Cooperation and Development) to follow up with a detailed study of how such a system of indicators might work.

Canada was one of twenty-four signatories to the Declaration of The Hague, March 1989, which calls for an international convention on climate change and stronger mechanisms to ensure international cooperation to protect the environment. Although the Declaration does not contain any "operational" promises it expresses the intention of the participants to take measures to save the atmosphere and calls on other countries to do the same thing. The Declaration includes three principles: a reinforcement of UN powers and the creation of a new institutional authority (either by the strengthening of existing institutions or by the creation of new ones) for the purpose of protecting the atmosphere; the granting of specific competences to the International Court of Justice in The Hague related to control and enforcement decisions made by the UN; and "fair and equitable aid" to developing countries which would have difficulty complying with the efforts to protect the atmosphere (Declaration of The Hague 1989).

Prime Minister Brian Mulroney also supported the Langkawi Declaration on the Environment at the October 1989 Commonwealth Summit in Kuala Lumpur, in which leaders from North and South called for cooperation between developing and industrialized countries to resolve environmental problems.

International Agreements and Programs

Canada is already a signatory to several important international agreements and involved in a number of international programs on the environment. These agreements cover ozone depletion, pollutants in acid rain and smog, and transboundary movement of hazardous wastes.

The Montreal Protocol on Substances that Deplete the Ozone Layer, 1987, committed countries to reduce their use of CFCs (chlorofluorocarbons, which contribute to both the greenhouse effect and to the destruction of the ozone layer in the upper stratosphere) by 50 percent by 1999. The agreement also provides for trade sanctions against countries which fail to sign the agreement or which deny their obligation to protect the global environment. The protocol has been agreed to by sixty-two countries and ratified by thirty-six countries and the European Community. In February 1989 Canadian Environment Minister Lucien Bouchard announced that Canada would reduce its use of CFCs by 85 percent by 1999, thus exceeding the targets of the Montreal Protocol. The European Community's twelve member nations went even further and agreed in March 1989 to eliminate completely by the year 2000 the production and use of CFCs. The move came amid reports of higher levels of chemicals than expected in the Arctic atmosphere.

In March 1989 the London Conference on "Saving the Ozone Layer" was attended by 123 countries, including Canada. This conference emphasized that the rate of ozone depletion was far more rapid than had been thought earlier, and produced a consensus that the ultimate objective had to be the elimination of the production and consumption of all ozone-threatening chemicals. The conference also stressed the link between ozone layer depletion and global warming, and the special threat that climate change presents for low-lying countries.

In May 1989, eighty-six countries, including the thirty-six initial signatories to the Montreal Protocol and fifty countries attending as observers, decided at a UNEP-sponsored forum in Helsinki, Finland, to eliminate production of CFCs and other chemicals which threaten the ozone shield by the year 2000. The accord also called for industrialized countries to create a special United Nations fund to help developing countries industrialize without CFCs, and a working group has been established to elaborate the details of this fund. Norway's environment minister took the lead by pledging 0.1 percent of his country's gross national product to this fund if other countries would follow suit (UNEP 1989).

Canada is also a signatory to the 1988 Sofia Protocol under which emissions of nitrogen oxides (one of the acids in acid rain which can react with hydrocarbons to produce ozone in the lower atmosphere) are frozen at 1987 levels. In addition, Canada signed the Basel Convention on the Transboundary Movement of Hazardous Wastes, which provides for the treatment of hazardous wastes as close as possible to the source, and allows shipment of hazardous wastes only to countries with adequate treatment facilities. The Convention was approved on March 22, 1989, with more than 100 countries and the European Community attending. The Convention was signed by thirty-five states—of which half were developing countries—and will go into effect when it has been ratified by twenty countries.

The fifty-three page Basel Convention contains twenty-nine articles and six annexes. The principal points of the agreement are as follows: 1) a signatory state cannot send hazardous waste to another signatory state that bans imports of it; 2) a signatory state cannot ship hazardous waste to any country that has not signed the Convention; 3) every country has the sovereign right to refuse to accept a shipment of hazardous waste; 4) before an exporting country can start a shipment on its way, it must have the importing country's consent in writing; 5) no signatory country may ship hazardous waste to another signatory state if the importing country does not have the facilities to dispose of the waste in an environmentally sound manner; 6) when an importing country proves unable to dispose of legally imported waste in an environmentally acceptable way, then the exporting state has a duty to take it back or to find some other way of disposing of it in an environmentally sound manner; 7) each signing nation must require that all cross-border shipments be packaged and labelled properly and that all companies transporting or disposing of hazardous wastes have official authorization to handle wastes; 8) the Convention states that "illegal traffic in hazardous waste is criminal." The Convention also sets up a secretariat to supervise and facilitate its implementation, and asks that less hazardous waste be generated and that what is generated be disposed of as close to its source as possible (*Environmental Policy and Law* 1989: 38-9).

Some developing countries worry that the Treaty gives nations receiving hazardous wastes little in the way of enforcement mechanisms and makes it hard for them to force a nation that exports waste to adhere to the Treaty provisions. They charge that the Treaty had been watered down and will not stop waste traffic from the industrialized world to impoverished Third World nations desperate for hard currency. Some environmental groups also argue that the Treaty was worse than nothing because it has so many loopholes and such vague language that widespread abuses could continue in the movement of hazardous wastes (*New York Times* 1989b). The Treaty's defenders, however, argue that it will put an end to the present lawless situation and may result in a sharp reduction of transboundary movement of hazardous waste—although there is no guarantee that this will happen. In time the Treaty will, in its turn, be strengthened, and its ultimate goal is to make the movement of hazardous waste so costly and difficult that industry will ultimately find it more profitable to reduce (and recycle) the production of hazardous chemical wastes.

With regard to climate change and global warming, Canada is an active participant in the UN's Intergovernmental Panel on Climate Change (IPCC). The IPCC's mandate is to provide a firmer assessment of the scientific basis for climate change, including the impact of emissions of greenhouse gases on the earth's radiation balance and the environmental and socio-economic consequences of climate change, and to formulate "realistic response strategies for the management of the climate change issue" (UNEP 1988). The IPCC has established three subgroups: the first is undertaking a comprehensive review of the state of knowledge of the science of climate change, with special emphasis on global warming; the second is reviewing programs and conducting studies of the social and economic impacts of climate change; and the third is developing and evaluating possible policy responses by governments for the purpose of delaying, or mitigating, the adverse impacts of climate change. The subgroups are preparing reports to be tabled at the second World Climate Conference in Geneva in 1990. Canada is a member of working groups two and three.

In addition to its work in the IPCC, Canada is the largest single contributor of development assistance to the Third World in the forestry sector ($120 million a year), including programs aimed at preserving and restoring tropical forests. It is also encouraging the World Bank to make protection of the environment a top priority in economic development projects that it funds.

Regional and Bilateral Cooperation

While pursuing what might be described as an "international" approach to global environmental problems, Canada has also responded positively to regional and bilateral initiatives intended to promote environmental cooperation among the circumpolar states (Denmark, Finland, Iceland, Norway, Sweden, Soviet Union, United States, and Canada). In part, this activity reflects the recognition that the Arctic is a unique natural environment characterized by low solar energy, low temperatures, unique ecosystems, biological and physical processes that differ from those of temperate latitudes, and small permanent populations with distinctive cultures and economies. At the same time, the circumpolar states share common concerns about the Arctic environment, threatened as it is by long-range transportation of pollutants and toxins which are changing the Arctic ecosystem, entering the food chain, and threatening the health and survival of native peoples; by air pollution, including ozone layer depletion and Arctic haze; and by marine pollution in the form of oil spills, industrial discharges, and other harmful occurrences.

The Finnish government has been active in promoting cooperation on environmental issues among the circumpolar states by calling for a special coordinated regional approach to environmental issues. The Finnish proposal is somewhat controversial, because non-Arctic states which have scientific programs in the Arctic or other interests in the region have sought to be included in activities which relate to the Arctic environment. Moreover, the scientific community is opposed to the idea of forming an exclusive Arctic club, on the grounds that this might create unnecessary barriers to the dissemination of scientific knowledge and hinder research on the region's ecosystem. Notwithstanding these concerns, representatives of the eight Arctic countries agreed to meet at Rovaniemi, Finland, at the invitation of the Finnish government, from September 20 through September 26, 1989, for the Consultative Meeting on the Protection of the Arctic Environment. Two working groups were established at the meeting: one to review the state of the environment in the Arctic and the need for further action; the second to consider the existing international legal instruments for the protection of the Arctic environment and the possibilities for future cooperation. The first working group agreed that a series of reports on the state of the environment be prepared, concentrating on the main pollutants in the different parts of the ecosystem and that national and international monitoring systems operating in the Arctic be strengthened in order to develop a common strategy on sustainable development for the Arctic. The second group considered the adequacy of current bilateral and multilateral agreements pertaining to the protection and preservation of the Arctic environment. The group also discussed the controversial issue of participation of representatives of non-Arctic states in future cooperation on the Arctic environment. Although some non-Arctic countries do have active scientific programs in the Arctic and are also sources of some kinds of Arctic pollution, it was concluded that Arctic countries should continue to work together to address issues of common concern. This would not preclude non-Arctic states from being invited as observers to future meetings or participating in other ways. Task forces were also established at the meeting to prepare reports for the proposed Ministerial Conference on the Arctic, to take place in the spring of 1990 (Embassy of Finland, 1989).

While generally supportive of multilateral approaches to environmental problems in the Arctic, Canada has also begun, somewhat belatedly, to upgrade its bilateral ties in the region. During his November 1989 visit to the Soviet Union Prime Minister Brian Mulroney signed a number of agreements on Arctic cooperation with the Soviets. The General Agreement on Arctic Cooperation puts on a higher footing Canada's existing agreement on cooperation, the 1984 Protocol on Scientific Exchanges, while also expanding the subject areas that are covered within the environmental category. The new Canada-U.S.S.R. Agreement on Cooperation in the Arctic and the North contains three programs covering science and technology, economics, and social and cultural issues (Office of the Prime Minister 1989d). There are also several protocols in a separate Environmental Cooperation Agreement, which call for greater levels of cooperation on environmental matters between the two countries over the next four years (Office of the Prime Minister 1989e). The Protocols cover exchanges of information on environmental issues in Canadian and Soviet environmental programs generally, agreed exchange of findings on such items as Arctic and northern development, environmental emergency responses, protection of marine and freshwater areas, waste management and disposal, and environmental training and education. Two Memoranda of Understanding have also been signed: one covering cooperation on atmospheric environmental programs such as climate analysis, measurement of ozone, methane and greenhouse gases, research and monitoring of acid rain, Arctic haze, climate change and air pollution (Environment Canada 1989b); the other Memorandum covers cooperation on water research in five areas: pollution problems in the lakes and inland seas, chemical effects in rivers, toxic chemicals in aquatic systems, pulp and paper toxins, problems of ice floes in northern rivers, and permafrost (Environment Canada 1989c).

Canada and the Soviet Union have also taken preliminary steps to limit oil spill possibilities in the Arctic. Under a Memorandum of Understanding on Arctic Marine Pollution, which was also signed on the Prime Minister's trip to the Soviet Union, the two governments have agreed to exchange information on environmental legislation, pollution prevention policy, pollution monitoring, pollution prevention measures in northern communities, clean-up capabilities, and research and development results. The agreement further provides for exchange of ice-breaker captains, the presence of observers at clean-up operations in the event of an oil spill, as well as personnel, specialized equipment, and financial and logistical support in the event of an oil spill (Office of the Prime Minister 1989f).

Canada's most important bilateral environment concerns continue to be with the United States. Ottawa has long sought a special agreement with the U.S. to control emissions causing acid rain. During his visit to Ottawa, which took place shortly after his inauguration, President Bush indicated that he would conclude an acid rain accord with Canada after Congress had approved legislation he would soon be tabling to address the problem. On June 12, 1989, the president announced proposals to reduce emissions which cause acid rain, urban ozone and toxic air pollution. The proposals, the first major overhaul of the Clean Air Act to be proposed by an administration in over a decade, called for a 10,000 million ton reduction in sulphur dioxide emissions by the year 2000, a two million ton reduction in nitrogen oxides, a 40 percent reduction in emission of volatile organic compounds which cause urban smog, and a reduction of 75 to 90 percent in toxic atmospheric emissions. These reductions are also aimed at curbing an increase in global warming resulting from fossil fuel combustion. The proposal also called for the use of alternative fuels by one million vehicles by 1997. Alternative fuels, while reducing ozone precursors, will also reduce the toxic aromatics which come from conventional gasoline. The president submitted the comprehensive Clean Air Bill to the Congress on July 21. In addition, the president proposed US $710 million in FY (fiscal year) 1990 for the Clean Coal Technology Program, intended to encourage development of new technologies to reduce sulphur dioxide and nitrogen oxide emissions, while still allowing coal to play a role in the country's energy future. The administration also approved action to increase corporate average fuel efficiency (CAFE) standards for automobiles to 27.5 miles per gallon. The action is intended to reduce oil imports and reduce the contribution of automobile emissions to global warming (White House Press Office 1989).

Canada has welcomed the administration's introduction of the Clean Air Bill, which goes some distance towards meeting Canada's objective of a 50 percent reduction in cross-border pollution.

Conclusion

Though modest, and perhaps inadequate by some standards, the international initiatives and programs described in this chapter are helping to lay the foundations for more comprehensive agreements and strategies to address the problems of air and water pollution, global warming, and climate change. Canada has been active and supportive, but its commitment to, and involvement in, these international programs will soon have to be backed up by actions on the domestic front. Right now Canada is one of the most profligate consumers of energy and fossil fuels, with the highest per-capita energy consumption of the countries in the Organization for Economic Cooperation and Development. Canada is also the world's largest producer of municipal solid waste and the smallest recycler among industrialized nations. Every day the average Canadian throws out almost 2 kilograms of garbage, compared to an average of 1.1 kilograms for West Germans and Japanese. Along with the United States, Canada shares the blame for having the largest polluted bodies of freshwater, the Great Lakes, in the world. Overharvesting of forests threatens one of Canada's greatest natural resources. The long-term destruction of the prairie soil base, caused by intensive cultivation practices, is also raising serious questions about the sustainability of Canada's agricultural base. Poorly managed offshore fisheries, which have resulted in drastic declines in nearly all commercial fish stocks, threaten another vital natural resource. The health of Canadians is also increasingly threatened by the alarming accumulation of dioxins and other toxic chemicals and gases in our air, water, and food.

While it undoubtedly has been and will continue to be useful for the country to play its traditional role of taking part in multilateral discussions on important environmental issues, Canada has nevertheless failed to take action or recognize urgent environmental problems at home. As owner of almost one-tenth of the world's fresh water supply and occupier of one-tenth of the world's real estate, Canada's first responsibility to the global commons is its own backyard. In the case of the environment Canada's traditional role as "helpful fixer" should begin at home.

Notes

[1] I would like to thank Ian Cameron for research assistance in preparing this paper.

References

Canada. 1988. Environment Canada. *Conference Statement.* "The Changing Atmosphere: Implications for Global Security." Toronto, Canada, June 27-30.

——. 1989a. Environment Canada. *Release.* "International Environmental Action." November 9-10.

——. 1989b. Environment Canada. *News Release.* "Canada and the U.S.S.R. to Cooperate on Atmospheric Environmental Programs." November 20.

——. 1989c. Environment Canada. *News Release.* "Water Research Agreement Signed with U.S.S.R." November 20.

——. 1989d. Office of the Prime Minister. *Release.* "Canada and the U.S.S.R. Sign an Agreement on Cooperation in the Arctic and the North." November 21.

——. 1989e. Office of the Prime Minister. *Release.* "Environmental Cooperation Agreement Signed by Canada and the U.S.S.R." November 21.

_____. 1989f. Office of the Prime Minister. *Canada and the U.S.S.R. Take Steps to Limit Oil Spill Possibilities in the Arctic.* November 21.

Davidson, Al and Tony Hodge. 1989. "The Fate of the Great Lakes" *Policy Options* 10, no. 8 (October 1989): 19-26.

Declaration of The Hague. 1989. *Communiqué*, March 11.

Embassy of Finland. 1989. *Report of the Consultative Meeting on the Protection of the Arctic Environment.* Rovaniemi, Finland, September 20-6.

Environmental Policy and Law. 1989. "Basel Convention: International Agreement on Hazardous Wastes." 19, no. 2: 38-40.

Flavin, Christopher. 1989. *Slowing Global Warming: A Worldwide Strategy.* Worldwatch Paper No. 91. Washington, D.C.: Worldwatch Institute, October.

Graedel, Thomas E. and Paul J. Crutsen. 1989. "The Changing Atmosphere." *Scientific American*, 261, no. 3 (September): 58-69.

Mintzer, Irving M.., 1987. *A Matter of Degrees: The Potential for Controlling the Greenhouse Effect.* Research Report No. 5. Washington, D.C.: World Resources Institute, April.

Schneider, Stephen H. 1989. "The Changing Climate." *Scientific American*, 261, no. 3 (September): 70-9.

Statement of the International Meeting of Legal and Policy Experts. 1989. *Protection of the Atmosphere.* Ottawa. February 22.

New York Times. 1989a. "Key Sections of the Paris Communique by the Group of Seven." July 17: A10.

_____. 1989b. "U.N. Conference Supports Curbs on Exporting of Hazardous Waste." (Stephen Greenhouse) March 23: A1, B11.

United Nations Environment Programme (UNEP). 1988. *Report of the First Session of the WMO/UNEP Interngovernmental Panel on Climate Change (IPCC).* TD, no. 267. Geneva: World Climate Programme Publication Series, November.

_____. 1989. "Helsinki Declaration on the Protection of the Ozone Layer." OzL.Pro,1/L.1/Appendix 1, May 5.

White House Press Office. 1989. "Fact Sheet on Bush Adminstration Environmental Initiatives." September 18.

Wilson, Edward O. 1989. "Threats to Biodiversity." *Scientific American*, 261, no. 3 (September): 108-17.

Vancouver Sun. 1989. "To Save a Planet Polluted." (Bruce Hutchison). November 21: A19.

12 Overseas Development Assistance: the Neo-Conservative Challenge

Robert E. Clarke

In 1987 Canada introduced a new strategy for its overseas development assistance (ODA) program. This strategy emerged from a process of wide public consultation and parliamentary inquiries and study. In 1986 the Simard-Hockin Report had asserted that the government's aid activities should be better integrated with Canadian foreign policy and that international development should become "a Canadian vocation" (Special Joint Committee 1986: 88). This sentiment was repeated in the report of the House of Commons Standing Committee on External Affairs and International Trade, *For Whose Benefit?* (House of Commons 1987a). This Committee, chaired by William Winegard, held public hearings across Canada, visited several countries receiving Canada ODA and devoted nearly a year to studying the issues. The Committee report concluded that the purposes of Canadian ODA were confused and that the order of priority among political, commercial and development objectives had become unclear. It offered a detailed set of recommendations, some of which attempted to define the Canadian vocation of international development by clarifying Canadian interests in ODA and by stipulating the purposes of development assistance. The Committee described Canadian national interest in ODA as threefold: "Humanitarian, ... to alleviate human suffering and promote social justice; political, ... to increase stability and peace; and economic, to support the economic growth of developing countries" (House of Commons 1987a: 7). The report further stipulated that "the primary purpose of ODA is to help the poorest countries and people. ODA must strengthen the human and institutional capacity of developing countries to solve their own problems in harmony with the natural environment" (House of Commons 1987a: 12).

This lengthy process of consultation led to the publication by the government of its official ODA strategy in the document *Sharing Our Future* (CIDA 1987b). These new initiatives would, according to Minister Landry, establish that "Canadians care." This strategy set new criteria of eligibility for aid which widened the scope of the program (Rudner 1989). It asserted that human rights issues would be carefully assessed in determining a country's eligibility for aid. Moreover, a number of initiatives would be taken to improve aid delivery. Staff and decision making of the Canadian International Development Agency (CIDA) would be decentralized to bring the administration of the program closer to Third World recipients. Human resource development would become the "lens" through which all aid programming would be considered. The role of women in development and environmental issues would be incorporated into the Agency's program. The restrictions which had tied a great deal of procurement to Canadian sources would be loosened. The new strategy would seek to foster partnerships between Canadian individuals, groups, organizations and firms on the one hand and their Third World counterparts on the other to undertake various development activities. In addition, CIDA would devote resources to developing an extensive outreach program to better inform the Canadian public about the work of the Agency.

As a cornerstone of this new policy CIDA established a new ODA charter, which articulated the guiding principles on which all activities of the agency would be premised. This charter affirmed that all activities would (1) put poverty first; (2) help people to help themselves; (3) maintain development priorities; and (4) encourage partnerships (CIDA 1987b: 23).

At the time that this strategy was put forward there was little public criticism of its initiatives. While the strategy is not based on any particular theory or paradigm of development and while there are some anomalies, for the most part it does reflect the dominant development ideology shared by a wide segment of Canadian society. The wide consultation process exposed the authors of the policy to the key elements of this ideology and they successfully integrated its values into their policies.

The Dominant Ideology

Canadian society, like all societies, can be characterized as exhibiting a number of differing ideologies. These ideologies are widely shared sets of ideas, values, beliefs and perceptions through which members of the society interpret their social world, their history and current social events. The dominant ideology is that set of ideas and values which are widely shared by the majority of the members of a society (Marchak 1988). In Canada, the views embodied in liberalism, social democracy and classical conservatism are all contained within this dominant ideology.

The dominant Canadian ideology legitimates private property rights while recognizing that such rights must be restricted in the interests of the wider community and social harmony. It accepts the profit motive while at the same time valuing altruism and other attitudes limiting the operation of that motive and, thereby preventing it from completely dominating the social system. It encompasses the view that the rewards that individuals receive for work may vary in accordance with such social factors as education, skills or talent, but it strongly rejects any view that differential rewards can or should be based on gender, ethnicity, religion or other non-economic ascribed characteristics of individual Canadians. The ideology tends to explain social action in terms of individuals, or of non-class groups (ie. men-women, ethnic groups or interest groups), rather than in terms of social classes. It asserts that social mobility is possible with sufficient application of hard work. Education is emphasized as the key to enable people to move up the stratification ladder. Incorported in the ideology is a notion that social progress is possible; Canadian society is portrayed as moving toward a better future which will be more egalitarian. This better society will, the ideology asserts, be achieved through a process of gradual evolution.

Aid Policy and the Dominant Ideology

The reflection of this Canadian dominant ideology can be seen in many aspects of the new aid policy. The policy encourages the participation of profit-making businesses in Canadian development activities while, at the same time, emphasizing a continuing important role for government. The policy strongly encourages recipient governments to support private sector development and the development of profit-making enterprises within the framework of a mixed economy. In the ODA charter, and in a number of the policy initiatives in *Sharing Our Future*, there is an emphasis on the alleviation of poverty and support for activities which will lead to greater equality. The specific focus on activities in the field of women and development reflects a concern about contributing to greater equality and the rejection of differences of status based on ascriptive criteria. The policy emphasizes the role of self-help within the framework of a market (or increasingly market-oriented) economy. It gives a strong priority to the development of human resources through education and skills training, as a means of achieving poverty alleviation and greater upward social mobility. The policy reflects the core values of the dominant Canadian ideology, inherent in its fundamentally optimistic orientation to change, its vision that a better society can be achieved and its view that this will be achieved in a series of incremental steps.

The congruence between this policy and the dominant Canadian ideology is further confirmed by the results of a national public opinion poll, commissioned by CIDA and undertaken in December 1987. This poll confirmed widespread support among Canadians for Canada's ODA program and policy. Only 18 percent of those queried thought that the Canadian government was spending too much money on ODA while a majority (66 percent) thought that Canada should be among the more generous donor countries in the world (CIDA 1988: 11). There were 48 percent of Canadians who identified poverty and hunger as the most important problems facing the world and, in accordance with the dominant ideology, education was ranked as the most important factor affecting development. Of the sample 46 percent thought that in aid-receiving countries the most critical problems were the absence of adequate food, shelter and medical treatment; however, 31 percent identified the lack of good basic education systems as the most critical problem. The vast majority of Canadians (75 percent) considered that aid should go to create longer-term economic and social progress in recipient countries. Their response to questions concerning the way in which aid should be spent indicated the importance of dominant ideology values. Two-thirds of the sample indicated that aid money should go first to poor countries and those that respect human rights, but that it should not be restricted to countries which have democratic governments. Respondents considered that clear instructions should be given as to how the aid should be used, although no conditions should be applied which would require the recipient country to use the aid to buy Canadian products or services.

The responses to this poll reflect clearly the widespread adherence to the dominant ideology and the application of core values of this ideology to the public's views about aid policy. In light of these congruencies it is not surprising that this policy finds wide acceptance among the Canadian community.

The Rise of Neo-Conservative Ideology

During the 1970s and early 1980s the world economic system experienced a major structural crisis. By the mid-1980s many of the key centres of this system had managed to restructure critical economic and social processes, so that capital accumulation had been re-established and social order assured. This period saw a declining use of traditional Keynesian economic management techniques. In the course of a number of different struggles capitalism has been able to reform itself, recover its dynamism and regain social control over the changed system. It has achieved this by decreasing the number of people who are beneficiaries of the system while at the same time creating an interconnected network of the remaining beneficiaries in all parts of the world (Castells 1987). The transnational corporation has been the institution which provides the basis for this network and it has been at the centre of this transformation.

As neo-conservative hegemony has established itself in a number of countries, a new model of economic growth has emerged. This new model is a substantial departure from the Keynesian welfare-state capitalism that emerged after the depression of the 1930s and on which much of Canada's dominant ideology is built. Most countries in both the North and the South, including Canada, are now reorganizing around this new model. The neo-conservative paradigm has received substantial support from economists and is increasingly invoked by business and government alike.

The neo-conservative ideology invokes austerity and monetarism as means to control inflation. It attacks wages, working conditions and social benefits in order to reduce labour costs, and advocates increasing the profitability of firms through lay-offs, reduced working time, technological innovation and increasing work pace. Neo-conservatism encourages the restructuring of industrial sectors by disinvestment from those industries deemed less profitable, and investment in new activities. It encourages shrinkage of the public sector which is thereby, increasingly rendered unable to meet social needs, even while police and military forces grow. Its application has seen a tremendous increase in the informal sector, the internationalization of the economy, and greater control of raw materials and energy prices by the core capitalist economies (Castells 1987).

The neo-conservative ideology has found a growing number of adherents in Canada. Whether its popularity has been the result of diffusion of its fundamental ideas from the United States (Marchak 1988) or a response to changes in the nature of the contemporary Canadian productive system (Howlett and Brownsey 1988), the ideology is taking on an increasing significance in the context of Canadian politics. The growth of a government agenda influenced by this ideology can be seen both in the government attack on ODA in the budget of 1989 and in the increasing advocacy of structural adjustment programs within CIDA.

The Neo-Conservative Budget of 1989

In their two terms in office the Mulroney Conservatives have had to balance their traditional base of support, which includes many constituents who subscribe to the core values of the dominant ideology, with that group of neo-conservative ideologues who have become prominent within the party in recent years. The increasing importance of neo-conservative ideology is reflected in the federal budget of April 1989.

The first budget of the Conservatives' second term reflects many aspects of the neo-conservative ideology. The document called for sharp cuts in federal spending and a variety of tax increases, all undertaken with the stated goal of reducing the federal deficit. The budget proposed the continuing privatization of Air Canada, cuts in the federal subsidy to VIA Rail passenger service, a reduction in federal commitments to day care, cuts in transfer payments to the provinces which are used for health care and education, and an attack on the principle of universal old age security and family allowance benefits (*Globe and Mail* 1989a, 1989b).

Among the largest reductions in the 1989 budget were cuts to Canada's ODA allocations. It became clear from this budget, which focused on measures reputed to be deficit-reducing, that overseas development assistance had become vulnerable. The cut in Canada's ODA was to be about $1.8 billion over the next five years (*Globe and Mail* 1989c). ODA received a disproportionate amount of the total budget cuts. While foreign aid spending represents about 3 percent of total government spending, Table 12.1 indicates it bore 23 percent of the cuts for the first year of this budget and 17 percent for the second year.

Table 12.1
Share of Total Government Spending and
Percentage Share of Cutbacks

Program spending	Share of 1988-89 expenditures	Share of cutbacks 1989-90	1990-91
Transfer to Persons	40.0	0.0	10.3
Transfer to Other Govts	24.3	17.2	24.3
Government Operations	16.2	3.2	3.5
Major Subsidies/Transfers	11.2	12.2	4.4
Defence	11.1	37.2	29.4
Crown Corporations	4.4	7.0	10.7
ODA	2.8	23.3	17.3
Totals	100.0	100.0	100.0

Source: The North South Insitute 1989.

Since the Conservatives came to power in 1984 aid has fallen in proportion to the Gross National Product (GNP), a common ratio used by donor nations to make comparisons. As Table 12.2 illustrates, Canada continues to rank only seventh among major donor countries when ODA is measured as a percentage of GNP. In the 1989 budget the government appears to have abandoned earlier, internationally accepted targets for ODA growth to 0.7 percent of GNP by 1990. The date to achieve this target had been previously rolled back twice by the Mulroney government, first to 1995 in the budget of November 1984, and then to the year 2000 in the budget of February 1986. In the 1989 budget the government appears to have abandoned this target altogether. No mention is made of it and as a result of the cuts Canada's ODA will fall to 0.43 percent in 1989-1990. This is a lower level than that which existed when the Mulroney government took office. It now appears that, instead of reaching 0.6 percent by 1995, Canada's aid spending will reach only 0.475 percent by 1995-1996. This is just barely above the 1987 level of 0.47 percent. By the year 2000 the level will have reached only 0.5 percent (North South Institute 1989).

Table 12.2
Relative Aid Performance, 1988
(In Rank Order of Top Seven Donors)

Countries	Aid as a Percentage of GNP
1. Norway	1.10
2. Netherlands	.98
3. Denmark	.89
4. Sweden	.87
5. France	.72
6. Finland	.59
7. Canada	.49

Source: OECD 1989.

The manner in which CIDA has applied the cuts across its programs also reflects its recognition of the importance of the new neo-conservative constituency. While most CIDA divisions have to absorb cuts of about 13 percent, the Industrial Cooperation Branch which funds business development and trade-related Agency initiatives, had its budget increased by 19 percent. At the same time CIDA increased funding to the Agency's publicity program by 13.4 million dollars.

The impact of the budget cuts on the Agency's other development partners, such as non-governmental organizations (NGOs), has been particularly devastating. The level of the cuts was a relatively small 3.2 percent, in recognition, no doubt, of the fact that these organizations can mobilize a very vocal constituency, but they have had a particularly severe impact because of the small and already austere budgets of these organizations. The distribution of the reductions on the NGOs has ranged from 50 percent (in the case of a pool of funding for university cooperation and freezes on funding for many of the smaller NGOs), to 7.4 percent in the case of CUSO, Canada's largest volunteer organization. These cuts have meant that dozens of projects have been cancelled, Canadians who were to have worked overseas have remained at home and numerous programs have been shelved (Canadian Council for International Cooperation 1989).

Despite the magnitude of these budget cuts and the wide impact on many aspects of Canada's ODA there was little public outcry following the cuts. The Canadian Council for International Cooperation orchestrated a national "save ODA" campaign but relatively few people or organizations were in fact mobilized.

Structural Adjustment—the International Neo-Conservative Agenda

During the early 1980s, while Canada's economy was passing through a period of high unemployment, inflation and low growth, many Third World countries were moving closer to the brink of disaster. Many of these countries found that their optimistic forecasts of take-off and development had proven false. Burdened with "high real interest rates, unfavourable terms of trade and the slow growth of world trade" (Bienefeld 1989: 135), many as the decade progressed, found themselves overwhelmed by crippling levels of debt. In the context of the new capitalist hegemony, the countries of the North, working through the international financial institutions, sought to influence the domestic policies of the indebted countries. Their action took the form of encouraging so-called "structural adjustment" by imposing conditions on loans and aid transfers to these countries.

Structural adjustment programs require that, to be eligible for loan rescheduling and some kinds of aid, indebted countries have to restructure their economies in accordance with requirements set out by the international financial institutions. The required conditions are based on initiatives that open these countries to world capitalism. They are the international expression of the neo-conservative ideology. Restructuring usually requires the recipient countries to adopt a package of policy changes which involves across-the-board economic liberalization, enhancement of market forces wherever possible, a reduction in the role of the state and an increase in the economies' openness to external trade, capital flows and other economic inputs (Helleiner 1989: 108). These measures may well lead to capital flight, recession and capital concentration, as there will be a disengagement from local economic activity directed at the local market. What little growth there is under these conditions will arise from industries dependent on low wages and the external market. The state is dramatically weakened and government programs become increasingly dependent upon foreign loans.

> The economic package produces economic disarray—it destroys the endogenous basis of economic development, it produces fundamental dislocations in the structure of the State, and what is more important it produces a situation of de facto trusteeship by the IFIs (International Financial Institutions) and several bilateral donors (Chossudovsky 1989: 4).

In human terms, reductions in government spending are usually applied to education, health care, food subsidies and public services. The implementation of such a program is very likely to result in increased poverty, greater hardship for the poor and a decline in the effectiveness of democratic institutions necessary for genuine development to take place (George 1988).

Structural Adjustment Gains a Canadian Ally

Through its representative at the International Monetary Fund (IMF), Marcel Massé, Canada has been a strong supporter and advocate of structural adjustment programs. For example, Canada has been instrumental in organizing a structural adjustment package for the small South American country of Guyana. The problems of Guyana are illustrative of the challenges faced by other small, heavily indebted Third World states. With a GDP of $310 million in 1987 the country had experienced an average decline in GDP in real terms of 6 percent per year between 1980-1987 (*Globe and Mail* 1989d). The country has experienced severe shortages of staple foods, power outages, abandoned schools, factories and clinics, and a rising rate of infant mortality. It owes U.S. $1.2 billion on its international loans, $120 million of this to the IMF and $36 million to the World Bank. In order to arrange further borrowing Guyana must first clear its debts with these agencies.

Canada has been instrumental in setting up a program of debt relief and supports for Guyana. At the International Monetary Fund Mr. Massé organized a consortium including the United States, France, West Germany, and Trinidad and Tobago, to provide nearly $300 million over three years. The funds will be used to help pay the $120 million due to the IMF and to cover essential import needs. In order to receive this aid the government of Guyana must agree to implement a program of structural adjustment involving austerity and liberalizing economic reforms approved by the IMF. This program calls for an exchange rate devaluation of 70 percent, numerous price increases and only slight wage increases (*Globe and Mail* 1989e, 1989f).

The implementation of this austerity program sparked massive strikes in the two major export industries (bauxite and sugar) as well as angry protests from churches and other groups. Canada's role in imposing this package was condemned by demonstrators staging protests before the Canadian High Commission in Georgetown. Both

Canadian and Guyanese commentators have argued that the scheme being imposed by the International Monetary Fund will not work, that it may well provoke more turmoil and further unrest, and that it will most certainly make conditions worse for Guyana's poor majority, the young, the elderly and women (*Globe and Mail* 1989e, 1989f, 1989g,1989h).

Structural Adjustment Comes to CIDA

In September of 1989, shortly after engineering the Guyanese program, Mr. Massé became the president of CIDA. In a speech in November 1989 Mr. Massé said, "structural adjustment looks more relevant with each day that passes" (Massé 1989: 1). He told his audience that "CIDA has taken the leap of faith and plunged into the uncharted seas of structural adjustment.... Structural adjustment figures among the priorities for Canadian development assistance" (Massé: 4). While CIDA has over the years made some contributions to debt reduction for heavily indebted countries these have been in the form of forgivable loans and the conversion of loans to grants (CIDA 1987b: 57). It appears from the Guyanese case that stringent conditionality will now be emphasized and endorsed in the Canadian program. It is difficult to predict how these new initiatives will serve the major goals to which CIDA subscribed in the new aid policy outlined above. As increased poverty and hardship for the majority appear to result from structural adjustment initiatives an emphasis by the Agency on supporting such initiatives may make it more difficult to implement the policy.

Canada's ODA into the 1990s

The CIDA policy statement of 1987 set out a progressive future for Canadian ODA, a future in which the elimination of poverty would be the first priority, self-help would be encouraged, development priorities would be maintained and partnerships would be fostered. These are goals which reflect the aspirations of most Canadians regarding our role in international aid activities and values that are central to the Canadian dominant ideology. It is because this dominant ideology is so widely shared and has been reflected in aid policy that this program has consistently received substantial public support. It was this ideology which was reflected in the public consultations which led up to the adoption of the new CIDA policy in 1987.

1989 saw two major challenges to the promise of this policy, both of which have a basis in neo-conservative ideology. While this is a relatively new ideological phenomenon in Canada it has gained a number of adherents among federal Conservatives. Both the cuts in the 1989 budget and the rise within CIDA of an emphasis on the use of ODA policy to support structural adjustment are manifestations of this ideology.

The budget cuts clearly put the objectives of austerity and federal deficit reduction before the maintenance of Canada's commitment to development assistance. Furthermore, these cuts may be only the beginning, despite the strong support among Canadians for a progressive aid program and the fact that the neo-conservative ideology is new and not widely shared. It has been demonstrated by the experience in 1989 that the constituency supporting ODA is not easily mobilized. While External Affairs Minister Joe Clark asserted that he entered the Cabinet's 1990 budget negotiations with the position that ODA should not receive additional cuts in the 1990 budget he may find it difficult to stand firm (*Globe and Mail* 1990). In a context where further spending cuts are a priority, and particularly in the wake of the furor over the Goods and Services Tax, ODA may appear to be an easy target.

The second challenge—the increased advocacy of structural adjustment by CIDA—may be equally difficult to meet. Large scale bureaucracies are relatively impervious to public pressure, particularly in situations in which they are taking up a new ideology which is widely advocated by authoritative and powerful international agencies. As the costs in human suffering and world disorder, resulting from the imposition of structural adjustment programs, become more evident, CIDA will be faced with some strategic decisions. The credibility of our aid motives will be questioned and Canada's international reputation as an innovative and compassionate donor will be at risk.

Canada's ability to meet its commitments to the alleviation of poverty in the Third World, and the effectiveness of its efforts there, are seriously challenged by the growing influence of neo-conservative ideology on funding, policy and programs. Concerned Canadians must find ways of reasserting the core values of the dominant ideology in policy decisions on development assistance. Canadians have over the years developed a number of very vibrant partnerships with counterparts in the Third World. As our Third World partners struggle against both massive debt and the crippling policies imposed by international financial institutions and development agencies we can work together with them, through our extensive network of non-governmental organizations and institutions, to find new social and economic strategies which may yield socially and economically viable and democratic futures. In so doing we may learn from them strategies which will help us to achieve the same kind of future for Canadians.

References

Bienefeld, Manfred. 1989. "A Time of Growing Disparities." In *Canada Among Nations 1988: the Tory Record*, edited by Brian W. Tomlin and Maureen Appel Molot. Toronto: James Lorimer & Co.: 125-148.

Canada. 1986. Parliament. Special Joint Committee of the Senate and House of Commons on Canada's International Relations. *Independence and Internationalism*. Ottawa: Supply and Services.

_____. 1987a. Parliament. House of Commons. 1987. Standing Committee on External Affairs and International Trade on Canada's Official Development Assistance Policies and Programs. *For Whose Benefit?* Ottawa: Queen's Printer.

_____. 1987b. Canadian International Development Agency (CIDA). *Sharing Our Future: Canada's International Development Assistance*. Ottawa: Supply and Services.

_____. 1988. CIDA. *Report to CIDA, Public Attitudes Toward International Development Assistance*. Ottawa: Ministry of Supply and Services.

Canadian Council for International Cooperation. 1989. Media Kit, ODA Campaign. Ottawa: Canadian Council for International Cooperation.

Castells, Manuel. 1987. "High Technology, World Development and Structural Transformation: The Trends and the Debate." In *The Political Economy of North South Relations*, edited by T. Miljan. New York: Broadview Press: 11-38.

Chossudovsky, Michel. 1989. "Third World Structural Adjustment." Unpublished paper presented at the International Colloquium on Structural Adjustment and Social Realities in Africa at the Institute for International Development and Cooperation, University of Ottawa. Ottawa, November 17.

George, Susan. 1988. *A Fate Worse than Debt* London: Penguin Books.

Globe and Mail. 1989a. "Budget raises taxes and scuttles subs."
  April 27.

———. 1989b. "Budget highlights." April 27.

———. 1989c. "Foreign aid declines annually since 1984." April 29.

———. 1989d. "Economic aid plan for Guyana last hope of recovery."
  September 5.

———. 1989e. "Canada putting together rescue package to help
  Guyana clear up arrears with IMF." March 21.

———. 1989f. "Canada's praise for austerity move sparks protest in
  Guyanese capital". April 19.

———. 1989g. "Canada drawing criticism for role in Guyanese
  austerity program." May 3.

———. 1989h. "Guyana austerity plan will provoke turmoil, opposition head says." October 4.

———. 1990. "1989 bad for most, group says." January 17.

Helleiner, G.K. 1989. "Conventional Foolishness and Overall Ignor-
  ance: Current Approaches to Global Transformation and Development." *Canadian Journal of Development Studies* X(1): 107-118.

Howlett, Michael and Keith Brownsey. 1988. "The Old Reality and
  the New Reality: Party Politics and Public Policy in British
  Columbia 1941-1987." *Studies in Political Economy.* 25: 141-176.

Marchak, Patricia M. 1988. *Ideological Perspectives on Canada.* Third
  Edition. Toronto: Mc-Graw Hill, Ryerson Limited.

Massé, Marcel. 1989. "Adjustment in Perspective." Unpublished paper
  presented at International Colloquium on Structural Adjustment
  and Social Realities in Africa at the Institute for International
  Development and Cooperation, University of Ottawa, Ottawa,
  Ontario, November 17.

North South Institute. 1989. "The 1989-90 Federal Budget and the
  ODA Cuts." Press Release. Ottawa.

Organization for Economic Cooperation and Development. 1989.
  Development co-operation in the 1990s. Paris: Organization for
  Economic Cooperation and Development.

Rudner, Martin. 1989. "New Directions in Canadian Development
  Assistance Policy." In *Canada Among Nations 1988: The Tory
  Record*, edited by Brian W. Tomlin and Maureen Appel Molot.
  Toronto: James Lorimer & Co.: 149-168.

13 Canada and Southern Africa 1989: Autonomy, Image and Capacity in Foreign Policy

Chris Brown

> Canada is ready, if there are no fundamental changes in South Africa, to invoke total sanctions against that country and its repressive regime. More than that, if there is no progress in the dismantling of apartheid, relations with South Africa may have to be severed absolutely.
> — Prime Minister Brian Mulroney, speaking to the United Nations General Assembly, October 23, 1985

Although events in southern Africa were often pushed off the front pages of Canadian newspapers by the momentous happenings in Eastern Europe and elsewhere, 1989 was nonetheless a year of dramatic change in that region. The most important developments were in Namibia and South Africa. In Namibia, the long-delayed transition to independence began at last. After a calamitous beginning, and despite much fear and suspicion on all sides, the United Nations (UN) independence plan appeared to reach a successful climax with the election of a constituent assembly in November. In South Africa, the eleven-year reign of P. W. Botha came to a sudden and acrimonious end. His successor, F. W. de Klerk, fresh from electoral victory, appeared to breathe new life into the apartheid reform process by allowing the first public anti-apartheid demonstrations in years and releasing eight major political prisoners.

For Canada, the changes in southern Africa represented both a vindication of, and a challenge to, long-established policies. With some justification, Canada could claim that it had contributed, in its own small but not insignificant way, to the coming independence of Namibia and the acceleration of change in South Africa. At the same time, however, the rapid pace of change often caught Canadian policymakers flat-footed, exposing the sometimes yawning gaps both between rhetorical proclamation and concrete policy and between avowed policy goals and actual capacity to pursue them. Instead of being able to claim credit for foreign policy successes, therefore, the Canadian government frequently found itself struggling to explain foreign policy failures. This chapter analyzes the "successes" and "failures" of Canadian foreign policy toward southern Africa in 1989, focusing on Namibia and South Africa. The key concepts used in the analysis are autonomy, image and capacity.

In many respects, southern Africa is a unique foreign policy field for Canada. The abomination of apartheid gives the region political and moral salience for many Canadians, yet Canada's economic, cultural and historic ties to southern Africa are relatively few. As a consequence, Canadian foreign policymakers have a relatively high degree of autonomy in formulating policy toward southern Africa.

In the past, as others have argued, this autonomy allowed Canada to develop a progressive image at home and abroad with regard to southern Africa (Freeman 1986). The peak period for Canada's positive image probably came between 1985 and 1987, when Prime Minister Brian Mulroney took the lead in the Commonwealth, and at other international fora, in calling for concerted international action against South Africa. The Prime Minister's bold statement before the United Nations General Assembly, quoted above, epitomized the rhetoric of the period.

Image, to be sustained, requires action leading to desired results. In the 1985-87 period Canada was able to match rhetoric with policy action, thereby justifying its progressive image. Since that time, however, Canada's lack of capacity to produce results has been increasingly exposed. Two separate but related processes are at work here. First, it has become harder to match rhetoric with new policy actions, since Canada has now reached the point where further official sanctions against South Africa will have real domestic economic costs. Second, it has become increasingly clear that achieving Canada's goals requires concerted multilateral action, which so far Canada has been unable to promote. As a consequence of these two processes, the distance between the government's rhetoric on southern Africa and the results of its policies has widened, leading to the development of a major credibility gap. This chapter describes how this credibility gap worsened in 1989, beginning with the events in Namibia.

Namibia

Events in 1989

A former German colony, Namibia was ruled after 1915 by South Africa, at first legally under a League of Nations and (then a) United

Nations mandate, subsequently illegally, after the mandate was withdrawn in 1966. The major black nationalist movement, the South West Africa People's Organization (SWAPO), began fighting a guerilla war against South African occupation in 1966; by 1989 this war had cost over 10,000 lives and generated approximately 50,000 refugees. In 1978, the Security Council passed Resolution 435, which established a framework for Namibian independence; it had been negotiated by the so-called "Contact Group"—the five Western members of the Security Council at the time (Canada, France, United Kingdom, United States, and West Germany). Despite initial acceptance of Resolution 435, South Africa blocked its implementation with a number of provisos, and particularly by insisting that Namibian independence could not proceed as long as there were Cuban troops in neighbouring Angola. Finally, in 1988, American-mediated talks between Angola, Cuba and South Africa produced a series of regional peace accords in which the parties agreed to the simultaneous withdrawal of the Cuban troops and implementation of Resolution 435, beginning on April 1, 1989.

Resolution 435 called for the creation of a United Nations Transition Assistance Group (UNTAG), consisting of up to 7,500 soldiers and 1,500 police and civilian personnel. A detailed timetable was established for a twelve-month transition to independence. The key steps in the transition were a ceasefire and the election of a constituent assembly, which would then write the constitution for an independent Namibia. The cost to the UN of the entire process was estimated at over U.S. $700 million. Significantly, the transition was to take place under the direct supervision of the Administrator-General for Namibia who had been appointed by South Africa. UNTAG, instead of directly controlling the process, was to observe its implementation and, ultimately, to certify its acceptability. A final key provision of the plan was that the independence constitution as a whole had to be approved by a two-thirds majority of the constituent assembly.

Implementation of Resolution 435 in 1989 began with a dispute over money. Under American pressure to economize, the Security Council agreed to reduce the military component of UNTAG to 4,650 troops and to cut its budget to U. S. $416 million. The wrangling over the budget so delayed the formation of UNTAG that, as April 1 approached, its deployment was two to three weeks behind schedule and it had no personnel on the ground in the crucial northern war zone.

This delay nearly proved fatal as, on April 1, instead of a ceasefire coming into effect as scheduled, the heaviest fighting of the entire war broke out. Part of the explanation for this unexpected outbreak of hostilities lies in the fact that SWAPO, not having been a party to the peace accords, had never made an explicit commitment to withdraw its troops to bases in Angola. As a result, in a decision that combined inexplicable naiveté with a desire to demonstrate that it really did have fighters inside Namibia, SWAPO sent up to 2,000 guerillas across the border on April 1 in search of non-existent UNTAG personnel to whom they could surrender. What they found instead were trigger-happy South Africans. Six weeks later, when the ceasefire was finally established, up to 300 SWAPO and 30 South African soldiers were dead.

This event set the tone of hostility and suspicion for the rest of the year. South Africa repeatedly tried to use its control of the transition process to deny SWAPO a two-thirds majority in the assembly and to help its preferred party, the Democratic Turnhalle Alliance (DTA). The UN, for its part, had to use the threat of scrapping the entire process to force South Africa to observe the letter and spirit of Resolution 435. Issues for dispute between South Africa and the UN included the demobilization of South Africa's dreaded Koevoet anti-insurgency unit; the extent and timing of the repeal of apartheid laws; the definition of "political," as opposed to "criminal," prisoners to be released; the method of voter registration; the qualifications for eligible voters; the rules governing electioneering; and the method for casting and counting ballots. Furthermore, although not directly part of the UNTAG process, South Africa's decisions to sell off Namibian government assets, slash budgetary support to the Namibian administration and establish a border post at its enclave of Walvis Bay, all moves clearly calculated to contribute to the "neo-colonization" of Namibia, also caused concern among international observers.

The election itself was held over a five-day period from November 7 to 11. Over 97 percent of the 701,483 registered voters cast their ballots under the watchful eyes of the world, amid only scattered reports of irregularities. At the end of the day, UN Special Representative Martti Ahtisaari was therefore able to declare proudly that the vote had been both free and fair. The results allowed most of the parties to claim at least a partial victory. SWAPO, with 57 percent of the votes and forty-one of the seventy-two seats in the assembly, was the clear winner, but it fell seven seats short of the two-thirds majority necessary for complete control. The DTA, for its part, garnered 29 percent of the votes and twenty-one seats, while six of the eight minor parties split the remaining ten seats.

As the year ended, therefore, the constituent assembly was starting to write a new constitution in time for independence in March 1990. Sceptics pointed out that the prospects for independent Namibia were bleak indeed. Years of South African rule had left Namibia under-developed and dependent. The vast majority of its black citizens were impoverished, while the white minority, comprising less than 10 percent of the population, controlled most of the wealth and owned half the land. Dependence on South Africa was almost total; it was symbolized by the galling fact that the only deep-water port on the Namibian coastline, Walvis Bay, remained firmly in South African hands. All these problems, however, awaited the future.

Canadian Responses

Canada has never had extensive economic or other links with Namibia and what links there were have declined over time. In the 1970s, a few major Canadian companies, among them Falconbridge, Noranda and Rio Algom, were active in Namibia, primarily in the mining sector. During the 1980s, most of these companies pulled out, ostensibly in response to declining market conditions, though public pressure to disinvest undoubtedly also played a role. The last major Canada-Namibia economic linkage, the processing of Namibian uranium from the giant Rossing mine by the Crown corporation Eldorado Nuclear, came to an end during 1988.

As a consequence of this lack of direct Canada-Namibia economic ties, the main domestic influence on Canadian foreign policy with respect to Namibia has come from a wide range of anti-apartheid, church and developmental non-governmental organizations (NGOs). These groups have consistently urged the government to take a firmer, more active, stand against South Africa's illegal occupation of Namibia and in favour of SWAPO. Similar pressures have come internationally from Third World states in the Commonwealth and at the United Nations, which have also urged Canada to use its influence with the United States and other countries which are members of the Organization for Economic Cooperation and Development (OECD) to get them to toughen their own policies.

The Canadian government, unconstrained by any domestic economic repercussions of its Namibian policy, has had the autonomy required for responding positively to these demands. It has attempted to define for itself an activist stance on Namibia, particularly the role of an "honest broker" between Third World and OECD interests. At the same time, it has used Namibian policy as a means of reconfirming its commitment to multilateralism in general and to the UN in particular. In the past, especially as a member of the original Contact Group and as an outspoken opponent of American efforts to link Namibian independence with Cuban troop withdrawal from Angola, Canada has been fairly successful in establishing a "progressive" image at home and abroad with regard to Namibia. During 1989, however, despite the fact that Canada made a major contribution to UNTAG, the lustre of its image faded to some degree. This can be attributed to its inability to exert influence on key issues and its unwillingness to abandon multilateralism and take a firm position in favour of SWAPO.

Canada displayed its eagerness to play a role in Namibia by pledging support to UNTAG well in advance of any formal request for help. In the end, Canada's contribution to the transition process, both bilaterally and through UNTAG, was substantial. For UNTAG, Canada contributed $15 million in budgetary support, 257 logistics personnel for the peacekeeping force, one hundred police monitors from the Royal Canadian Mounted Police, 4,000 ballot boxes, an expert on computerized election results from Elections British Columbia, and fifty election monitors. Canada also established an official observer mission, provided $2 million for refugee repatriation, and promised bilateral aid to independent Namibia. Canada's contribution to the transition process was, in sum, undeniably substantial and, as such, contributed significantly to its overall success. As a welcome side-effect for the government, domestic media coverage of Mounties and election monitors in the Namibian bush provided much favourable publicity.

Nonetheless, the year was characterized by bickering over Namibia between the government and NGOs, several of whom sent their own observer missions to monitor the transition process. The NGO team that received the most publicity was one sent in August by the Canadian Council for International Cooperation, headed by former Conservative Cabinet Minister Flora MacDonald. Criticism by this team and others focused on two concerns.

First, the government was accused of being unwilling or unable to effect changes to remedy key weaknesses in the transition plan. On the issue of UNTAG's budget and force size, for instance, Canada's much-vaunted "seat at the table" in the Security Council proved meaningless in the face of American pressure to economize. Similarly, during the many South African-UNTAG disputes, Canada's voice was rarely influential.

Second, Canada was accused of masking an indifference to South African manipulation of the electoral process behind a guise of multilateralism and impartiality. During a meeting with SWAPO Secretary-General Andimba Toivo ya Toivo in March, External Affairs Minister Joe Clark made it clear that the need to be impartial took precedence over Canada's long-standing ties to SWAPO and that, as a consequence, SWAPO could expect no Canadian assistance of any kind during the transition. In a manifestly unequal situation, responded the critics, impartiality amounts to support for the powerful, in this case South Africa. Canada's response to the fighting in April appeared to be a case in point; Clark blamed SWAPO for crossing the border, rather than South Africa for initiating hostilities, even though by this time UN Secretary-General Javier Perez de Cuellar had declared that the SWAPO guerillas had had no "offensive intent" (*Globe and Mail* 1989a). Similarly, the critics argued that Canada could have taken a far firmer stand on issues such as intimidation by Koevoet and South Africa's economic manipulations.

Whatever the merits of these arguments, it is clear that Canada's effort to project itself as a "friend of Namibia," to use a phrase from an External Affairs press release (Department of External Affairs 1989), were only partially successful in 1989. Despite a substantial contribution to UNTAG, Canada, because of the limited influence it could exercise within a multilateral framework, and its unwillingness to step outside the role of impartial peacekeeper, was unconvincing in the role of First World crusader on behalf of the oppressed of the Third World. A similar credibility gap was even more apparent in the case of South Africa.

South Africa[1]

Events in 1989

As a system of institutionalized racism, apartheid is unique. In the words of the Eminent Persons Group (EPG), which was created in 1985 by the Commonwealth to explore the possibility of a negotiated settlement in South Africa, apartheid "is awesome in its cruelty. It is achieved and sustained only through force, creating human misery and deprivation and blighting the lives of millions" (Commonwealth Secretariat 1986).

The dynamics of apartheid can perhaps be best understood as the product of a three-cornered system of relationships between closely connected variables—resistance, reform/repression, and sanctions. Black resistance is the dynamic element in the triangle. As resistance increases, it prompts reform/repression and inspires sanctions. Reform/repression is a two-pronged government response to resistance; it comprises an attempt to blunt some resistance by changing the form of white domination without altering its content, while simultaneously crushing the remaining resistance. The mix between reform and resistance in this response partially conditions both future resistance and future sanctions. Sanctions is a word used here to connote a wide range of official and private measures, including disinvestment, trade embargoes and boycotts. As sanctions are imposed, they inspire further resistance and also increase the pressure on the government for more reform/repression.

As 1989 approached in South Africa, the latest phase of this triangular dynamic had been developing for almost five years. The current wave of resistance began with the formation in 1984 of the United Democratic Front (UDF), a group which subscribes to the multiracial principles of the long-banned African National Congress (ANC). In the face of the UDF's success in its campaign to make the black townships of South Africa "ungovernable," the government imposed a State of Emergency in 1985, while simultaneously continuing to search for a political formula that would bring some "moderate" blacks into the system of white domination. The deaths, detentions and bannings occasioned by the State of Emergency (over 3,500 deaths and 35,000 detentions by mid-1988) filled the television screens of the world in 1985 and 1986, prompting an unprecedented wave of sanctions. In response, and as the sanctions began to bite, the government stepped up repression and imposed almost total censorship. In the short run at least, this strategy worked. With the UDF and other organizations banned, and with reporting of dissent censored, domestic resistance slackened after 1987 and the momentum for new sanctions disappeared.

By the beginning of 1989, therefore, a sort of uneasy equilibrium had been reached in South Africa. Surveying the scene, President P.W. Botha would have had little reason to guess that 1989 would see the ignominious end of his political career and the acceleration of resistance and reform/repression under his successor, F.W. de Klerk. For Botha personally, the beginning of the end came with a stroke on January 18. When the severity of Botha's condition became apparent, his cabinet and caucus colleagues in the ruling National Party rebelled against him. He was forced to resign his party leadership in February and the Presidency in August, both in favour of de Klerk.

The crisis in the National Party and the expectation of an election later in the year heated up the simmering black resistance. A hunger strike among detainees spread rapidly, eventually forcing the government to release most of the 1,000 people still in detention. More significantly, the banned UDF resurfaced in the form of the Mass Democratic Movement (MDM), an intentionally amorphous organization that nonetheless successfully mobilized protest during the run-up to the election. In a deliberate imitation of a famous campaign directed by Nelson Mandela for the ANC in 1952, the MDM encouraged people to defy selected apartheid laws. The first target for defiance—segregated hospitals—was particularly well chosen, as the sight of hundreds of black patients presenting themselves for treatment at whites-only hospitals focused the world's attention on unreformed apartheid.

Pushed aside by the MDM's defiance campaign was the election itself, finally set for September 6. In the race for the all-powerful white chamber of Parliament, the National Party faced the staunchly pro-apartheid Conservative Party on its right and the newly-united left in the form of the Democratic Party, which established a milestone in white politics by campaigning on a platform calling for equal political rights for all. As in its successful 1987 election campaign, the National Party presented itself as the party of moderate reform standing between these two "extremes."

In the final weeks of the campaign, de Klerk promised reform and practised repression, much as Botha had done before him. To protect his left flank, he promised renewed reform if elected. To protect his right flank, he cracked down on MDM protests as the campaign wound down. In fact, on election day itself, the police shot twenty-nine demonstrators, the greatest one-day death total since the 1960 Sharpeville Massacre. This prompted the anti-government *Weekly Mail*

(1989) to announce the election results with the following headline: "Nats 93, Cons 39, Dem 33, Wounded 100, Dead 29."

Returned to power with a reduced majority, de Klerk soon made good on his promise of further reform. First, he gave permission for some demonstrations, with the result that South Africa soon witnessed the biggest protest marches in its history. Second, in October he released eight major political prisoners, most notably former ANC Secretary-General Walter Sisulu, and hinted that he might later release ANC leader Nelson Mandela. Third, de Klerk promised several reforms to apartheid law. He promised to scrap the Separate Amenities Act, which permits municipalities to segregate public facilities such as washrooms and parks, and he moved to amend the Group Areas Act to allow selected integrated residential neighbourhoods. Finally, and perhaps most significantly, de Klerk moved to dismantle the State Security Council, an advisory body which under Botha had usurped much decision-making authority from Cabinet and Parliament.

None of de Klerk's actions or promises amounted to a fundamental change in white domination, but nonetheless it was clear that he had gone much further than Botha would ever have done. He had also shown during the final week of the election campaign that he, too, could unleash the forces of repression. The question at the end of 1989 was whether the reform was genuine or whether, as with Botha, repression was the true face of the man.

Canadian Responses

Canadian economic ties to South Africa, though greater than those with Namibia, are not extensive. Table 13.1 presents data on Canadian corporations with investments in South Africa, while Table 13.2 presents trade statistics. As can be seen from the tables, Canadian economic ties to South Africa declined during the 1980s. As of the end of 1988, only one-sixth of the Canadian corporations which had South African investments at the beginning of the decade still held them; the book value of Canadian investment in South Africa had declined from $257 million to $70 million. According to the official 1988 report on the Canadian Code of Conduct for companies doing business in South Africa, businesses had severed their links because "(a) their operations were unprofitable; (b) their major business in the United States was threatened by maintaining South African links ... and (c) in light of the foregoing reasons they were not prepared to put up with the hassle from domestic anti-apartheid forces" (Small 1989). On the trade side, total two-way flow of goods and services declined by almost 50 percent between 1980 and 1988. One way of putting Canada-South Africa economic ties in perspective is to note that, in 1988, trade with South Africa accounted for less than one-tenth of one per cent of Canada's global total.

Table 13.1
Canadian Corporations with Operations in South Africa

	1981	1988	% Change (1981-88)
Number of Firms	36	6	-83
Value of Direct Investment (millions of dollars)	257	70	-73
Number of Employees	25,000*	5,084	-80

* This figure is an approximation derived from the figures for 1985, the earliest year for which such data are available.
Source: John Small, *Report on the Administration and Observance of the Code of Conduct Concerning the Employment Practices of Canadian Companies Operating in South Africa, 1988*. Ottawa: Department of External Affairs, May 1989.

Table 13.2
Canadian Trade with South Africa
(customs basis, thousands of dollars)

Year	Imports	Exports	Total
1980	355,530	202,526	558,056
1981	402,723	239,300	642,023
1982	218,718	213,787	432,505
1983	194,143	165,764	359,907
1984	221,830	201,871	423,701
1985	227,734	150,916	378,650
1986	328,991	151,529	480,520
1987	100,166	102,629	202,795
1988	156,723	139,268	295,991
% Change 1980-1988	-56	-31	-47

Source: Government of Canada, *Summary of Canadian International Trade*. Ottawa: Statistics Canada, various years.

Since business ties were not extensive and were declining, the Canadian government has been relatively unconstrained by economic considerations in developing policy toward South Africa, although, as will be discussed below, there are limits to this autonomy. Therefore, just as with Namibia, the main domestic influence on South African policy has come from the NGO sector. A multitude of anti-apartheid, church, labour and other NGOs has consistently urged the government to impose mandatory and comprehensive sanctions. Though there have been voices raised on the other side of this debate, the weight of public opinion has consistently been in favour of strong measures against apartheid, as was even demonstrated by a 1989 poll paid for by the South African embassy in Ottawa (*Globe and Mail* 1989b).

Indeed, the Conservative government has used its policy-making autonomy to stake out a strong anti-apartheid position. What is striking about the decision-making process in recent years is the extent of leadership by the prime minister. Especially in the 1985-87 period, as Canadians recoiled in horror from the nightly scenes of repression in South Africa on their television screens, Brian Mulroney took the lead in establishing an activist stance on South Africa. Apartheid, he argued, was one area where Canada could make a difference. The extent of Canada's commitment was such that, if no change occurred in South Africa, Canada was willing to impose mandatory sanctions and cut all diplomatic ties. This bold proclamation henceforth became the measure of Canada's sincerity on apartheid.

Much of the international context for Mulroney's crusade has been provided by the Commonwealth. At the Commonwealth Heads of Government Summit in Nassau in 1985, Mulroney helped put together the agreement to establish the Eminent Persons Group. When the EPG mission ended in failure in 1986, Canada enthusiastically implemented the full package of sanctions agreed upon in Nassau (see Table 13.3 for a listing of major Canadian measures against South Africa). At the 1987 Commonwealth Summit in Vancouver, the split over sanctions between Margaret Thatcher and the rest of the Commonwealth was fully revealed. Great Britain, which had refused to implement most of the Nassau package, and which in any case regarded the European Community as the more important model for its sanctions policy, provided trade statistics suggesting that Canada's sanctions rhetoric was hollow hypocrisy. Canada retorted with statistics of its own and proposed the formation of a Commonwealth Committee of Foreign Ministers on Southern Africa (CCFMSA), which would be delegated to pursue action against South Africa between summits. Britain refused to participate in this committee; Canada was made the chair, thus allowing Canadian officials to claim that Canada had assumed the moral leadership of the Commonwealth.

Since 1987, the CCFMSA has met regularly under the chairmanship of External Affairs Minister Clark. Despite this, as Table 13.3 makes clear, almost no new sanctions have been imposed by Canada. In part, this loss of momentum can be attributed to the dynamic of resistance-reform/repression-sanctions discussed above. As the South African government has successfully crushed dissent, and as the whole issue of apartheid has faded from the media spotlight, public pressure for sanctions has lessened in Canada. Accordingly, the prime minister's leadership on the issue has slackened, leaving decision-making on South Africa to Joe Clark and the officials at External Affairs. Although Clark's personal commitment on the issue is undoubted, the fact remains true that without leadership from the prime minister it has become more difficult to adopt new sanctions.

A further cause of the loss of momentum can be attributed to the fact that Canada has adopted all the "easy" measures; any new ones will have a negative domestic economic impact. Many of Canada's early actions either actually benefited the Canadian economy, or else had no impact on it. For example, banning the sale of South African Krugerrands boosted sales of Canada's own Maple Leaf gold coin; banning the import of agricultural commodities had little impact as alternate sources of supply were readily available; and banning direct air links was meaningless since no such links ever existed.

Today, such easy options no longer exist, at least in the realm of trade embargoes. The major commodities Canada imports from South Africa—specialized steel alloys and special wood pulp, for instance—are impossible to obtain at competitive prices elsewhere. Cutting this trade would force closure of Canadian manufacturing plants using these commodities as inputs, for example, a pulp mill in Cornwall, Ontario employing 600 people. On the export side, the main commodity Canada sends to South Africa is sulfur, which is used to produce fertilizer. Alternative markets for sulfur might be found, but an embargo would nonetheless be politically risky, both because the mineral is produced primarily in Alberta, where a government-induced market disruption would hardly be popular, and because much of the sulfur is actually destined for South Africa's black-ruled neighbours, where it is a vital agricultural input.

Table 13.3
Canadian Corporations with Operations in South Africa

1961
—Led movement for South African withdrawal from Commonwealth

1963
—Introduced voluntary arms embargo

1972
—Banned funding of sporting links

1977
—Imposed mandatory UN arms embargo
—Limited sporting contacts
—Downgraded trade promotion

1978
—Established Code of Conduct for Canadian firms in South Africa

1985
—Strengthened Code of Conduct
—Tightened arms embargo
—Abrogated double taxation agreement
—Terminated export promotion
—Further limited sporting contacts
—Introduced voluntary ban on sale of Krugerrands
—Introduced ban on loans to the public and private sectors in South Africa
—Introduced voluntary ban on sale of oil products
—Applied embargo on direct air links
—Established register of measures adopted by Canadians to fight apartheid
—Established program for education of South African blacks

1986
—Ended Canadian government procurement of South African products
—Introduced voluntary ban on tourism promotion
—Cancelled accreditation of non-resident South African attachés to Canada
—Introduced voluntary ban on new investment or reinvestment of profits
—Banned import of agricultural products
—Banned import of uranium, coal, iron and steel
—Curtailed consular services in South Africa

1988
—Banned all South African athletes from competing in Canada
—Introduced program to combat censorship in South Africa

1989
—Tightened ban on loans
—Tightened ban on export of strategic materials

Unable to impose new sanctions, the Canadian government found itself subject to a string of embarrassments in 1989 as it struggled to live up to the inflated expectations created by Mulroney's 1985 UN speech. The first set of embarrassments occurred at the third meeting of the CCFMSA in Harare in February. Preliminary 1988 trade statistics released just prior to the meeting showed a 68 percent increase in imports from South Africa and a 44 percent rise in exports to South Africa over 1987. Although the government could properly argue that these figures were less meaningful than they might appear—the increases largely reflected price changes rather than volume increases and the small totals involved produced dramatic changes in percentage terms—the damage to Canada's reputation as a sanctions leader was nonetheless substantial. New Democratic Party MP Howard McCurdy echoed the feelings of many when he called the trade rise a "slap in the face" and charged that the government had "a commitment to hypocrisy rather than action" (*Globe and Mail* 1989c).

At the CCFMSA meeting itself, Canada's reputation was further damaged when it was announced that the Bank of Nova Scotia intended to make a $600 million loan to Minorco, an off-shore subsidiary of the giant South African conglomerate, Anglo-American. External Affairs Minister Clark was left to explain lamely that this action violated the spirit, but not the letter, of Canada's voluntary ban on private sector loans to South Africa, and was therefore acceptable. Rev. Alan Boesak, a leading South African anti-apartheid activist, called the proposed loan a "vast betrayal" of South Africa's black population (*Africa Research Bulletin* 1989a).

As the fourth meeting of the CCFMSA in Canberra approached in August, the Canadian Council of Churches chastised the government for its "lax" policy on South Africa and urged comprehensive mandatory sanctions. Joe Clark was forced to agree that there had been no fundamental changes in South Africa but retorted that the call for mandatory sanctions was "outdated." He argued instead that the new goal was to "widen, tighten and intensify" existing sanctions (*Globe and Mail* 1989d). At the meeting itself, in an effort to demonstrate continued Canadian leadership, Clark led the call for a focus on so-called financial sanctions. In particular, the Foreign Ministers agreed that the Commonwealth should put pressure on banks not to reschedule US $8 billion of South African government debt due in June 1990. Later, Clark announced that he had assurances from twelve of the fourteen major banks involved that "they would be seeking the highest possible interest payments and the fastest possible repayments" (*Globe and Mail* 1989e).

In fact, the focus on financial sanctions handed the South Africans a major propaganda victory over Canada and the Commonwealth. Immediately prior to the Commonwealth Heads of Government summit in Kuala Lumpur in October, South Africa announced that it had managed to reschedule its debt on favourable terms. Arriving at the summit, an embarrassed Mulroney was at a loss to explain what had happened, though his officials pointed accusatory fingers at Margaret Thatcher, whose government had made no effort to pressure British banks to cooperate. This episode failed to dissuade Mulroney from declaring, however, that he had "staked out for my successors the high moral ground" of opposing apartheid unequivocally and that, "when the question is asked by a new South Africa, 'where did Canada stand and who stood for us,' the word Canada will come back" loud and clear (*Globe and Mail* 1989f).

The tensions between Thatcher and Mulroney over South Africa reached a boiling point when Thatcher released her own declaration on sanctions at the end of the conference, contradicting many key points of the agreed Commonwealth statement which she herself had signed. Mulroney denounced Thatcher for undermining Commonwealth co-operation, while Thatcher found it "astounding and appalling" that Mulroney would suggest that she should not explain her position publicly (*Globe and Mail* 1989g). In commenting on this "sandbox spat," the *Globe and Mail* opined that, if Thatcher had "wilfully put herself on the wrong side of morality and history," Mulroney's grandiose claims were "pompous, self-serving and hypocritical" (*Globe and Mail* 1989h). The only concrete result of the summit was the renewal of the mandate of the CCFMSA for six months, though it was unclear what changes were expected to occur in South Africa in that time.

Conclusion

At least since 1985, Canada has taken a very strong moral stand against apartheid and has led the international fight for sanctions against South Africa. Significant measures were imposed by Canada in the 1985-87 period and the Commonwealth, with Canada taking the lead, set the agenda for much of the world-wide sanctions movement. Since 1987, however, Canada has found it increasingly difficult to impose new measures of its own or to convince its more influential allies, especially Great Britain, to follow its lead. Canada has therefore found itself in a very exposed position, proclaiming moral leadership but unable to deliver results. In 1989, the consequence was a series of embarrassments, which made the government appear ineffectual and hypocritical. The irony in this perception was that the government's inflated claims for its policies obscured the fact that by 1989 the sanctions imposed by Canada and other countries were indeed beginning to have an impact, as no less an authority than the Governor of the South African Reserve Bank candidly admitted (*Africa Research Bulletin* 1989b).

On Namibia, the government did not get itself into nearly as much trouble in 1989. Even here, however, inflated assertions of Canada's willingness and ability to act as an advocate for Third World interests obscured an otherwise praiseworthy role in contributing to the success of the transition process.

In sum, a lack of direct economic ties has given Canadian policy makers the autonomy to stake out strong moral positions on southern African affairs. In the past, these positions have allowed the government to cultivate a progressive image at home and abroad as a leader in the struggle against apartheid. More recently the government's rhetoric has unfortunately run ahead of its capacity to impose new sanctions of its own and of its ability to convince its more influential allies to follow its lead, thus creating a major credibility gap. As a result, in 1989 the real successes of Canadian policy on southern Africa were obscured by the rhetorical failures. Sadly, the prime minister's exaggerated claims for Canada's role made at the Commonwealth summit suggest that the temptation to substitute rhetoric for analysis on southern Africa is still all too prevalent.

Notes

[1] In February 1990 President de Klerk announced a series of reforms including the unbanning of the ANC and other political organizations, the release of Nelson Mandela and other political prisoners, and the relaxation of the State of Emergency.

References

Africa Research Bulletin. 1989a. "Canada's Embarrassment." March 31: 9465-9466.

_____. 1989b. "Surviving Sanctions." February 28: 9429.

Canada. 1989. Department of External Affairs. "Namibia: Clark Welcomes Refugee Repatriation and Urges Full Release of Detainees." News Release No. 144 Ottawa, June 15.

Commonwealth Secretariat. 1986. *Mission to South Africa: The Commonwealth Report.* London: Penguin Books.

Freeman, Linda. 1986. "What's Right with Mulroney?: Canada and Sanctions, 1986." *Southern Africa Report.* October 1986: 3-8.

Globe and Mail. 1989a. "SWAPO broke accord, Clark acknowledges." (Paul Koring) April 7.

_____. 1989b. "Canadians oppose sanctions, embassy says." (Howard Ross) August 9.

_____. 1989c. "Trade rise 'slap in face' to apartheid opponents." (Charlotte Montgomery and Susan Delacourt) January 27.

_____. 1989d. "Apartheid foes betrayed by Ottawa, churches say." (Howard Ross) August 18.

_____. 1989e. "South Africa sidesteps short-term debt squeeze." October 20: 3.

_____. 1989f. "Mulroney takes credit for anti-apartheid push." October 21: 4.

_____. 1989g. "Thatcher's action called threat to Commonwealth cooperation." October 24: 4.

_____. 1989h. "Preening and Posturing on South Africa." October 24.

Small, John. 1989. *Report on the Administration and Observance of the Code of Conduct Concerning the Employment Practices of Canadian Companies Operating in South Africa, 1988.* Ottawa: Department of External Affairs.

Weekly Mail (Johannesburg). 1989. "Nats 93, Cons 39, Dem 33, Wounded 100, Dead 29." Sept. 13-19.

14 Canada and Central America

Tim Draimin and Liisa North

Central America's civil wars became a major international issue in the 1980s. The radical nationalism of the Sandinista Revolution in Nicaragua and the eruption of civil war in El Salvador and Guatemala were perceived by Washington as manifestations of Soviet-Cuban expansionism in the Western hemisphere. The resultant U.S. policy of military "roll-back" became in turn the catalyst for a new Latin American assertiveness centred on the principles of self-determination and non-intervention. Latin American nations—especially the regional middle powers—entered the international diplomatic stage with a cohesion and boldness that had yet to be witnessed.

The deterioration in U.S.-Latin American relations and the eventual international isolation of the United States led the Bush administration to adopt the trappings of multilateralism and to tone down the rhetorical war of the Reagan years. However, as the decade drew to a close, no fundamental changes in Washington's policies towards Central America had been initiated. The trade embargo against Nicaragua, an unwillingness to dismantle the Contras, massive military assistance to El Salvador, the advocacy of reliance on market forces to resolve the region's economic problems, and accusations of combined Soviet and Cuban interference all continued, even as the Central American nations attempted to maintain the momentum of the peace process propelled by the Esquipulas II accord of August 1987. Finally, the apparent incapacity of the United States to reorient its foreign policy in the hemisphere towards diplomatic channels and away from military action was dramatically illustrated in the closing days of 1989 by the U.S. invasion of Panama, which exacerbated regional tensions and animosities once more.

The makers of Canada's policy toward the region were caught between the Latin American advocacy of peace through negotiations and the U.S. goal of military victory over revolutionary forces. Ottawa agreed with Latin American peacemakers that Central America's conflicts derived essentially from historic problems of social and economic inequity and political oppression rather than Soviet-Cuban expansionism. More importantly, U.S. policy towards the region violated the fundamental tenets on which Canadian foreign policy has rested: respect for international law, the peaceful resolution of disputes, the principle of self-determination, and recourse to multilateral institutions; it threatened an escalation of military conflict and direct U.S. military intervention—both of which would have a destabilizing impact in the hemisphere; and it produced enormous refugee outflows that became a contentious domestic issue in Canada. All of this, in turn, generated a high level of media and public attention as well as informed demand for a foreign policy clearly independent of the United States—Canada's principal ally and trading partner but also the principal obstacle to the resolution of the Central American crisis.

   This chapter first examines the efforts of Latin American countries to obtain negotiated solutions to the conflicts in the region. It then turns to an analysis of the various aspects of Canadian policy, focusing on diplomacy, development assistance, and peacekeeping; given limitations of space, refugee policy will be mentioned only briefly. The concluding remarks will attempt to sketch the basic hemispheric issues confronting Canada in the 1990s.[1]

The Latin American-Led Peace Process

In sharp contrast to Washington, the Latin Americans—whether or not they liked what they saw—viewed the Sandinista Resolution in Nicaragua and the emergence of revolutionary movements elsewhere in Central America as manifestations of popular demands for long-overdue reform of archaic, inequitable socio-economic structures and political institutions. For them, the conflicts in the region derived from the history of what Enrique Baloyra has called "reactionary despotism" (Baloyra 1983) and from the U.S. role in the maintenance of the "despotic" regimes that had imposed a particularly inequitable economic modernization model on the region's societies (Maira 1983).

   Not only Cuba, but also U.S. allies—Costa Rica, Panama, and Venezuela—gave the Sandinistas much military and diplomatic assistance in their struggle against the Somoza family dynasty. Latin American countries also rejected the Carter administration's efforts to prevent the dissolution of the dictator's National Guard in the course of the Sandinistas' final offensive.

Disagreements between the Latin Americans and the United States deepened into near confrontation with the inauguration of President Reagan in 1981. The principal Latin American democracies saw the United States behaving like an imperialist bully, exacerbating a series of difficult but manageable conflicts to the point of converting them into a protracted major crisis. Following real, though problematic, movement towards multilateralism and consultation during the Carter administration, the unilateralist posture of the Reagan White House, and its penchant for military rather than diplomatic solutions, appeared to be a regression to the worst moments in U.S.-Latin American relations. Latin Americans perceived the U.S. recourse to military force—the organization of the contras, the mining of Nicaragua's harbours, the sharply increased military assistance to El Salvador, the war games in Honduras—as a threat to the "national security of all of the countries of the continent," and they rejected any consideration of the "East-West thesis" as a potential legitimization of "the supposed right of the great powers to divide Latin American territory into zones of influence according to the dynamic of their respective interests" (Garcia 1987: 17).

To take Mexico as an example, although its active support of the Sandinistas and calls for a negotiated settlement in El Salvador were in contradiction with the Reagan administration's crusade in Central America, most notably in the early 1980s, its foreign policy was not out of line with Latin American reactions in general. Of course, those reactions were not unanimous. But as civilian governments replaced military dictatorships in South America, consensus on the desirability of negotiations widened. Thus Argentina, Brazil, Peru, and Uruguay formed the Contadora Support Group in 1985 to back the peacemaking efforts of Colombia, Mexico, Panama, and Venezuela, which had established the Contadora Group early in 1983.

The Contadora and Support Groups' peace proposals, all of which involved the dissolution of the Contras, were consistently opposed by the United States which, until 1987, succeeded in maintaining three of its four regional allies—Costa Rica, El Salvador, and Honduras, but not Guatemala—on board (see Chronological Table). However, by that year, the economic, political, and human costs of the regional conflicts had mounted to such a point that even those small and highly dependent nations became willing to contest U.S. policy. Despite strong pressure from the White House, President Oscar Arias of Costa Rica insisted on pursuing his peace plan and a difficult process of de-escalating a regional conflict was set into motion with the signing of the Esquipulas II accord on August 7, 1987 (Chace 1987).

The accord's call for the termination of external support for all "irregular forces and insurrectionist movements" fighting against established governments applied, most particularly, to the U.S.-financed Contras. Esquipulas II also committed the Central American nations to resolve domestic conflicts by taking steps towards social and political democratization and negotiations with opposition groups; to form National Reconciliation Commissions to promote dialogue and verify compliance with the terms of the accord; to work towards regional solutions to refugee relief and resettlement, the revitalization of economic cooperation, and the organization of a Central American parliament. Finally, it stated that the support of the international community was essential for converting the accord into reality.

CHRONOLOGICAL TABLE
THE CENTRAL AMERICAN PEACE PROCESS:
SELECTED LATIN AMERICAN INITIATIVES AND
U.S. REACTIONS

August 1981:
Mexico and France recognize the Salvadoran revolutionary opposition as a "representative political force" and call for negotiations.

September 1982:
Presidents of Mexico and Venezuela send letter to U.S. president Reagan, offering to mediate between Honduras and Nicaragua.

January 8-9, 1983:
Foreign ministers of Panama, Mexico, Colombia, and Venezuela meet on the Panamanian Island of Contadora and sign "The Contadora Declaration," a general statement of principles for building peace in Central America.

September 7, 1984:
Central American and Contadora Group foreign ministers meet and issue the draft "Contadora Act on Peace and Cooperation in Central America." It is accepted by Nicaragua and the other Central American countries also indicate their willingness to sign it.

October 20, 1984:
Following a visit by Secretary of State Schultz to Central America, the foreign ministers of Costa Rica, Honduras, Guatemala, and El Salvador meet in Tegucigalpa to discuss September 7 draft and issue (with Guatemala abstaining) the "Revised Tegucigalpa Draft of the Contadora Act." Nicaragua objects to the revisions.

July 27, 1985:
At the inauguration of Peru's President Alan Garcia, "The Lima Declaration" is signed and results in the formation of the Contadora Support Group composed of Argentina, Brazil, Peru, and Uruguay.

September 12, 1985:
Second Contadora draft treaty is presented. It is rejected by Nicaragua.

February 10, 1986:
Secretary of State Schultz meets with the Contadora and Support Group foreign ministers and rejects their request to delay the U.S. government's plan for U.S.$100 million in new aid to the Contras.

June 5-6, 1986:
Contadora and Support Group nations meet in Panama to prepare new draft treaty which they call "the last version." It is accepted by Nicaragua but criticized by Costa Rica, El Salvador, and Honduras.

January 17-20, 1987:
Efforts to revive the Contadora process draw in the Secretaries-General of the United Nations and the Organization of American States (OAS). The United States opposes their initiatives.

February 15, 1987:
Costa Rican peace plan prepared in consultation with El Salvador, Honduras, and Guatemala is announced by President Arias and supported by Democrats in the U.S. Congress.

August 7, 1987:
Esquipulas II accord (a modified version of the Arias plan) is signed by the five Central American presidents. An alternative plan submitted earlier by the United States is not considered.

January 14-16, 1988:
The report of the International Verification Commission (CIVS), set up under the terms the Esquipulas II accord, states that ending U.S. aid to the Contras is the "indispensable requirement" for the success of the accord. The CIVS (composed of the foreign ministers of the Contadora and Support Group nations and the Central American five) is subsequently dissolved at the behest of El Salvador, Guatemala, and Honduras.

November 29-December 4, 1988:
Central American foreign ministers meet in Mexico at inauguration of President Salinas de Gortari to renew the peace process; they call for a new verification commission and a UN peacekeeping presence.

February 13-14, 1989:
Meeting in Costa del Sol, El Salvador, the presidents of the five Central American nations discuss the implementation of the peace accord, including the stationing of UN observers to verify the removal of the Contras from the Honduras-Nicaragua border. The bipartisan plan agreed upon by Congress and President Bush, however, continues to provide "humanitarian" assistance to the Contras.

August 7, 1989:
Meeting in Tela, Honduras, the presidents of the five Central American nations call for the creation of a joint UN-OAS International Support and Verification Commission (CIAV) to supervise the demobilization of the Contras by December 5, 1989.

December 12, 1989:
Meeting in San Isidro de Coronado, Costa Rica, the Central American presidents call for the channeling of all "approved" funding to the Contras through the yet to be created CIAV.

The Diplomatic Challenge and the Domestic Debate

As the Central American crisis deepened and the United States pursued its policies of "roll back" through "low intensity war," Canadian public concern grew and so did advocacy of a more independent foreign policy for Canada. But Ottawa, in the midst of free trade negotiations, avoided open criticism of U.S. policy, while at the same time seeking to identify itself, first, with the Latin American diplomatic initiatives oriented toward de-escalation and negotiations, and subsequently with the Esquipulas II process.

Central America became one of the most prominent foreign policy questions for Canadians during the 1980s. A well-articulated and well-informed network of institutions made it possible to mobilize more concern, and more public advocacy, with regard to Central American affairs than had been devoted to any other Third World issue. The network comprised a broad range of non-governmental organizations (NGOs), church agencies, labour groups, and academic circles. A 1984 Gallup poll disclosed that Canadians opposed U.S. policy in the region by a two-to-one margin. A poll commissioned by the government in 1987 revealed that over two-thirds of Canadians believed that Canada should pursue a foreign policy which would be more independent of the United States.

Parliamentary interest in the Central American crisis was reflected in the number of committees that addressed the issue and members of Parliament were impressed by the public response to their debates. In 1981-1982, members of the Parliamentary Sub-Committee on Canada's Relations with Latin America and the Caribbean expressed surprise at the interest manifested in its proceedings by communities across the country (SCEAND 1982). The Sub-Committee's final report recommended that Central America be recognized as a foreign policy priority. In 1986, the Special Joint Committee on Canada's International Relations reported that it had received more submissions on Central America than on any other subject (Special Joint Committee 1986a). In 1988, the proceedings of the House of Commons Special Committee on the Peace Process in Central America were closely monitored by human rights and religious groups, NGOs and labour organizations, and the academic community (House of Commons Special Committee 1988).

On the whole, the reports and recommendations of these three committees proposed initiatives which would have asserted Canada's position, over that of the U.S., more strongly than did those pursued by the government. The last of the three advocated strong diplomatic support for the Central American five, substantially increased development assistance, and participation in peacekeeping missions—proposals accepted by the government in principle.

In effect, public and parliamentary concern forced Central America higher on the Canadian government's foreign policy agenda than would otherwise have been the case. That concern also counteracted, to some extent, steady pressure from the United States and the fear harboured by Ottawa, from 1985 onwards, of upsetting the course of the free trade negotiations. At the same time, however, the accusations of free trade opponents that the agreement would infringe on Canadian sovereignty in international affairs provided an inducement for the government to highlight certain policy differences with the United States.

In short, the government felt constrained "to do something" to satisfy public demands and to support the Latin American middle powers in their quest for negotiated solutions. But fears of antagonizing the United States precluded assertively independent action. These contradictory pressures yielded the political and diplomatic balancing act summarized as "quiet diplomacy": expressions of sympathetic interest for, and willingness to assist in, peace promotion undertaken by Latin American countries—but only in a low-key and relatively passive fashion— combined with occasional polite expressions of discomfort with U.S. policy. On the one hand, government officials consistently expressed support for the Contadora-led negotiations process, stressed the indigenous social, political, and economic sources of the conflicts, and opposed militarization and external intervention in general. On the other, unlike the Latin Americans and also some European nations, Canada avoided criticism of the United States, the principal external actor and the country that consistently violated the very principles on which Canadian foreign policy stands. One academic expert spelled out the gap between appearance and reality in the following terms:

> Essentially, then, Canada would endorse unreservedly a mutually accepted agreement reached by the Contadora countries. If the ... [Contadora process] broke down, however, Canada would express public support for reconciliation while it quietly backed the United States.
> In the unlikely event that the United States intervened directly in the region, Canada might well express a certain amount of indignation, but ultimately would do nothing substantive (Lemco 1986: 16-17)

Nevertheless, Canada's support for the Contadora process was more than verbal. The government provided detailed technical advice on the security and control provisions of the Contadora treaty proposals. Canada supported partial peace efforts by witnessing negotiations between the Nicaraguan government and MISURASATA, the native peoples' organization that opposed the Sandinista government in the mid-1980s; and offered technical assistance in the design of a proposed Costa Rican-Nicaraguan joint border commission in 1986. Ottawa also refused to go along with the U.S. embargo of trade with Nicaragua and increased its development assistance to that country; it also voted in favour of the United Nations General Assembly resolution calling on the United States to comply with the June 1986 ruling of the International Court of Justice which demanded cessation of aid to the Contras and payment of reparations to Nicaragua.

However, while taking these helpful steps, Ottawa actually reduced its diplomatic representation in the region.[2] Moreover, it never actively sought out multilateral fora to express support for the peace process or to question U.S. actions. Unlike several other heads of state,[3] the prime minister never spoke out in the United States. Canada's declarations of opposition to third-party intervention and aid to irregular forces studiously avoided directly addressing U.S. funding of the Contras and the flagrant American role in the militarization of the region. A case in point was the prime minister's address to the Inter-American Press Association meeting in Vancouver in September 1986: Mulroney stated: "we do not approve of any country supplying arms to any faction in the area ... whoever the third party may be, and regardless of its legitimate interests in the area" (Office of the Prime Minister 1986b). The contrast with both the directness of Canada's response to the analogous situation in Southern Africa, and the candour of statements made by Contadora members and European nations, was notable.[4]

Ottawa's answer to requests for election monitoring in the region reflected the overall ambiguity of its policies. Nicaraguan invitations to furnish aid to send observers to its 1984 national elections were rejected and NGO observers' reports concerning the fairness of those elections were discounted by Ottawa. Still, in late 1989, the secretary of state for external affairs implicitly denied the legitimacy of those earlier elections when he expressed the hope that "Chile and Nicaragua" will soon make "the historic and brave transition from dictatorship to democracy" (*Nicaragua Election Observer* 1989b). Only when international support for Nicaragua's February 1990 elections had become overwhelming did Canada commit significant assistance (more than CAN $700,000) to that country's Supreme Electoral Council (CSE). However, it did not escape critics that, as in the case of development assistance, Western European contributions surpassed Canada's; West Germany, for example, provided $1.6 million (*Nicaragua Election Observer* 1989a).

Meanwhile, Canada sent official observer missions to El Salvador and Guatemala, providing a measure of legitimacy for their elections, but not much objective evaluation of them. The escalation of violence in El Salvador during the second half of 1989, following the inauguration of the government of President Cristiani (the candidate of the extreme right ARENA party, associated with death squads), eventually did lead Ottawa to endorse negotiations as a necessary step toward peace. However, Ottawa refused to comment on the U.S. military assistance that kept the war going.

The basic elements of a policy mix which would be compatible with a "quiet diplomacy" of attempting to satisfy both the United States and the Latin Americans were to be increased official development assistance (ODA) and participation in UN-sponsored peacekeeping. Both could be conceived in technical rather than political terms and both had the obvious attraction of being as unquestionable as "motherhood" to the Canadian public.

But without a coherent diplomatic position, increased ODA, as well as other policy initiatives, resulted in rather weak and muddled gestures. For example, during his November 1987 tour of Central America, Joe Clark, the Secretary of State for External Affairs, announced major new development assistance to Honduras precisely at a moment when Honduras, under U.S. and local military pressure, had done less than any other Central American country to comply with the August 1987 Esquipulas II peace accord that Canada was supposedly supporting. Meanwhile, no major assistance was announced for Nicaragua, although the country's compliance record was the best in the region. It was after that tour, and the public outcry over the ODA announcements, that the government established the Special Committee on the Peace Process in Central America.

Development Assistance for Whom?

Contadora and the Esquipulas II accord identified development assistance as essential for peace building, but at the end of the 1980s Ottawa had not responded fully to that challenge. ODA to Central America did increase in the 1980s, in a setting of controversy around the issues of country choices and programme focus. Both these issues, in turn, related to the broader issues of the importance that should be assigned to human rights considerations in the allocation of ODA, and the capacity and willingness of the different Central American governments to pursue development policies directed towards the alleviation of the inequalities that were at the root of conflict in the region.

By fiscal year 1987/88, total direct aid to the region had reached CAN $55.1 million. Although still a modest amount, this represented a sharp increase in money terms: more than double the CAN $22.1 million of 1981/82. In real terms (taking inflation into account), the increase was much less. Moreover, and most contradictorily, in view of the government's declarations of intent to increase ODA in support of Esquipulas II, assistance to the region during fiscal 1988/89 actually declined to CAN $50.7 (CIDA 1989).

Bilateral aid to Costa Rica and Nicaragua—Central America's most democratic societies—increased most rapidly. Honduras, however, where militarization caused a deterioration of the human rights situation, remained a key country in Canadian International Development Agency (CIDA) programming. El Salvador and Guatemala trailed behind, since bilateral assistance to both had been suspended in 1981.

Even the later, higher amounts of Canadian aid left Canada trailing fifth among Western donors to the region over the period 1981 to 1986 (OECD 1986, 1987, 1988). Ottawa lagged behind not only the United States but also West Germany, The Netherlands and Japan. Given Canada's location in the hemisphere, the ODA profile could only be interpreted as part of the generally cautious stance of the country's diplomacy resulting from the conflicting demands emanating from the United States and Latin American countries, and from the Canadian public.

Non-controversial ODA choices were not easily available to Ottawa. Canadians questioned the renewal of ODA to U.S. allies Guatemala and El Salvador and would not tolerate high-profile assistance to either country. Costa Rica, by Third World and regional standards, was relatively prosperous. Honduras' capacity to use increased aid effectively and honestly was questionable, especially in the light of the massive U.S. military and economic assistance programs in that country. Moreover, Honduras played host to the Contras.

While informed Canadians favoured substantially increased assistance to Nicaragua, the United States would have looked askance at such a move. Assistance was provided to that beleaguered nation but it did not respond to Nicaragua's increasingly urgent needs, as the Contra war destroyed clinics, schools, cooperatives, and infrastructure. Indeed, Canadian aid was modest in comparison to that of other Western donors (OECD 1986, 1987, 1988). Sweden alone provided in 1988/89 a development assistance package to Nicaragua of U.S.$31 million, more than four times the amount provided by Canada in that year.

The explanation for these differences may well lie in the presence of powerful social democratic parties—whether in or out of government—in several Western European countries. Although the relationships between the Sandinistas and the member parties of the Socialist International were often tense during the 1980s, social democrats, on the whole, saw the reforms sponsored by Nicaragua's revolutionary government as steps towards the resolution of the country's historic problems of social inequity and political repression, and therefore as a positive model for the region as a whole. Although the Canadian government too repeatedly stated that the roots of conflict in the region lay in social injustice and political repression, its ODA choices did not fully reflect that understanding.

Probably the most contentious of its ODA decisions was the renewal of bilateral assistance to El Salvador in 1985 and to Guatemala in 1987. Ottawa had suspended bilateral aid to both countries in November 1981 because of concerns about the safety of Canadian field staff, systematic patterns of gross human rights violations, and the political instability arising out of their civil wars. Termination of aid followed in the wake of the murder of a lay missionary from New Brunswick, apparently at the hands of Guatemalan security forces, and a monstrous escalation of death squad assassinations and military abuse in El Salvador.

To justify renewal, Ottawa argued that the human rights situation had improved significantly. But critics pointed to a continued pattern of gross violations, military abuse and dominance, and a lack of capacity or willingness on the part of the recipient governments to pursue redistributive reforms or to open up the political process—that is, to address the causes of war. Although, at the moment of renewal, Guatemala was highly supportive of the Esquipulas II endeavour and had earlier backed the Contadora process, neither that country nor El Salvador had made progress towards terminating its own civil war through dialogue. In fact, aid to El Salvador was renewed immediately after a series of highly questionable elections in which the left opposition parties could not participate.

As has been argued in a major study of Canadian aid to El Salvador, prepared by the Latin American Working Group (LAWG), the political implications of the renewal of aid to that country could not be denied. By "choosing to deliver Canadian aid through bilateral, government-to-government channels, and ... through the way the resumption of aid is explained, the Canadian government is taking a position on El Salvador—on the current political and human rights situation, on possible or desirable outcomes of the conflict ..." (*LAWG Letter* 1987: 11). The LAWG study argued further that the overwhelming presence of the United States in El Salvador distorted policy making to such an extent that any Canadian bilateral assistance program was rendered irrelevant at best, or, at worst, served to buttress U.S.-financed militarization. As an investigative report in *The New York Times Magazine* summarized the situation, "Instead of fostering reform, [one billion dollars in U.S. military aid] has been absorbed into a network of corruption and patronage that has grown up over a half a century, and has made the Salvadoran military an empire unto itself" (Millman 1989).

Indeed, the very high levels of corruption prevailing in the two countries, not only in military but also in civilian circles, were another major cause for concern among critics of the renewals. For example, the *Wall Street Journal* disclosed that a confidential U.S. State Department report on El Salvador documented "the diversion of U.S.$20 million intended for reconstruction ... to the private bank accounts of Christian Democratic activists and officials" (*Caribbean Insight* 1987: 11). The delivery of Canadian bilateral assistance to El Salvador was suspended again in November 1989, following the army's gruesome assassination of six Jesuit priests at the Central American University and the indiscriminate bombing and strafing of the capital's lower-income neighbourhoods with which the government responded to the fall offensive of the Farabundo Marti National Liberation Front.

Canada's ODA choices appeared to be constrained by other priorities—avoidance of irritation to the United States and, after the signing of Esquipulas II, maintaining acceptability to all five countries as a participant in planned peace observing missions. Two weeks after bilateral development assistance was renewed to Guatemala, that country's foreign minister, without the slightest embarrassment, returned the compliment by nominating Canada for participation in what was to become the United Nations Observer Group in Central America (ONUCA).

Refugee Policy: From Open to Closed Doors

As in the case of ODA choices, refugee policy, especially during the second half of the 1980s, provoked a great deal of controversy. The Canadian government first responded helpfully to the massive displacement of peoples from the region—by 1987, up to 18 per cent of the region's population may have been internally displaced or forced to flee to other countries. Between 1982 and 1986, approximately three thousand refugees per annum (mostly from El Salvador and Guatemala) were admitted to Canada under the terms of special programs. In addition, Canada provided assistance to the Central American work of the UN High Commission for Refugees and the International Committee of the Red Cross. However, when changes in U.S. immigration laws threatened thousands of undocumented refugees with deportation and triggered a massive influx of refugee claimants into Canada in late 1986 and early 1987, the government modified its refugee policy and proposed controversial restrictive changes to refugee law. These were passed by the House of Commons in July 1988, despite sustained public protest.

Peacekeeping: A Safe and Traditional Role

Technical advice on verification was provided by Canada to the Contadora Group in the preparation of the Group's draft treaties; similar advice was lent to Esquipulas II. By the end of the decade, Canada was deeply involved in peacekeeping as a member of the United Nations Observer Mission in Central America, together with Ireland, Spain, and Latin American countries. ONUCA was approved by the Security Council in November 1989, and given the task of monitoring compliance with the Esquipulas II accord's international security clauses. Ottawa pledged about 40 observers and eight light helicopters, crews and support staff for the U.N. security verification mechanism and, in early December, a nine-member advance party of Canadian military personnel left to join ONUCA in Tegucigalpa, Honduras.

These initiatives had broad public support and would significantly increase Canadian involvement in Central America. With Canadian observers on the ground, both the media and the public were likely to pay more attention to the region. The meagre Canadian diplomatic representation in Central America would also have to be augmented (Canada maintains diplomatic relations with all Central American states but has an ambassador only in San José, Costa Rica). Peace-keeping, however, can be undertaken as a "technical" matter without adopting a broader political and diplomatic stand that addresses the fundamental issues. Indeed, the adoption of a peacekeeping role can be used to justify "neutrality": how can a "neutral" peacekeeper decry U.S. intervention and financing of militarization?

In offering to take on peacekeeping functions, the government was apparently moving in this formalistic direction. Thus in November 1989, when asked about Canada's reaction to the suspension of the Sandinistas' unilateral cease-fire in the midst of escalating Contra attacks that were disrupting the preparations for the February 1990 elections, Secretary of State Clark contended that Canada did not have enough resources to ascertain whether the Contras were actually staging attacks in Nicaragua (Clark 1989). In effect, Clark ducked the controversial point of continued U.S. financing of the Contras. Similarly, as noted above, although Canada eventually came to advocate negotiations in El Salvador, it refused to criticize U.S. military assistance to that country, even as human rights violations multiplied and the civil war intensified in the fall of 1989. Interestingly, Spain, although also an ONUCA member, did not hesitate to publicly criticize Washington in that respect.

Conclusions

Canada's overall performance with regard to Central America could be described as a combination of modest involvement, good will and minimal initiative, accompanied by maximum promotion of its role at home to respond to domestic critics. It would be wrong to overestimate the influence that a middle power like Canada could have in a region like Central America. Nevertheless, Ottawa clearly held back from making a greater contribution than it actually provided by circumscribing the mandate for its diplomacy and limiting the resources committed. At the same time, events in Central America were the driving force behind Canada's tentative and erratic moves toward a stronger hemispheric focus in its foreign policy.

Canada's decision, taken in fall 1989, to join the Organization of American States (OAS) was criticized by some observers as yet another move to create the appearance of action in the hemisphere which had no real content. Whatever the pros and cons of joining, with membership a *fait accompli* the development of a coherent and independent foreign policy towards Latin America in general, and the Central American crisis in particular, became all the more urgent. As a *Globe and Mail* (1989a) editorial stated, "Until now, Canadian politicians have been more comfortable whispering their disapproval of U.S. policy in Central America or Cuba.... Now Canada must very publicly assert an independent policy or find itself dismissed as a characterless weakling." As Latin Americans looked towards Canada to become "a political ally to help them resist the heavy weight of U.S. influence" in the OAS, Ottawa would be faced with critical choices in the 1990s (*Globe and Mail* 1989b).

Indeed, the first critical choice came in mid-December 1989, when Ottawa's inauspicious response to the U.S. invasion of Panama was to "mindlessly link itself to its North American partner" (*Toronto Star* 1989). Instead of standing up for the principles of international law and non-intervention, Prime Minister Mulroney regretted, but endorsed, the military action as necessary. As the director of Washington's independent Council on Hemispheric Affairs noted, Canada's "support for intervention in Panama destroyed all illusions in Latin America that the Mulroney government was readying an independent course on hemispheric issues" (*Toronto Star* 1989).

Nevertheless, Latin American pressure for a more critical Canadian policy towards Washington, and an independent role in hemispheric affairs, will certainly grow, as will the pressures on Ottawa to commit more resources, increase the size of its diplomatic representation, and upgrade the region's profile at the Department of External Affairs and International Trade. It is the allies of the U.S., and Canada prominently among them as a hemispheric middle power, that have a special responsibility for weaning the United States away from its imperial stance and its penchant for military reactions to the conflicts that it faces in its relations with Latin America. Washington must be discouraged from further poisoning its relations with Latin America and thereby prejudicing its own long-term security and that of the hemisphere and the world as a whole. Perversely, it appears that the much improved U.S.-Soviet relations, and the de-escalation of conflict in other regions of the world where the superpowers were facing each other, may leave the United States more inclined to revert to its traditional pattern of crass intervention in its "backyard." That, in turn, could undermine Gorbachev's policies of opening up Soviet attitudes toward the West, since hard liners in the Communist party and in the civilian and military bureaucracies of the Soviet Union will certainly argue that the United States is not reciprocating and cannot be trusted.

As in the 1980s, so in the 1990s, Central America's conflicts and the U.S. involvement in them will continue to be a testing ground for Canada's hemispheric role. The fundamental issues will also remain the same: respect for international law, the peaceful resolution of conflicts, and the principle of self-determination, together with the design of international economic policies that could promote equitable development and democratization in the region. The 1980s demonstrated that Canada had not yet achieved the maturity needed for confronting these issues with a confident independent stance. Whether the country will do so in the 1990s is an open question.

Notes

[1] This chapter draws heavily from earlier works completed by the authors, especially from North (1990) (ed.), *Between War and Peace in Central America: Choices for Canada* (Toronto: Between The Lines).

[2] Canada withdrew its Ambassador from Guatemala in 1986; it now has only a chargé d'affaires there.

[3] Among them François Mitterand of France, Raul Alfonsin of Argentina, Felipe González of Spain, Oscar Arias of Costa Rica, and Miguel de la Madrid of Mexico.

[4] For example, Sweden's minister for foreign affairs stated: "American support to the Contras is obstructing ... a settlement and is in violation of the fundamental principles of international law on which Contadora's work is based" (Government of Sweden 1987).

References

Baloyra, Enrique. 1983. "Reactionary Despotism in El Salvador: an Impediment to Democratic Transition." In *Trouble in Our Backyard: Central America and the United States in the Eighties*, edited by Martin Diskin. New York: Pantheon Books.

Canada. 1982. Parliament. House of Commons. Report of the Standing Committee on External Affairs and National Defence (SCEAND), Sub-Committee on Canada's Relations with Latin America and the Caribbean. Ottawa: Supply and Services.

_____. 1986a. Parliament. *Independence and Internationalism.* Report of the Special Joint Committee on Canada's International Relations. Ottawa: Supply and Services.

_____. 1986b. Office of the Prime Minister. "Notes for Address by the Right Honourable Brian Mulroney, Prime Minister, before the Inter-American Press Association". Vancouver. September 15.

_____. 1988. Parliament. House of Commons. *Supporting the Five: Canada and the Central American Peace Process.* First Report of the House of Commons Special Committee on the Peace Process in Central America. Ottawa: Supply and Services.

_____. 1989. Canadian International Development Agency (CIDA). *Summary of Canadian Aid to Central America 1984-89.* Hull.

Caribbean Insight. 1987. 10, no. 12. December.

Chace, James. 1987. "The End of the Affair?" *New York Review of Books.* October 8.

Clark, Rt. Hon. J. 1989. Interview CBC Morningside. November 2.

Garcia, Medrano Renward. 1987. "Centroamerica: UN Memo Latinamericano." Action Committee for Socio-economic Development in Central America (CADESCA). mimeo.

Globe and Mail. 1989a. "Why Canada Belongs in OAS." (Editorial) October 28.

_____. 1989b. "Expectations high for Canadian role in OAS." (Linda Hossie) October 26.

Government of Sweden. 1987. Statement by the Minister for Foreign Affairs, Mr. Sten Andersson, on Contadora. Press Release, Ministry for Foreign Affairs. Stockholm, January 19.

Latin American Working Group (LAWG). 1987. "Taking Sides: Canadian Aid to El Salvador." *Letter.* X:1. December.

Lemco, Jonathan. 1988. "Canada and Central America: A Review of Current Issues." *Behind the Headlines.* XLIII:5. May.

Maira, Luis. 1983. "Reagan and Central America: Policy Through a Fractured Lens." In *Trouble in our Backyard: Central America and the United States in the Eighties,* edited by Martin Diskin. New York: Pantheon Books.

Millman, Joel. 1989. "El Salvador's Army: A Force Unto Itself." *New York Times Magazine.* December 10.

Nicaragua Election Observer. 1989a. "Aid for Elections is Key to Peace." 1. October 20.

_____. 1989b. "Challenges for Canada". 5. December 15.

North, Liisa, ed. 1990. *Between War and Peace in Central America: Choices for Canada.* Toronto: Between the Lines.

Organization for Economic Cooperation and Development (OECD). 1986, 1987, 1988. *Geographical Distributioin of Financial Flows to Developing Countries.* Paris: OECD.

Toronto Star. 1989. "Mulroney may regret toeing Bush line on invasion of Panama." (Larry Birns) December 24.